WHISKEY ★ AMERICA

THE ESSENTIAL GUIDE TO THE U.S. DISTILLING REVOLUTION

WHISKEY ★ AMERICA

THE ESSENTIAL GUIDE TO THE U.S. DISTILLING REVOLUTION

DOMINIC ROSKROW

MITCHELL BEAZLEY

An Hachette UK Company
www.hachette.co.uk

First published in Great Britain in 2018 by Mitchell Beazley,
an imprint of Octopus Publishing Group Ltd
Carmelite House
50 Victoria Embankment
London EC4Y 0DZ
www.octopusbooks.co.uk

This book was designed and produced by
White Lion Publishing, an imprint of The Quarto Group
The Old Brewery, 6 Blundell Street
London, N7 9BH
www.QuartoKnows.com

Distributed in the US by
Hachette Book Group
1290 Avenue of the Americas
4th and 5th Floors
New York, NY 10104

Distributed in Canada by
Canadian Manda Group
664 Annette St.
Toronto, Ontario, Canada M6S 2C8

ISBN 978 1 78472 435 1

A CIP catalogue record for this book is available from the British Library.

Printed and bound in China

10 9 8 7 6 5 4 3 2 1

Senior Editor: Elspeth Beidas
Editor: Henry Russell
Project Editor: Joe Hallsworth
Designer: Dean Martin
Production Manager: Rohana Yusof
Editorial Director: Ruth Patrick
Publisher: Philip Cooper
Group Publishing Director: Denise Bates

CONTENTS

INTRODUCTION

No country in the world is as diverse as the United States. From the Norse descendants in Minnesota to the Spanish-influenced residents of Texas; from the Irish diaspora of Boston and New York to the Mormons of Utah and the Amish of Pennsylvania, the nation is the broadest of broad churches.

With that diversity comes huge contradictions. What other country could serve up a political choice for its leader between a white American middle-class populist such as Donald Trump and a politically liberal metropolitan elitist such as Hillary Clinton? Or provide solace for tens of thousands of socially conservative God-fearing Christians, and yet be home to the largest hardcore porn industry on the planet? In America, you can bear arms in the street, but jaywalking is frowned upon. And nowhere does the American dichotomy reveal itself more than in the area of alcohol. America not only invented the cocktail, but it elevated it to a position in society where it symbolized class and sophistication. No other place can match New York, Chicago, and New Orleans (and, indeed, a host of other American cities) in the hedonistic pursuit of happy hour. America, with its huge mix of cultures and ethnicities, produces a vast range of different alcoholic drinks, and it produces them very well.

On the other hand, this is also the nation where a rich puritanical streak has drawn a cloud over the alcohol industry throughout its history, and a prohibitionary shadow has stalked it for as long as white settlers have lived in it. There is a view that America and not Scotland could have dominated the world of whiskey had it been allowed to—and the standard spelling of the word whiskey would have been with an 'e'— but the temperance movement put paid to that. Even today,

many counties in America remain dry, including Lynchburg, Tennessee, where one of the world's biggest-selling spirits is produced but cannot be consumed.

Even within the alcohol-tolerant part of America there are huge differences—and there is a chasm of difference between a style bar in Manhattan, and the rock and roll whiskey bar Delilah's in Chicago.

The contrast between the two worlds of whiskey was summed up for this writer in 2005 at the Kentucky Bourbon Festival, which takes place over a week in September, and is broadly based around Bardstown, which lies some 66km (40 miles) south of Kentucky's biggest city, Louisville.

It was about 10am on the Sunday morning of the festival and we arrived at the festival site to find it all but deserted, though there was one couple sat on a bench. She was breastfeeding, he was wearing dungarees, checked shirt, and cap. It turns out he had been practicing turkey calling. This is a spin-off sport from wild turkey hunting, which involves dressing up in camouflage, strapping yourself to a tree, and then impersonating a female turkey to attract a male turkey so that you can shoot it. It's a dangerous sport, partly because wild male turkeys get annoyed when they realize you're not a female, but mainly because wild turkey hunters have a habit of mistaking other hunters for turkeys, and shooting them.

But if you're good at turkey calling, you can enter competitions, some of which are televised, to be the best turkey impersonator, and you can win considerable amounts of money. It seems that our man, who goes by the competition name of Mother Clucker, was pretty good at it, and he also knew where everyone was.

'They will be here presently,' he said, 'but right now they're in the church. Round these parts folk sin pretty hard, and if you're gonna drink hard liquor on a Sunday afternoon, then you gotta pray on Sunday morning.'

Kentucky is on the frontline between traditional and liberal. To the Southern states it is in the North, to a Northern state it is in the South. Travel there, though, and you know it's in the South. The Ohio River is effectively the border, and everything about Kentucky, from grits to country music, and from accents to baseball caps, is Southern.

Then, of course, there's bourbon. While bourbon can be (and increasingly is) made anywhere in the United States, its spiritual home is Kentucky, and its capital is Bardstown. But the State has the same split between the Christian belt and the alcohol producers, retailers, bars, and consumers. Kentucky is a staunchly Republican state—it voted 66 percent for Donald Trump—and many of its counties are dry. Bourbon producers will tell you that only since the turn of the millennium has the whiskey industry recovered from the negative reputation it was historically saddled with. Whiskey tourism based around the world-famous distilleries scattered around the state is an even more recent phenomenon.

While researching this book, I traveled to Louisville for the first time in seven years, and was astounded by the transformation. Louisville is a liberal city, full of young hipsters and a cool food and drink culture. But when I met Mother Clucker in 2005, bourbon wasn't part of it. With the exception of the Bourbons Bistro, there were no bourbon restaurants pairing the state's rich and tasty food with the spirit. There was barely a reference to whiskey anywhere in the city.

An urban bourbon trail with just five members wasn't set up until 2008. Bourbon was almost a dirty word, and whiskey writers quit Louisville at the earliest opportunity, and headed out into the rural parts where bourbon is made.

How times change! Today the urban bourbon trail has more than 30 members, and its governing body is having to turn bars and restaurants away. The tourist folk will tell you that no bar hoping to survive in the city would be able to do so without offering a decent, if not extensive, bourbon list. There are many new whiskey visitor centers in the city, including the Evan Williams Bourbon Experience and the Jim Beam Visitors' Experience; posters along the streets promote the drink; old buildings in Whiskey Row, the traditional whiskey-producing district, are being refurbished as distilleries.

Nowhere is the change in attitude better demonstrated than at the Frazier History Museum. What was a struggling old-fashioned black-and-white photo venue has been totally transformed and, in August 2018, opened as an official starting point for both the urban and suburban bourbon trails, a one-stop shop for whiskey lovers to learn about bourbon, to plan their time in the State most effectively, and to further understand how whiskey weaves its way through Kentucky's turbulent history.

At the core of the new offering is a high-tech interactive 'education center' where visitors can use computer technology to trace bourbon family histories, and trace where the Beams, the Boones, and the Elijah Craigs fit into the whiskey story. A drab waste ground has been landscaped into a colorful tropical garden, packed with exotic flowers and stunning butterflies; bourbon has stepped out of its dungarees and into the finest tailor-made suits. All the dots have been joined up, so that from one central point the visitor can see bourbon in its geographical, historical, and social context, and get the bigger picture of Louisville's birth on the waterfalls of the Ohio, and its trading links to the Mississippi down to New Orleans.

Unsurprisingly, big money has contributed to this bourbon revolution, and the Brown Formans, Jim Beams, and Heaven Hills are all over the story. It would be remiss of a book such as this not to put the big companies into context and give them the credit they deserve. But they're not what this book is about.

The reason I went to Louisville was to catch up with Kentucky's new wave of whiskey distillers. It borders on sacrilege to say it, but I didn't even travel out to Bardstown. We're seeing a changing of the guard, and while Bardstown will jealously hold on to its title of bourbon capital of the world, I suspect we're seeing a bid by Louisville to go one better. This wonderful, characterful city is going all out to be the world's most important whiskey city. Indeed, only Dublin can give it a run for its money.

In Louisville, the sons and grandsons of distinguished Woodford Reserve master distiller Lincoln Henderson are making fine whiskey under the name Angel's Envy. In 2018, Michter's joined Old Forester on Whiskey Row, and just around the corner Peerless is making rye and bourbon by methods that contradict the accepted and traditional way of making bourbon in the state.

These distilleries are part of a national revolution in craft distilling—though neither Peerless nor Angel's Envy are that small—a movement that has resulted in hundreds of new distillers making not only traditional American whiskey but also developing their own take on styles such as single malt whiskey. Moreover, the micro-distilling boom seems to have unleashed the American entrepreneurial spirit. Creative and innovative new drinks styles—some are whiskeys, some are technically not—are bringing a fresh generation of drinkers to the whiskey category, and the temptation to give up stressful city jobs for stress-free and sedate distilling careers has attracted a glittering array of new distillers, many from the unlikeliest of backgrounds.

Kentucky has dominated this introduction, but it doesn't dominate this book. The craft distilling revolution is a national phenomenon, and it's evolving so rapidly that it would be impossible for anyone to keep up. Telling the story of the new wave of craft distilleries is like painting the Golden Gate Bridge—an endless job and you're bound to miss bits. But Whiskey: America has found distilleries with great stories in the snowy winter wastelands of Alaska, on the sun-scorched plains of San José, and just about everywhere in between.

Since 2008, distilleries making everything from absinthe to apple brandy have sprung up, and when it comes to whiskey, there are distilleries at every stage of the production cycle. Many have thought short-term and are trading moonshine and un-aged corn whiskey; others have met the definition of an American 'straight' whiskey, and are bottling at two years old. Others have put whiskey aside in warehouses and are preparing for the long haul.

We've even already reached the stage that American craft brewing reached a few years back: a fallout has begun; distilleries are shutting as well as opening as market factors kick in and the survival of the fittest gets under way.

There has been much debate about what the word 'craft' means. All whiskey production is artisanal by definition, and the brewing of grain followed by the distilling of the brewers' beer to make distilled grain spirit is done pretty much the same way (depending on the whiskey style) no matter how big the distillery. The finest bourbons are produced by large producers such as Buffalo Trace and Heaven Hill, and are none the worse for the size of the distillery. Conversely, a whiskey produced in a dustbin in a garden shed isn't necessarily good because it is produced on a small scale. Indeed, the chances are it won't be good at all.

Some of the new distilleries are sizeable—Balcones, Corsair, Angel's Envy are just a few of the new whiskey-makers producing large volumes of whiskey for export, and their whiskeys are excellent. But they are included here because they epitomize the values of the craft distilling movement.

When the first whiskeys from the new producers started to reach out across America, traditional producers either ignored them or criticized them. But now the situation has changed in two important ways. Firstly, many of those traditional distillers have taken an 'if you can't beat them, join them' attitude, and initiated whiskey-based projects of their own. Secondly, many of the new whiskeys have reached standards that are winning them fans not just in the United States, but across the world.

In *Whiskey: America* we look at the history and evolution of American whiskey, at the pioneers, at the first wave of new distillers, who started making different whiskey styles back in the 1970s, and mostly at the new micro-distilleries. We describe the taste of the best of the new whiskeys, and provide an introduction to some of the bars in America and elsewhere where the new wave of whiskeys can be enjoyed.

Whiskey: America is designed to help readers to orientate themselves in the potentially confusing modern world of craft distilling, and embolden them to explore the new products and outlets that are currently emerging all the time.

CHAPTER 1

AMERICAN WHISKEY HISTORY

There has been American whiskey for as long as there has been an America. George Washington owned a distillery, Abraham Lincoln extolled its virtues, and there was even a rebellion over a whiskey tax introduced to pay off the costs of the War of Independence. Bourbon got its name either from a County in Kentucky or a New Orleans street named in honour of the Frenchmen who helped the Americans in their struggle for independence. Many of the thousands of European migrants, many of them farmers, brought with them their distilling skills. Rye whiskey and then corn whiskey were shaped and improved in parallel with the civilization of American society.

RIGHT Whiskey Country: The beautiful
Cumberland Gap National Historical Park, on the
borders of Kentucky, Tennessee and Virginia.

THE EARLY PIONEERS

When we think of American whiskey, Kentucky and Tennessee first come to mind. Really, though, we should start at the beginning, in Virginia, Pennsylvania, and Maryland. And we shouldn't focus on bourbon, which is made with corn, but on whiskey made with rye.

Whiskey communities are farming communities. Across Ireland, Scotland, and Alpine Europe, and in Sweden, France, Wales, and England, farming is never far from a whiskey story. It's obvious when you consider that whiskey is made with grain, yeast, and water. Most early whiskey stories start with an individual making spirit, and the easiest way to source grain is to grow it yourself. Often not with the specific intention of making alcohol—in many cases, a surplus of grain grown for other purposes was used rather than allowed to go to waste.

It made sense economically to run excess grain into alcohol: the spirit fetched a higher price than the grain it was made from, and it was better for farmers to grow crops, make spirit and then swap it for quality footwear or clothing, rather than grow fewer crops and make bad shoes. It was this use of grain spirit as currency that shaped the early whiskey stories.

Later, people moved around the world in search of riches or to escape poverty and persecution. Famine in Ireland, land clearances in Scotland, and the Temperance Movement in Wales led many to seek new lives in North America, where a wave of immigration lasted from 1650 to 1800. Among the arrivals were farmers with distilling skills, including ancestors of Jack Daniel and Evan Williams.

The British and Irish weren't the only ones to head west. The Dutch, also skilled in distilling, started arriving in 1626 and settled along the Hudson River. Germans came too, among them the Boehm family, who landed after the War of Independence and started distilling in Maryland from 1795.

Many British and Irish settlers remained on the east coast in Virginia, Pennsylvania, Maryland, and North Carolina, where rye could be grown. The whiskey they produced was a rough, fiery, spicy spirit—the 'red eye' drunk by cowboys in Western movies.

In those early days, though, whiskey wasn't common. The pioneers fermented and then distilled fruit, particularly apples. Brandy was more popular than whiskey.

The period between 1775 and 1800 was crucial for the development of the Kentucky whiskey industry. Although settlers were flooding in from Europe, Kentucky County remained populated mainly by Native Americans until 1775, when the introduction of a policy that gave land to farmers who agreed to grow corn proved irresistibly attractive to many residents of Pennysylvania, Virginia, and North Carolina. The most famous of these early settlers was Daniel Boone, a founder of the State of Kentucky.

And so it was that farming helped to develop the land—it wasn't just corn that was grown, but also hemp and tobacco. And with the corn came the first versions of bourbon—a rough and ready corn whiskey that has nothing in common with today's spirit.

GEORGE WASHINGTON, VIRGINIA, AND WHISKEY

The shaping of America's fledgling whiskey industry had a lot to do with George Washington, the first President of the United States. In 1794, his government imposed a tax on alcohol to fund the debt incurred by the War of Independence.

The levy sparked what became known as the Whiskey Rebellion. Many of the protestors were war veterans. The demonstrations often turned violent. When the farmers of Pennsylvania learned that their counterparts in Kentucky County were evading the tax, many of them moved south to do likewise. Thus was created a concentration of whiskey-makers in the fertile regions south of Ohio.

It is ironic that Washington should have set off this chain of events, since he had provided whiskey as a tonic to his troops, and described the spirit as 'essential to the health of the men'. He even owned a distillery. He had purchased a plantation at Mount Vernon, in Fairfax County, Virginia, in 1761. At the end of the 18th century he began making rye whiskey in what became one of the biggest commercial distilleries of colonial times, with 50 mash tuns and five copper stills. It produced 50,000 liters (13,208 gallons) a year, which were sold un-aged on site and to local merchants. Washington's recipe was 60 per cent rye, 35 per cent corn, and 5 per cent malted barley.

Today, a replica of the distillery at Mount Vernon offers a visitor experience that includes tasting a rye made to the original recipe, served by workers dressed in period costume.

OPPOSITE LEFT An early advertisement for Belle of Nelson Old Fashioned Hand Made Sour Mash Whiskey. **OPPOSITE RIGHT** An antique print of Louisville from 1874. **BELOW** I predict a riot: Protestors tar and feather a tax collector during the Whiskey Rebellion in Pennsylvania 1790s.

KENTUCKY—A COMING OF AGE

Farther West, life remained tough for the early settlers, and their frequent skirmishes with Native Americans sometimes escalated into major armed confrontations. Yet slowly but surely, permanent European settlements were taking shape, and, with them, whiskey distilleries were beginning to emerge. One such place on the Kentucky River, originally established in 1775 and known from 1787 as Frank's Ford—later elided into Frankfort—quickly became a popular stopping point for travelers and grew into a wealthy town.

To this point Kentucky had been claimed by Virginia, but the people in the new settlements increasingly wanted to govern themselves. They were a long way away from Richmond, the state capital, the journey to and from which was along a route fraught with danger. They felt unable to protect themselves from Native American attack because they had to seek authorization from the Governor of Virginia to use the militia. And they wanted to be able to trade with settlements along the Mississippi River, which Virginia forbade them from doing.

During the 1780s there was a growing initiative for Kentucky independence. Eventually, after a decade of politicking and legal negotiations under the leadership of Daniel Boone, Kentucky became the 15th State of the Union in 1792. The state capital was Frankfort, which by this time had become a thriving city. Its prosperity spawned a distillery, Buffalo Trace, which in due course became a major producer of whiskey.

Kentucky's largest city, Louisville stands on a stretch of the Ohio River where a series of waterfalls prevents the smooth passage of shipping—early traders had to unload their boats and carry their goods past the rapids. And they would either have to carry their vessels, or hire other boats on the far side. Service industries grew up here as a result.

At the heart of Louisville was Whiskey Row, where liquor merchants traded and prepared their spirits for transportation down to New Orleans and beyond in charred barrels. Why the containers were charred is a matter of debate. One theory is that they were burned in order to banish the smell of fish, pickles, and other products that they had previously contained; another is that the barrels first used had been recovered from a warehouse fire. It is more likely that the technique was picked up from rum producers, who had long known that barrel-aging made their spirit smooth and mellow.

Bourbon as we know it today evolved in the 19th century, to a great extent due to the work of James Crow, who applied science to the spirit and brought consistency to it. He is credited with the introduction of the sour mash process to whiskey-making, though this, too, was already known to rum producers. Sour mash is the process of adding the remains of the previous distillation—a mix of grains stripped of their sugars and the grain swill—to the start of the next distillation. This minimizes the bacteria that can make the flavor variable. Crow also brought in innovations that controled acidity and unwanted chemical reactions in the bourbon-making process.

RIGHT Rest in peace: Oak barrels in a stone warehouse at Woodford Reserve Distillery

BOURBON TODAY

Bourbon is now made all over North America, but its roots remain firmly in Kentucky, which has the perfect environment for its creation. There's plentiful corn, of course. And calcium-rich water, which also produces strong-limbed racehorses. The long, hot summers and sharp winters are ideal for the liquor's maturation.

Kentucky bourbon has been successful ever since Evan Williams founded the state's first commercial distilleries. It will continue to prosper no matter how popular or numerous the new distillers become. Indeed, the industry currently struggles to meet demand. Maker's Mark 46, for instance, was launched eight years before there was enough of it to export to the United Kingdom.

Bourbon whiskey is protected by law, and the rules governing its production are stricter than those for any other spirit. Or at least they are in theory. In practice, some of the new distillers interpret what can and cannot be called bourbon very loosely.

By definition, bourbon is a spirit made in the United States from a fermented mash comprising at least 51 per cent corn. It must be distilled at no higher than 160 proof (80 per cent ABV) and put in virgin oak barrels at a strength of not more than 125 proof (62.5 per cent ABV). Whiskey can be called bourbon after only one minute in the barrel, but to be called straight bourbon it must be matured for at least two years.

The barrel can theoretically be made from any species of oak, but in practice it is American white oak that is nearly always used. The casks can be of any size, and the corn content may be, and normally is, rather greater than the stipulated minimum.

THE 'ORIGINAL' DISTILLERIES OF KENTUCKY

The principal difference between Tennessee whiskey and bourbon is that Tennessee whiskey is made using the Lincoln Process of 'charcoal mellowing'; admirers contend that this makes for a smoother and less bitter whiskey. The rules governing bourbon state that nothing can be included in the whiskey-making process that would significantly change the final flavor of the spirit.

OPPOSITE Maturing 1792 bourbon at the Barton distillery in Bardstown. TOP Testing their strength of bourbon at Barton on July 1, 2017. BOTTOM The Brown Forman Distillery in Louisville, Kentucky.

BARTON 1792 DISTILLERY
BARDSTOWN

This is nothing like the prettiest distillery in Kentucky, and it has a checkered past, having changed names as well as ownership twice in recent years. But it is a working distillery with a big job to do, and it is home to several of the nation's least glamorous but best-loved bourbons, including Very Old Barton and Tom Moore.

The name of the distillery is the same as that of its best-known brand, which in turn takes its name from the year Kentucky achieved statehood. Barton was for years the only working distillery in America's whiskey capital. Although it's no longer alone, it's the oldest working distillery in Bardstown, having been founded by Tom Moore in 1879. Many of its buildings were built in the 1940s, and the distillery boasts 29 barrel-aging warehouses. Recently opened to the public, the distillery now offers three tours: the Barton Tradition Tour, the Bushel to Bottle Tour, and the 1792 Estate Tour.

BROWN-FORMAN DISTILLERY
LOUISVILLE

The Brown-Forman Company owns Jack Daniel's. The name 'Brown' is synonymous with whiskey in Louisville, and it's fitting that the company's main bourbon distillery should be in the city.

Formerly known as Early Times, the distillery still produces a whiskey of that name, along with Old Forester and bourbon destined for Woodford Reserve. It was set up in 1870 by George Gavin Brown, a pharmaceuticals salesman who perceived a need for high-quality whiskey as a medicinal aid for various ailments. He teamed up with his half-brother and started to put whiskey in sealed glass bottles. Until that time whiskey was bought in barrels, and it was not uncommon for unscrupulous retailers to siphon off some of the whiskey and add water to the cask. The Browns thus ensured that their whiskey reached the buyers unadulterated.

Early Times is 79 per cent corn, 11 per cent rye, and 10 per cent malted barley. Old Forester is 72 per cent corn, a weighty 18 per cent rye, and 10 per cent malted barley. The rye content makes for a complex and spicy whiskey.

Different yeasts are used for each whiskey. Old Forester is matured in new oak charred barrels. Some of the Early Times spirit is matured in used barrels. It is therefore not a bourbon, and is described on the label as 'Kentucky whiskey'.

BUFFALO TRACE

FRANKFORT

Buffalo Trace occupies land originally settled in 1775 when Hancock and Willis Lee set up Leestown. The settlement became a stop for travelers and grew into a thriving community. Built in 1857 and originally called Ancient Age, this was the first distillery to use steam power in the production of bourbon.

Buffalo Trace produces the eponymous bourbon found in bars worldwide, premium brands such as Blanton's, and some of Kentucky's most iconic whiskeys: Van Winkle, Eagle Rare, and Sazerac Rye.

In addition to industrial-scale whiskey production, there is a small still where the distillers experiment, and a special warehouse for 'works in progress'.

Among the legends who have worked here are Colonel Albert Bacon Blanton (55 years' service); George T Stagg, whose name adorns one of the world's best bourbons; Pappy Van Winkle; and Elmer T Lee, who checked whiskey on the site right up to his death in 2013, shortly before his 94th birthday.

OPPOSITE LEFT Do the mash: The mash house at Four Roses Distillery. **OPPOSITE RIGHT** White oak barrels at Heaven Hill Distillery in Bardstown. **BELOW** Roll 'em out: Workers unload barrels at Buffalo Trace Distillery Frankfort, Kentucky.

FOUR ROSES
LAWRENCEBURG

It's traditional at the Kentucky Bourbon Festival to head out on the Friday morning to Four Roses for the annual 'Let's Talk Bourbon' event. If you're lucky, you'll get a fine late summer morning, when the lawns are covered with dew and sunlight filters through the trees. You can eat grits and crispy bacon, drink strong black coffee, and meet other bourbon lovers. It's a wonderful experience in one of the world's prettiest distilleries. Not that you'd recognize it as such; it looks more like a Spanish hacienda.

The bourbon's different, too, both from other bourbons and from the original Four Roses, which was a very ordinary blend before it was withdrawn from the domestic market.

Four Roses was bought in 2002 by Japanese company Kirin and relaunched in 2004 in America, where it battled hard to lose its old image. The key to doing that was getting folk to taste it. It was common to find master distiller, Jim Rutledge, manning Four Roses tasting stands in shopping malls.

Tasting is all it requires, because this distinctive floral bourbon is a delight. The standard version comprises ten individually produced bourbons that have been aged for five or six years. A small-batch version is made up of four of the ten whiskeys, and one of the whiskeys is selected for a single-barrel version.

HEAVEN HILL
LOUISVILLE

Heaven Hill produces some of Kentucky's most iconic whiskeys, including Evan Williams, Elijah Craig, and Rittenhouse Rye. Head out to Bardstown and you'll find the Heaven Hill visitor center and some huge warehouses. The distillery's not here though—a fire in 1996 destroyed it, and production is now at the Bernheim Distillery in Louisville.

Heaven Hill is still independently owned by the Shapiro family, who have made great efforts to raise the profile of Louisville bourbon, not least by opening the Evan William Experience in Whiskey Row, the attractions of which include an authentic speakeasy bar.

JIM BEAM

CLERMONT

Jim Beam is the world's best-selling bourbon, and in Kentucky only the name Boone is as famous as Beam.

Beam is an Anglicization of Boehm, the name of a family that traveled from Germany and settled first in Maryland, then moved to Kentucky.

The first Beam to distill was Jacob, in 1795, and his great-grandson David established a new distillery in the mid-1800s at Clear Springs, near what is now the Clermont Distillery. But it wasn't until the end of Prohibition in 1933 that Beam moved to its present site.

The current premises are home to the American Outpost, where visitors can look round the old Beam family home. Another visitor attraction has also been opened in Louisville.

The company was sold in 1967 to American Brands, which changed its name first to Fortune Brands, and subsequently to Beam Global.

In 2014, Japanese giant Suntory bought Beam to form Beam Suntory, which thus became the third biggest drinks company in the world.

The standard Jim Beam white label is matured for four years. The black label version is aged for eight years and is a beauty. In the early 1990s, Beam launched four small-batch whiskeys. The first to be released was Booker's, named after Jim Beam's grandson, the legendary brand ambassador Booker Noe.

Three more whiskeys were subsequently released: Baker's, named after relative Baker Beam; Basil Hayden's, named after Booker's cousin; and Knob Creek, matured for nine years, named after Abraham Lincoln's childhood home in Kentucky.

Beam is also responsible for producing three of the most iconic and respected whiskeys: Old Crow, Old Grand-Dad, and Old Taylor.

MAKER'S MARK
LORETTO

Maker's Mark is a young bourbon brand produced on one of the oldest whiskey-making sites. It's Kentucky's most southerly distillery, and the farthest away from Louisville. It is situated on land made up of extensive exotic gardens, and there is a sedate feel to it. On the road down to the creek from the distillery you'll find The Quart House, one of America's oldest remaining 'retail package stores'. Before Prohibition, local residents would come by horse and buggy to have their quart jugs filled directly from whiskey barrels stored here.

The bourbon produced on site is soft, sweet, and gentle. The recipe was created by Bill Samuels, Snr with a little help from his friends on Whiskey Row and at the Stitzel-Weller Distillery, which is now home to Bulleit and owned by Diageo, but which once produced the sort of wheated bourbons typical of Weller and Van Winkle. Samuels wanted to convert new drinkers, and to broaden his product's appeal to women, so it wasn't just the taste that had to distinguish it. Everything about the new Maker's Mark was unconventional, from the red wax sealing to the unusual name. Even the word 'whisky' sets it apart, because it's spelled without an 'e' as a respectful nod to the Scottish ancestry of the Samuels family.

Maker's Mark is made slightly differently from other bourbons. The distillery eschews the normal hammer to crush the hard corn, preferring a roller mill because it believes the hammer causes scorching of the grain, which imparts a bitter note. The spirit is put into the cask at a lower than normal 110 proof (55 per cent ABV). During maturation the barrels are rotated, a costly and time-consuming process.

For many years, this distillery made only one whiskey, and as part of the tour the guide would let visitors taste both a younger and an older version of the bourbon in an effort to demonstrate that six years is the only age that works for Maker's. An excellent new version of the bourbon was introduced in North America in 2010. Maker's Mark 46 is the standard whiskey with added spice. This is achieved by emptying the cask after several years of production, adding to the cask some seared French oak staves (with the stave toasting level of 46, hence the name), and then refilling the cask with Maker's.

A new visitor center was added to the distillery at the start of the new millennium, and among the attractions was the opportunity to purchase a bottle with a personalized label and a wax seal.

WILD TURKEY

LAWRENCEBURG

The 21st century has been remarkably kind to whiskey, and few varieties of the liquor have surfed the wave more successfully than Wild Turkey.

For many years this iconic bourbon seemed to be treading water, living off past glories and its reputation as a heavyweight whiskey, relying on the legendary status of its master distiller, Jimmy Russell, but appearing increasingly out of touch with the rapidly changing world of spirits.

That all changed in 2009, when Gruppo Campari bought the brand from Pernod Ricard, which had owned it since 1980, and set about reshaping it. Campari has an admirable track record when it comes to buying whiskey brands. It seeks out distilleries in which independent family values are important, and then invests in them without interfering, enhancing their principal assets while leaving day-to-day operation to the established management.

Wild Turkey now has state-of-the-art facilities and a new bottling and packaging plant. A total of $100 million has been spent on it.

The whole Wild Turkey range was given a thorough packaging overhaul, and the famous 101 whiskey was joined by a softer, more mainstream 81 proof version to appeal to a new generation.

The key issue for Wild Turkey is that it has always been a big, flavor-rich bourbon, and Campari has respected and even encouraged that. Its core is unchanged, despite the change of ownership. There are now two master distillers named Russell—Eddie now has the same title as his father—and the whiskey is as good as ever.

The new distillery is one of the biggest in North America. It occupies 12,500 sq m (134,000 sq f) and can produce a staggering 50 million liters (11 million gallons) of spirit a year—more than twice its former capacity. (In addition to the Wild Turkey products, Campari's SKYY vodka is bottled here after being shipped from Illinois.)

Wild Turkey doesn't disclose its mash bill, but Jimmy Russell has suggested that the corn content is in the low 70s, which is less than that of any other bourbon. With the exception of its rye, all whiskeys are made to the same grain mash bill. The spirit is put into the cask at just 110 proof (55 per cent ABV), because, according to Russell, less of the flavor is lost that way.

ABOVE Real wild one: The iconic Wild Turkey 101.
OPPOSITE LEFT Oak barrels at Woodford Reserve Distillery. **OPPOSITE RIGHT** Woodford Reserve's unique pot stills.

WOODFORD RESERVE

VERSAILLES

Woodford County is everything you might expect Kentucky to be. Traditional homesteads with trimmed lawns and perfectly maintained gardens are scattered across it, white fences surround bluegrass fields, and within them the healthiest pedigree horses you will ever see canter in graceful splendor.

Woodford Reserve occupies a site by Glenn's Creek. It was here that Oscar Pepper hired James Crow, the man who would create the framework for modern bourbon.

The distillery, called Labrot & Graham until 2003, is beautiful and sedate. The tour is relaxed, and the site has been developed to accommodate visitors.

Wisely, owners Brown-Forman have not turned Woodford Reserve into a bourbon-producing museum. Master distiller Chris Morris acknowledges the past, but honors Crow's memory by adopting his experimental approach through bottlings that explore different parts of the whiskey-making process. These have included a bourbon made using four grains instead of three; a whiskey finished in a Sonoma-Cutrer wine cask; a sweet mash whiskey in which the backset was not added to the distillation; and a 'four-wood' bourbon.

This distillery differs from others in Kentucky because it uses pot stills, as they do in Scotland, rather than column stills. These have enabled Morris also to make two single malts.

The smallest of the 'traditional' distilleries, Woodford Reserve is genuinely 'small batch', making just 40 to 50 barrels of whiskey a day.

THE 'ORIGINAL' DISTILLERIES OF TENNESSEE

The principal difference between Tennessee whiskey and bourbon is that Tennessee whiskey is made using the Lincoln Process of 'charcoal mellowing'; admirers contend that this makes for a smoother and less bitter whiskey. The rules governing bourbon state that nothing can be included in the whiskey-making process that would significantly change the final flavor of the spirit.

ABOVE Let it burn: Piles of maple wood ready for burning at the Jack Daniel Distillery. **OPPOSITE TOP** A matter of taste: sampling spirit at the Jack Daniel Distillery. **OPPOSITE BOTTOM** By George: The general store at the Dickel distillery.

JACK DANIEL'S
LYNCHBURG

Jack Daniel's enjoys a cult status that few other drinks can match. At the headquarters in Lynchburg there is plenty of branded merchandise on sale in a visitor center that features a courthouse and a square of shops and cafés. The distillery itself is vast, but visitors see little of the vast maturation warehouses or the bottling halls. What the tourist gets shown is more theme park than whiskey distillery.

You do get to see the original water source for the distillery in a small cave, however, as well as various statues, and the safe that Jack Daniel is said to have kicked, thus sustaining the injury that would eventually result in his death. There is also a chance to see the spirit dripping through almost 3m (10ft) of charcoal before it's put into barrels. Every drop of the millions of gallons of Jack Daniel's made every year must undertake this journey. Another highlight of the tour is a visit to where maple wood is burned to produce the charcoal, which, once cooled with water, is added to the vats and spirit is filtered through it. It is replaced every three months.

In every other way Jack Daniel's is produced as bourbon on a vast scale. The still house is a seven-story building. There were 16 fermenters on site, and 4 copper column stills, but more than $100 million has been spent recently on expansion so that number has increased. Jack Daniel's famous Old No. 7 is the distillery's main product, but in recent years there has been more focus on Gentleman Jack and the company's single-barrel range. Brand extensions include the flavored spirits Tennessee Honey and Tennessee Fire.

GEORGE DICKEL
CASCADE HOLLOW

George Dickel distillery today is sited about 1.5km (1 mile) from the site founded in 1877 by Dickel himself. The distillery was called Cascade, and the whiskey was originally called Cascade Tennessee whiskey. However, since Dickel died in 1894 the bottles have always borne his name.

The State of Tennessee outlawed whiskey in 1910, and the distillery was closed. The business moved to Louisville, Kentucky. The names Dickel and Cascade were acquired eventually by national drinks company Schenley Industries, and in the 1950s the owners decided to bring the Dickel name back to Tennessee, building a new distillery there in 1958. The brand is now owned by Diageo.

THE FIRST WAVE OF CRAFT DISTILLERS

The first drips of the current distilling revolution can be traced back to 2003; in 2007 the trickle turned in to a stream; in 2011 the stream became a flood.

Before then the American whiskey landscape was well and truly dominated by Kentucky and Tennessee, but some other distilleries across the United States have been offering something new and different to drinkers since before the current cart boom. This first wave of craft distillers had to battle against the odds to produce and establish whiskeys that had no precedent. Every one of them has survived and prospered by creating impressive and original produce.

ABOVE The Anchor distillery. **OPPOSITE TOP** Old Potrero Straight Rye Whiskey. **OPPOSITE BOTTOM** The stillroom at Anchor.

HOTALING & CO.
SAN FRANCISCO

If micro-distilling has a father figure, it's Fritz Maytag. He has retired now, and he sold his business in 2010, but his legacy lives on through a range of almost-impossible-to-find but fantastic whiskeys made to historical recipes.

Maytag bought the Anchor Steam Brewery in San Francisco in 1965 and started distilling in 1994. The distillery, tucked away at the back of the brewery, makes a renowned gin named Junipero.

Its whiskeys are all barrel-strength and made with 100 per cent rye. Old Potrero Single Malt No. 1 is matured for a year in new, uncharted barrels, and is rich and oily; Old Potrero Single Malt Rye is matured for three years in new charred-oak barrels; and Old Potrero Hotaling's is perhaps the most complex of them all, an oily monster bursting with citrus notes and fresh grains.

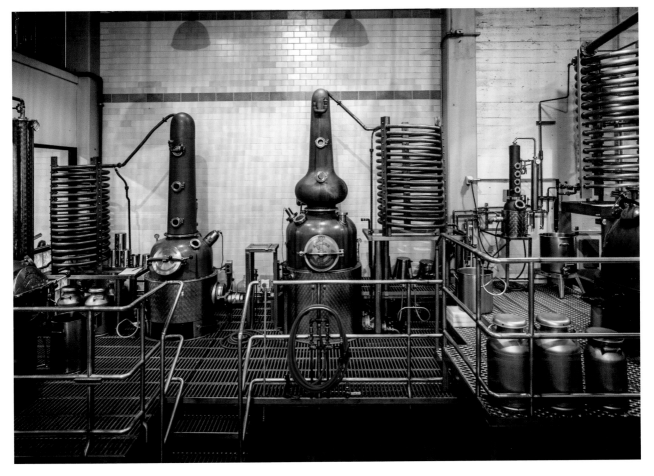

CHARBAY WINERY AND DISTILLERY

ST HELENA, CALIFORNIA

The winery was founded by Miles Karakasevic, another legendary figure in the history of the American craft distilling industry, and the baton was picked up by his son, Marko. The distillery was added in 1999, and since then releases have been sporadic but markedly original. The first was a four-year-old 'whiskey' named Double Barrel Release One—an early example of how craft distillers in America are operating at the margins, because most definitions of whiskey would exclude a spirit made with hops.

In 2013, a whiskey was released which had spent six years in charred new American oak barrels and a further eight years in stainless steel—so strictly a six-year-old whiskey. Other releases include a 'whiskey' distilled from stout, and a whiskey matured for 21 months in French oak.

At the end of 2017, a 16-year-old spirit was released, again made from beer; this was described on the label as 'hop flavored whiskey'.

ABOVE The Charbay whiskey range. **BELOW** The Charbay Distillery. **OPPOSITE** The Clear Creek Distillery.

CLEAR CREEK DISTILLERY
PORTLAND, OREGON

Steve McCarthy set up the Clear Creek Distillery in 1985 to make a range of European-style spirits. But his McCarthy's Oregon Single Malt Whiskey is one of the earliest examples of American craft distilling and remains one of the very best. It's a bold and unique whiskey that is as far removed from bourbon as it's possible to get.

It is made from an unhooked, peated wash made by a local brewery, and is distilled in a Holstein pot still. The spirit is matured in various woods for at least three years.

EDGEFIELD DISTILLERY
PORTLAND, OREGON

McMenamin's Edgefield contains many things within its 30 hectares (74 acres): a hotel, a winery, a brewery, and a cinema; it also has its own golf course. In addition to all this, it has a distillery making a large range of spirits, including several whiskeys, and has a history stretching back to 1998. The most famous of its products is Hogshead Whiskey, which proudly steers away from the whiskies of Scotland, and the whiskeys of Ireland and Kentucky. The company owns a second distillery: Cornelius Pass, which opened in 2012.

ST. GEORGE SPIRITS
ALAMEDA, CALIFORNIA

St. George Spirits was set up in 1982 by Jörg Rupf, who has been variously described as a maverick and a genius. It makes an amazing absinthe, a chili vodka, and some very tasty gins.

Its whiskeys are highly impressive and well made. A favorite is Baller, which amply demonstrates the innovation that micro-distillers are capable of bringing to the world of whiskey. It is made with 100 per cent American barley, and distilled in eau de vie pot stills. It is aged for three to four years in used bourbon casks and French oak wine casks, as well as filtered through maple charcoal. It is finished in casks that had held house-made umeshu (a Japanese style of plum liqueur made entirely from California-grown ume fruit). Distiller Lance Winters describes Baller as 'a California take on the Japanese spin on Scotch whisky'. Now that's really something different.

TRIPLE EIGHT DISTILLERY
NANTUCKET

Alongside Nantucket Vineyard and Cisco Brewery, Triple Eight Distillery opened in 2000, and makes a range of spirits and liqueurs including a bourbon. But its reputation has been built around Notch (as in 'not Scotch'), a malt whiskey matured in a mixture of barrels previously used to store bourbon, Cognac, Sauterne, various other types of wine, port and sherry.

The original Notch was released as an eight-year-old but there is a ten-year-old expression and the 12-year-old has won a Liquid Gold award and received a score of 96.5 in Jim Murray's *Whisky Bible*.

Triple Eight has been looking to other malt-making American distilleries with a view to launching an American blended malt whiskey.

STRANAHAN'S
COLORADO

The company says that the Stranahan's distillery was forged by friendship and fire and it was. Firefighter Jess Graber and brewer George Stranahan struck up a friendship after the former was called out to a fire at the latter's premises. Their mutual love of whiskey led to Stranahan's single malt, which is made differently from the whiskies of Scotland.

The distillery has also released a number of special malts matured in ex-sherry, ex-wine, ex-rum, and ex-tequila casks.

OPPOSITE The impressive distillery at St. George Spirits in Alameda, California.

TRADITIONAL STYLES OF WHISKEY AND HOW THEY ARE MADE

In this book we examine American micro-distilling and some of its main practitioners. Many of them are operating at the margins, experimenting with different methods, and exploring new flavors. Some of the new spirits stretch existing definitions of what whiskey is, and some step way over the mark. That's not necessarily a bad thing, as long as we remember where the traditional lines are drawn.

It may be that the new 'whiskey' styles will eventually form a drinks category of their own, distinct from what currently constitutes whiskey. So it's worth pausing to look at what the traditional styles are, and how they are made.

There is no universal agreement as to what constitutes whiskey, although most would define it as a spirits drink distilled from grain and made from grain, yeast, and water.

From that definition, whiskeys from different parts of the world go in different directions. Scotland, Ireland, and America have their own definitions of the different styles of whisky/whiskey they produce. Scotland's definitions of what may be called a single malt whisky or a blended malt whisky have been adopted by all European producers. For instance, whisky must be matured for a minimum of three years in Europe. Distillers in other parts of the world accept that rule.

But not in America. It is one of whiskey's great ironies that the rules governing the production of bourbon, rye, and wheat whiskey are some of the world's most stringent, and yet spirits may be called whiskeys with very little or even no maturation in wood. While there are many positive sides to craft distilling, a few of the new producers are flying under the radar and muddying the waters. The term 'flavored whiskey' is used in America but would not be acceptable in Europe.

There are ways around the rules without breaking them. The Copper & Kings Distillery in Louisville makes brandies, apple brandies and absinthe, and has distilled craft beers. Its Brewskey is described, not as whiskey, but as 'spirits distilled from grains with hops. Finished in oak barrels'.

The emergence of new distilleries in Tennessee raises a question. If a whiskey produced in the state doesn't use the Lincoln County method of charcoal filtering, can it be called a Tennessee whiskey, or should it be 'whiskey from Tennessee'?

TOP Jim Beam's beer and spirit still. **BOTTOM** Washbacks at Maker's Mark. **OPPOSITE** Copper pot stills at Town Branch Distillery in Lexington, Kentucky.

BOURBON

The principal grain in bourbon is corn or maize—at least 51 per cent, normally more. A small amount of the recipe will be malted barley, because this acts as the catalyst for alcohol conversion. A third grain, normally wheat or rye, is also included. There have been examples of four- or even five-grain whiskeys. These may still be bourbons as long as the corn content is above 51 per cent. The grain must be cooked before being mashed. This is done in a number of ways, but often in what are effectively over-sized pressure cookers.

Corn is cooked first, at the highest temperature. Then the heat is reduced and rye or wheat added, and finally, at an even lower temperature, malted barley.

Distillation takes place in a still known as a column still, a continuous still or a Coffey still. As one of these names implies, it is a continuous process, and up to five stills can be operated in tandem.

The round stainless steel stills may be huge. Interspersed down the inside of the still is a series of copper plates, which are perforated to allow spirit and liquid to pass through them.

Alcohol is obtained by passing steam under pressure at high temperatures up the column, where it meets the unfiltered mash. The alcohol evaporates, with the most volatile spirits rising as vapor, and the others passing down the column and being collected.

The process is repeated a second time, and may be repeated two or three more times until the spirit, now drinkable alcohol, is collected.

The first still is known as the beer still; the second distillation is carried out in a doubler. The liquid here will have a strength of mid- to high-60s ABV.

Some distilleries replace the doubler with a thumper, so named because of the sound made when the vapors make contact with the hot water.

The spirit, known as white dog, is now put into a new barrel made of white oak that has been charred or toasted over fire, and the level of charring or toasting will vary depending on the bourbon being made.

Nothing may be added to the spirit at any point.

OTHER GRAIN WHISKEYS

The mash for making American whiskey can be made up of any combination of grains, but in every case there must be a minimum of 51 per cent of one type of grain if the whiskey is to be described as bourbon (corn), rye, wheat, or oat whiskey.

Micro-distilling has seen some exciting developments to the mix of grains: both Adnams in England and Pun in Italy have made Triple Grain whiskies; Ireland's Teeling Whiskey has played with its mash bills, and there are four- and five-grain whiskeys in existence. In America, grains such as quinoa and triticale have been used successfully to make whiskey.

All grain whiskeys must be matured in new white oak barrels that have been charred or toasted. That maturation spell does not have to be two years, but at least two years' maturation is required to merit the term 'straight whiskey'.

BELOW No grain, no gain: Display of grains that go into the mash bill at Woodford Reserve. **OPPOSITE** Moonshine runs from the still at Casey Jones Distillery in Hopkinsville, Kentucky.

CORN WHISKEY AND MOONSHINE

Corn whiskey is different from bourbon for three reasons. Firstly, the corn content must be 80 per cent or more. Secondly, corn whiskey doesn't need to be mauled in a barrel at all, and if it is, it's normally for a short time, typically no longer than six months. Thirdly, if a barrel is used for maturation it must be un-charred or must have been used previously.

Many micro-distillers are making what they are calling moonshine, but to all intents and purposes these are corn whiskeys that have not been matured in wood. The whole concept of modern moonshine is a misnomer because the name correctly refers to a whiskey distilled secretly and illegally to avoid taxes.

Most modern moonshine, then, is un-aged corn whiskey or white whiskey, produced legally.

To make corn you need to malt it, which means getting it to grow and then stopping the process by heat. Next the corn is mashed, heating it so that enzymes from the malt begin to convert from starch to sugar. Yeast is added to ferment it. This may take two weeks. It is distilled in the same way as bourbon, on a continuous or column still. Collect the finished product of the distillation process, and then distill it a second time. This increases purity. Then it should be matured in used or un-charred oak casks for as long as desired.

SINGLE MALT WHISKEY

Single malt whiskey is made with malted grain. Most commonly that grain is barley, but some whiskeys are made with 100 per cent wheat and 100 per cent rye; these may also be described as malt whiskeys. The word 'single' refers to the fact that the drink is all made at one distillery, and is not a reference to the number of casks or types of casks used in the production. Most single malt whiskeys comprise liquor from several casks.

MAKING MALT WHISKEY WITH BARLEY

Firstly, the barley must be malted, and that is done by steeping the grain in water two or three times, thus tricking it into growing.

Next the grain is allowed to germinate. Effectively the kernel of the grain is broken down so that shoots can start to grow. But this in turn allows access to the starches and enzymes contained within the grain.

Germination takes from five to nine days, depending on the time of the year, the local climate, and the temperature in the malting room. It's a fairly consistent process in Scotland, but the diversity of climates in North America significantly affects the amount of time required.

When the grain reaches the optimum point of germination—that is, when the rootlets are about three-quarters the length of the grain—growth is halted by spreading the grain over a perforated floor and passing heat through it from below. It is at this stage that peat fires may be used to impart smoky flavors.

Next the grain is mashed in order to remove soluble sugars and enzymes.

The dried grain is crushed into flour, known as grist, before hot water is added, then allowed to rest for a while before the liquid is drained off. A second wash is carried out at a higher temperature, and then again the liquid is siphoned off. Now only a small quantity of sugars is left in the grain, so normally a third wash of even hotter water is added. This time, though, the liquid is siphoned off separately. It is cooled and added back into the first wash of the next run. The liquid collected in the first two mashes is known as wort. It is brown and sweet and may be used for cattle feed.

Yeast is added to the liquid; it feeds on the sugars, creating alcohol and carbon dioxide. This can be a dramatic and violent process, and fermentation may last from 40 to more than 100 hours depending on the distillery. The resulting liquid is a form of beer, but differs from commercial beer in that it has a sour taste. The liquid, known as wash, will have an alcoholic strength of between 7 and 11 percent ABV and it is now ready for distillation.

Distillation is the separation of alcohol from water by using heat. Alcohol has a lower boiling point than water, so when it is heated it will turn to spirit and travel up and away from the water. Traditionally a pot still, which is effectively a giant kettle, is used for this purpose. The still is always heated from below.

TOP A barrel is filled with new make spirit.
BOTTOM A bottle of whiskey produced at Maine Craft Distilling in Portland. OPPOSITE Small batch: The whiskeys proceed at George Washington's Mount Vernon distillery.

Distilleries normally have a pair of stills or multiples of two. There are two types: the larger wash still, and the spirit still. They are nearly always made of copper, a metal that conducts heat, is pliable and easily shaped. It is also rough, with the result that, as the spirit passes over it, it will trap heavier, fattier, and often unpleasant elements in the spirit.

The size and shape of the still are crucial to the sort of spirit the distillery is making. The greater the contact between the copper and the spirit, the lighter the spirit, because the greater the quantity of impurities, fats, and other compounds that will be removed. A long, tall still will allow only the light spirit to rise all the way up it. Small, squat stills produce more robust, oilier whiskeys.

The wash is placed first in the wash still and heated. The alcohol, with a lower boiling point than water, evaporates, and the spirit travels up the still until it reaches the lyne arm. From there it enters a condenser, where it is converted back into liquid and collected in a receiving tank. At this point the liquid has an alcoholic strength in the 20s.

A second distillation now collects a proportion of spirit to put into casks to mature into whisky. The first spirits off the still are the strongest, most dangerous, and foulest-tasting, so they are taken away and collected in a holding vessel. The length of time of this first stage will vary from distillery to distillery. This first spirit is known as the heads or foreshots.

Eventually, as the strength of the spirit falls, the distiller will collect the heart of the run over a period of hours until the liquid becomes too weak. The unwanted surplus is collected in the same way as the initial part of the run. Such residue is known as the tails or the feints.

The more times you distill, the more alcohol will be separated from water, so the stronger the spirit. Extra distillation makes the spirit lighter and more fragrant.

The spirit collected is clear and has a high alcoholic strength. The common view is that the ideal casking strength is 63.5 per cent, so water is added to the spirit prior to it being put into the cask. This figure is not a legal requirement. At this stage the liquid—known as 'new make' in Scotland and 'white dog' in America—may not yet be called whiskey.

CHAPTER 2

THE CRAFT REVOLUTION

We live in an increasingly stressful world, and more and more people are turning their backs on it for their own health and well being. Turning to craft products was a logical and obvious way to do that. In the field of alcohol, it all started with beer, as Americans switched from bland Bud to extreme IPAs and German and Belgian-style lagers. The production of whiskey, distilled from hopless beer, was a logical next step. And this being America, all sorts of spirits, which would not be called whisky in Europe, have brought new drinks styles. It's still early days, but we're witnessing a new world order for the category.

WHY DID THE AMERICAN CRAFT REVOLUTION HAPPEN?

America didn't invent craft distilling, but no one developed it quite like the United States.

Historically the most sedate of spirits, whiskey does tradition better than any other drink. Nowhere is this more noticeable than in Kentucky, where the bourbon distilleries breathe heritage, and the huge maturation warehouses are a constant reminder that fine bourbon has brought prosperity to the State for generations.

Kentucky's whiskey-makers are proud of their history and of having brought a modest spirit to worldwide attention.

No one's in a hurry here because you can't rush fine bourbon. And even as the spirit has grown in popularity and production facilities have been expanded, the process of making whiskey has remained unchanged.

Contrast that with the growth in micro-distilleries. If Kentucky's distilleries are like huge, slow cargo boats traveling up and down the Ohio River, then the new craft distillers are motorboats, zipping this way and that, churning up the calm waters. How is it that a community that barely existed a few years ago can produce whiskeys that already have admirers everywhere?

In truth, the clues were there, from the boom in craft brewing which preceded the distilling trend by a few years. Almost overnight America went from nation dominated by uninspiring lagers to the brewing equivalent of hot chili sauces.

It wasn't just about exciting beers, either, although that was what drove it. The United States seemed to have an unquenchable thirst for knowledge, for exploring new tastes,

and for resurrecting long-forgotten brewing styles and giving them a 21st-century makeover.

Micro-distilling is on a different scale, of course. It's more expensive to invest in equipment, and there are licencing problems. But the concept of producing a spirit and bottling it has fired the imagination of hundreds of people. Scores of new distillers have brushed the obstacles aside, and with the support of organizations such as the American Distilling Institute and the American Craft Spirits Association, they are now making everything from absinthe to apple brandy.

Unsurprisingly, many of the new distillers have opted to make vodka and gin. These are relatively easy to make, and do not require maturation in high-quality barrels. In the early part of the millennium, finding quality wood was a problem. When the whiskey industry was struggling, demand for barrels fell, and much of the supportive industry disappeared. When whiskey came back into vogue, timber merchants and barrel makers had to be found, and the process was slow. There was a widely held view that it wouldn't be a fall in demand from consumers that would halt the whiskey boom, but rather a shortage of casks.

That situation has been rectified, but medium-sized companies may still find themselves squeezed by the biggest producers, who have secured their supply of new barrels at larger discounts.

Can the craft distilling movement be sustained? Undoubtedly yes. As we shall see, 'micro-distilling' and 'craft distilling' are umbrella terms, and some of the more ambitious distillers are growing into major companies. Which raises questions: can Balcones still be considered a craft distiller if it has expanded and is conquering markets across the world? Is Tuthilltown Spirits any less of a micro-distillery because it is now owned by Scottish William Grant & Sons?

WHAT IS CRAFT OR MICRO-DISTILLING?

Wikipedia defines a micro-distillery as 'a small, often boutique-style distillery established to produce beverage grade spirit alcohol in relatively small quantities, usually done in single batches (as opposed to larger distillers' continuous distilling process)'.

The last part is inaccurate, because whether a whiskey is distilled in batches or as part of a continuous distilling process has nothing to do with size, and everything to do with the style of whiskey being made. Glenlivet and Glenfiddich might be amused to hear their output of 10–12 million liters (2.6 million–3.1 million gallons) of malt spirit a year described as micro-distilling.

There are other problems with the definition. What are 'relatively small quantities', and what does 'boutique-style' actually mean? Many of the biggest distillers create their new whiskeys on small craft stills, experimenting with flavors and fine-tuning their creations before they are put into production. The craft version and the big still version are exactly the same.

BELOW LEFT Like father, like son: Matt Kozuba, left, and his father, Zbigniew "Papa" Kozuba at Kozuba & Sons Craft Distillery. **BELOW RIGHT** Fermented wort in the hybrid copper still at Kozuba & Sons Craft Distillery. **OPPOSITE** The stills at Kozuba & Sons Craft Distillerynumerous.

It would be ridiculous to include Jim Beam or Jack Daniel's in the category of micro-distilling, but what about Woodford Reserve? Angel's Envy and Michter's, both sizeable distilleries, would easily make the cut.

Size of distillery cannot therefore be core to our definition. Although the word 'craft' implies an aspect of quality, it can't be totally about quality. You can't argue that Elijah Craig or Knob Creek aren't high-quality whiskeys. They are, but they are not craft products.

We make more progress with our definition when we look the word 'boutique' up in the dictionary. The word can be used to mean 'a business serving a sophisticated or specialized clientele'.

This is better. This definition nods toward the concept of size, but makes it an issue of demand as well as supply. The business could still be 'boutique' even if it grew to service a great increase in demand.

This works for a definition of craft or micro-distilling, too. If someone produces a whiskey that becomes popular so that the business has to grow to meet demand, then, under our definition, this remains a craft operation, provided that no compromise is made on quality, and there is no sellout of the producer's original ideals.

Perhaps then, a craft distillery can be defined as 'any distillery that starts out as an independent boutique operation with the intention of making a bespoke and individual spirit, and which stays true to the ideals of creating premium and quality spirits no matter what happens to it'. That fits the American craft brewing industry. There are countless examples of beers that were created by craft breweries but were bought up by huge brewers and are now presented as craft products but taste nothing like the original beers.

We can hope that this will not happen to craft whiskey, and so far it hasn't.

It's early days for the craft distilling movement, and no doubt many of the distilleries featured in this book will follow Tuthilltown Spirits and Westland and sell their businesses to international drinks companies. But so what? If the new whiskeys stay faithful to the ideals from which they were created, and investment makes them more readily available, then more of us have the chance to taste them.

WHY HAS THERE BEEN A BOOM IN MICRO-DISTILLING?

Micro-distilling has been at the center of a perfect storm for the last few years. The desire to make spirits has found a welcome audience in a growing number of consumers who are not only open to new drink products, but who also have taken the concept of bespoke and boutique products to their hearts.

We need to get a sense of perspective. Craft distilling represents a relatively small but growing segment of the drinks market. Never have the global brands been more powerful, and a glance over the spirits shelves of any supermarket shows that on one level little has changed. The biggest names are all present and correct, and global companies are spending millions on promotion of their star performers worldwide to make sure they stay there.

The changes may be small, but there has been change. Our leading retailers are adept at taking advantage of any

OPPOSITE TOP A column still at Key West Distilling. **OPPOSITE BOTTOM** All white: Alcohol pouring in test jar at Key West Distilling. **BELOW** An increasing number of craft distilleries are using pot stills for single malt whiskey.

trend, and increasingly we're seeing some craft brands joining the big boys on the shop shelves.

A selection of gins in particular is today considered essential for a drinks merchant, both in the off trade and in bars, hotels, and restaurants. It will take longer before the leading micro-distilling whiskey brands reach the High Street, but already a large number of pubs and bars stock small brand world whiskeys and take pride in turning the spotlight on them.

Much of this is because of the Internet and the growth in social media. Never has the world been smaller as a result, and never have we been more traveled or culturally aware.

But that access to information and experience has resulted in a growing number of people turning their backs on homogenization and globalization, and increasingly consumers are looking for brands with a unique selling point.

Consumers turning their backs on global brands will seek out anything that can demonstrate its provenance and heritage. This doesn't mean that the item in question must have a long history, and indeed, many of the new distilleries make a virtue of the fact that they are the first to operate from their location. But consumers want to hear a good backstory, and are drawn to brands that are uniquely tied to their locality, whether it be through the name, some ingredient in the spirit, or through re-creating a long-forgotten local drinks style.

The Internet provides the platform to search out such brands, and the distillers now have an opportunity to promote their spirits and emphasize what makes them different and special. It is possible to find a market without having to compete with multi-million dollar marketing budgets.

Word of mouth is still a powerful tool, and the Twittersphere is as good a medium as any through which to reach people and let them know about exciting new spirits.

The world of drinks is adapting to the changes in society generally. People are better traveled than ever before, and they have been introduced to exotic foods with extreme flavors. They have discovered drinks in the farthest corners of the world, and even in more popular travel destinations they have come to realize that the brand on the supermarket shelf

back home is a poorer or duller or less authentic version of the drinks on offer at the holiday bar.

We are more health-conscious, too, and are choosing to drink less, but better. The modern consumer will seek out premium drinks and not demur over the price. But they want to be sold the offering. It's not about cheap, it's about value for money, so customers expect their bar staff to sell their products to them. They want an anecdote or a backstory. This has raised the level of professionalism across the drinks trade.

People's desire to discover something first so that they can tell everyone else about it, mixed with the fun of trying new flavors, has created a new phenomenon: it's not just drinking that is a hobby these days, it's seeking out the best spirits to drink.

While all spirits have benefited from this perfect alignment of trends and attitudes, whiskey has one other advantage: it is very much in fashion. For a generation of people currently in their twenties, whiskey was not their fathers' drink. Their fathers drank vodka and lime, rum and coke, or pre-mixed spirits. So a new generation has rediscovered whiskey, and is making it its own. This is fertile ground for craft distillers, who can slake the thirst of whiskey's new drinkers with new and bespoke products.

The polarity of cocktails and the growth of mixology haven't hurt either. There's nothing a cool bar person likes more than to provide a customer with a drink made with a craft whiskey and home-made bitters. The growing number of consumers prepared to explore new spirits, drinks and whiskeys provides the incentive for bartenders to create increasingly sophisticated and stylish drinkers—music to any micro-distiller's ears.

Never has there been so much interest in the subject. The Internet has any number of forum sites to discuss all styles of whiskeys and bourbons. Tasting clubs are commonplace; the bigger companies spend big sums to woo the whiskey bloggers, and conduct online tastings with a hashtag for everyone to use to share the event.

America is perfectly placed to benefit most. Someone once said that the difference between a British producer and an American one is that a Briton will invent something and then seek out a market for it. An American producer, on the other hand, will look for a gap in the market and then create something to fill it. At this point, there are plenty of gaps, and a growing audience prepared to create even more. The American craft distilling story is still in its infancy.

OPPOSITE The impressive still room at High West Distillery.

THE GLOBAL PICTURE

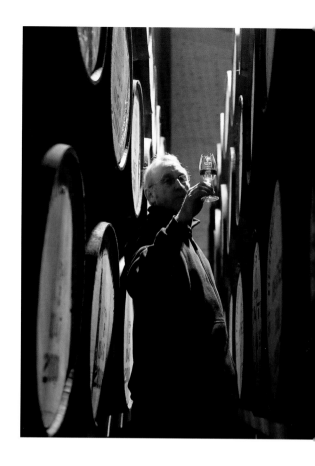

In 2009, Diageo opened its 'super distillery' Roseisle in Morayshire, Scotland, a plant that can produce 12 million liters (2.65 million gallons) of spirit each year.

From its first day of operation, the big demand was not for single malts, but for blended whiskies such as the company's highly successful Johnnie Walker. And as drinkers across the world sought to move to more premium whisky, they eschewed single malts and chose an older and better Johnnie Walker blend instead. Finally Diageo presented a graph showing how much whisky they would need in a few years' time. It was a lot more than they had, even with the increased output from Roseisle.

Such is the nature of making single malt whisky in Scotland: it's impossible to respond quickly to increased demand. Once all the year's three million liters (790,000 gallons) of Talisker have gone, they have gone. You can build an extension to the distillery, but even when that's complete, the standard Talisker is ten years old.

That creates a problem, and one that the bigger suppliers have fixed. They have encouraged new territories to buy in to blends. You can grow a blend far more easily, because when the Talisker dries up it can be replaced in the blend by another malt. There may be some differences, but if you're drinking Johnnie Walker in Mexico how do you know that they're drinking something slightly different in Massachusetts, especially when you mix it?

But to grow your blended whisky, you have to move single malts into them, and that creates shortages. Malts disappear or become very expensive. That creates an opportunity for micro-distillers to step into the breach.

ABOVE Art in a glass: The English Whisky Company brought whisky back to England for the first time in more than 100 years. **OPPOSITE TOP** St George's makes a range of whiskies including spirit made with peated malt. **OPPOSITE BOTTOM** The still room at Bushmills.

And that's exactly what they did. Across the world, craft distillers started producing whisky to satisfy domestic demand. It wasn't easy—with the exceptions of the United States, Canada, and Ireland, any distillery choosing to make whisky does so in the shadow of a large Scottish cloud. Scotland has a 1,000-year head start, and the bar is set high. But many of the new breed have been successful.

Different distillers take different approaches. Many Australian distillers, making big, beefy whiskeys full of taste and often bottled at barrel strength, irreverently crash the whiskey party, bringing fresh thinking to it. They have raised questions about the relevance of age to maturation, citing the heat and climactic extremes in Australia, and drawing attention to accelerated maturation. They have a point: Indian and Taiwanese whisky can be amazing at just four or five years old, and many American distillers don't need lessons on how their environment affects the way wood interacts with spirit.

Sweden brings science to the table, breaking down Scottish single malts and seeking to replicate them. They do this with the finest wood, some of it from countries such as Hungary and Russia, oak not used in Scotland. And they seek out rare and old grains which they believe might produce better quality spirit, even if the yield is lower. The Swedish distilleries currently bottling whiskey—Mackmyra, Spirit of Hven, Smögen, and Box—have all made excellent whiskies, and there are plenty more to come.

Between these two extremes, many other whiskey-makers are producing liquor on stills of varying shapes and sizes. In France and Belgium, England and Wales, and in the Netherlands, there are world-class whiskies being made.

It's in these countries that the debate as to what is and isn't a micro-distillery is brought into sharp focus. St George's Distillery, the first new whisky distillery in England for more than 100 years, makes a little over 100,000 liters (26,000 gallons) a year. But it is big enough to offer visitors a tour, and to have a shop, café and newly built restaurant and functions facility. Penderyn Distillery in Wales was making 90,000 liters (24,000 gallons) of spirit a year, but that has now been expanded to 300,000 liters (79,000 gallons). Nevertheless, the distillery's still on the same rural site as it always was, and the capacity is nothing compared with even modest-sized distilleries in Scotland and the United States.

THE OPPORTUNITY FOR AMERICAN CRAFT DISTILLERS

Different distillers have different aspirations and intentions. Some will be content to produce no more than a few barrels a year and sell them locally or offer them to friends. Others will have bars, restaurants, and hotels, and will make spirits to service their own trade outlets.

Whiskey may be a central focus or a spirit that is made all year round. But other distilleries will slot whiskey into a portfolio of spirits, and will make whiskey only sporadically. For a large number of distillers export isn't an option, either because they do not have the distribution networks or they know from the outset that their products will have nothing more than parochial appeal.

For many, though, there is an irresistible challenge to create a whiskey that is both commercially successful and internationally acclaimed. The likes of Corsair, Balcones, Tuthilltown, Westland, and Michter's are already well along this road. One of the great joys for a fan of what we might term New World Whiskey is attending The Whisky Show which takes place in London every October, and there seeing each year more American craft distillers join the likes of The NZ Whisky Company, Distillerie Warenghem, Amrut, and Starward to rub shoulders with the greatest names of American, Scottish, Irish, and Japanese whiskey.

Some of the newer craft distillers are evolving into brand ambassadors for their whiskeys, whilst other distillers are taking on the business side of their companies. Some are making important decisions over the investment, expansion, and distribution of their whiskey. But whatever their role, they have ensured that whiskey across the world is in an exciting phase of its history.

LEFT Tuthilltown Spirits, now owned by William Grant & Sons. **BELOW** Tuthilltown's Hudson Whiskey is exported across the world.

Has the United States got anything new to add to the party? Most certainly yes, and never more so than in the field of American single malt whiskey. Admittedly, it's still early days, and much of their whiskey is work in progress. Who knows what some of the products will taste like after they have been matured for several years?

Undoubtedly, by using American barley and woods often associated with the production of bourbon, wheat, and rye, American distilleries are capable of producing high-class single malts that are full of flavor, well made and with attitude aplenty—but which taste nothing like Scottish whisky.

That's what Sweden, Australia, and India are doing too— and it's possible that the United States is in the process of creating what will effectively be a brand-new category for whiskey. Now that's exciting.

CHAPTER 3

CRAFT PRODUCERS

In a period of no more than 15 years, America has evolved from a country of less than 10 bourbon producers in Kentucky and a smattering of independent producers scattered across the country, to one where the number of distilleries is 1,500 and climbing. Not all of them are making whiskey, but there are very few States—if any—that don't have a craft whiskey-maker. Many of the new craft producers have moved on from making craft beer and have their own bar or restaurant. But distillers come from all walks of life—from wealthy whiskey enthusiasts to city professionals looking for a new challenge.

AMERICA'S BEST CRAFT DISTILLERIES

The growth of American craft distilling has been astounding. In 2007, the whiskey map of the United States featured no more than a handful of distilleries in Kentucky, with a few others scattered across the country. Most whiskey was corn-based, with a smattering of oddball spirits from the likes of Anchor Distilling and St. George Spirits.

Within a decade, that all changed beyond recognition. The American Distilling Institute welcomed its 1,000th member in 2016, and every week since then the total has increased. Not all the distilleries are making whiskey, and some are making a very basic white form of it. Nevertheless, the number of distillers turning their hand to grain spirit is astounding.

When applied to distilled spirits, 'craft' has a special meaning. The alternative term, micro-distilling, reinforces the notion that 'craft' implies 'small', but this need not be the case at all. The process of distilling whiskey spirit to an acceptable standard is the same in a garage as it is in large purpose-built premises. Take Buffalo Trace, a huge distillery making vast quantities of spirit. It has a tiny experimental still where new whiskey styles are created, and if they're deemed good enough, the levels of raw materials are ramped up and the new spirits are produced in exactly the same way but on a much bigger scale. So it is that the likes of Balcones, Corsair, Angel's Envy, Tuthilltown, and Kentucky Peerless may be considered craft distillers even though they're growing into big businesses with international distribution and networks of ambassadors and marketing folk to promote them.

Craft whiskey, then, is about attitude and about a vision that is maintained, no matter how big a company grows or how many times it changes hands. The largest companies have recognized this and, where they have become involved, have left the distillery staff to get on with the job.

The following pages contain a selection of America's top craft distilleries.

PORT CHILKOOT

LOCATION HAINES, ALASKA **FOUNDED** 2013 **WHISKEY STYLES** BOURBON, RYE **VISITOR FACILITIES** TASTING ROOM ALL YEAR ROUND, WITH REDUCED HOURS IN WINTER

Husband-and-wife team Sean Copeland and Heather Shade have built their distillery from scratch in what was most recently the bakery of Fort Seward, and before that an army outpost for half a century. It's an other-worldly place, above the town of Hines, which is situated on the edge of America's longest and deepest fjord.

The couple imported a still from Louisville. Now they're producing a range of spirits, including an award-winning gin and an absinthe based on a recipe from the 18th century. Heather's a former National Park Service biologist, so she brings a scientific approach to her role as head distiller. 'Our spirits taste like nothing else because they come from a place like nowhere else,' she says.

Port Chilkoot's Boatwright Bourbon is aged for two years in charred white oak barrels, and the unique changes in barometric pressure in the region contribute to a unique Alaskan flavor: 'So when the skies turn cloudy we smile. We figure that someone up there really loves great bourbon.'

The couple also make rye whiskey. Wrack Line Rye is made with 70 per cent organic rye. The couple say it's a bit drier than the distillery's bourbon, but it is ideal for making classic cocktails such as Old Fashioneds and Sazeracs.

3 HOWLS

LOCATION SEATTLE **FOUNDED** 2013 **WHISKEY STYLES** BOURBON, RYE, HOPPED WHISKEY, SINGLE MALT **VISITOR FACILITIES** OFFERS TOURS FOR INDIVIDUALS AND GROUPS. BOOK THROUGH WEBSITE

3 Howls is situated in a 465-sq-m (5,000-sq-ft) warehouse in the industrial heart of Seattle, but the name of the distillery comes from the Scottish whisky island of Islay. It is there that one of the distillery's three founders and owners, Will Maschmeier, first heard the story of the Cù-Sìth (pronounced *koo-shee*). Legend has it that this giant creature—a shaggy dog or wolf—is a harbinger of death that roams Scotland's highlands and moors, howling three times before taking souls to the underworld.

3 Howls makes a full range of spirits, all of them beautifully packaged, and they include a whiskey made with hops, giving it a citrusy, flowery, and spicy flavor with some pine notes.

The single malt whiskey is made with a range of grains including chocolate malt and a peated malt imported from Scotland. All three of the owners, Will, Craig Phalen, and Warren Strasen, are actively involved in the distillation process.

HERITAGE DISTILLING CO.

LOCATION GIG HARBOR, WASHINGTON
FOUNDED 2012 **WHISKEY STYLES** RYE, BOURBON, BLENDED WHISKEY **VISITOR FACILITIES** TOURS ARE ON SATURDAYS, OR WEEKDAYS BY APPOINTMENT

Justin Stiefel was destined to run a distillery. He distilled his first batch of booze in 1987 when he was in seventh grade in Spokane, and thereafter his interest became his ambition: he is now owner of the Heritage Distilling Co.

Since those heady school days, Justin has acquired a chemistry degree, a law degree, and a distilling licence, and now he's in business. Success has been rapid—the distillery marked its second anniversary in 2014 by moving into a bigger waterside site—and every year the distillery's spirits have picked up clutches of awards.

Heritage's Brown Sugar Bourbon is exactly what its name suggests, and the distillery makes a wide range of other whiskeys, including Elk Rider Blended Whiskey, which combines grain and malt whiskeys made at Heritage with Elk Rider Rye Whiskey, which is deliberately smooth and spicy and bottled at 92 proof (46 per cent ABV).

BAINBRIDGE

LOCATION BAINBRIDGE ISLAND, WASHINGTON
FOUNDED 2009 **WHISKEY STYLES** SINGLE GRAIN,
ORGANIC **VISITOR FACILITIES** TOURS AND
TASTINGS ALL YEAR-ROUND

This distillery is the source of one of the most unusual and exciting whiskeys in the world of craft distilling: Bainbridge Yama Mizunara Cask, a single-grain whiskey matured in Japanese mizunara oak. This wood is seldom employed, even in Japan, and Bainbridge was the first non-Japanese distillery to use it. The wood was sourced direct from Japan and then fashioned into small casks. It imparts an exotic, incense-like spiciness to the finished product, and reflects Bainbridge's impressive attention to detail.

Every phase of the production process, from choosing the grain to maturing the spirit, is done on site, and the distillery is quite deliberately 'small batch.'

Bainbridge also makes Bainbridge Battle Point Organic Wheat Whiskey, a single-grain whiskey, which is fermented on estate-grown soft white wheat utilizing a unique combination of yeasts usually employed to make Irish and Scottish whiskies. It is double-distilled and aged for two years in new, No. 3 charred, 45-liter (10-gallon) American white oak barrels. The distillery claims that the resulting whiskey is rich and complex, with notes of vanilla, eucalyptus, and sherry, and a lingering finish with a bit of salt-air brine.

Bainbridge makes all its spirits using organic ingredients, arguing that this ensures the highest quality. Distilling organic spirits is significantly more difficult than making spirits using conventionally grown crops and genetically modified yeasts and enzymes, but the distillery believes firmly in no pain, no gain: 'We feel that the trade-off is worth it,' says a spokesman.

COPPERWORKS

LOCATION SEATTLE, WASHINGTON **FOUNDED** 2013
WHISKEY STYLES SINGLE MALT **VISITOR FACILITIES**
OFFERS TOURS AND TASTINGS OF VARIOUS SPIRITS;
THE DISTILLERY CAN BE HIRED FOR PRIVATE EVENTS

Copperworks was founded in 2013, but it has gone through the gears quickly, making a tasty, balanced, and flavorsome whiskey almost at its first attempt. This remarkable success is attributable at least in part to the diverse but relevant backgrounds of the three founders. Friends Micah Nutt and Jason Parker have long had an interest in brewing. Micah had started home-brewing in the 1980s, and even built his own fully automated brewery. Jason was the first brewer at Pike Place Brewery in 1989, and subsequently worked at various other breweries. When legislation was passed allowing distilling in Washington State the two men decided to try their hands at that process too. They were joined by Jeff Kanof, who was an attorney before he got a taste for distilling.

The distillery's single malt whiskey is its sixth release. It combines seven barrels of Copperworks whiskey matured in new American Oak with a half-cask of whiskey matured in a used Oloroso sherry cask. The result is whiskey with a nose of dried fruit, especially cherry and orange. The flavor has notes of leather, almond paste, and additional dried fruit, with a finish of slight walnut and leather notes.

This whiskey has been making a significant impact, not only on the market in Washington but also on the international stage. Reviewing it in his 2018 *Whisky Bible*, Jim Murray praised it lavishly: 'Copperworks has raised the game considerably,' he wrote, 'A three-course single malt if ever there was one.'

The Copperworks distillery is something of a rare phenomenon: a business that is both of the moment and one to keep an eye on in the future.

OOLA DISTILLERY

LOCATION SEATTLE, WASHINGTON **FOUNDED** 2010
WHISKEY STYLES BOURBON, SINGLE MALT, HYBRIDS
VISITOR FACILITIES THE TASTING ROOM IS OPEN
TUESDAY TO SATURDAY, TOURS ARE HELD ON
SATURDAY AFTERNOONS OR BY APPOINTMENT

OOLA epitomizes everything that is good about innovative and creative craft distilling. In addition to making single malt whiskey and bourbon, it has what it terms its Discourse Whiskey Series. It is under this umbrella that distillery owner Kirby Kallas-Lewis introduces what he calls 'conversations' between different whiskey styles. The first release, for instance, was a four- or five-year-old bourbon further matured in a Cabernet Sauvignon French oak barrel. The second, the Discourse Smoked Whiskey, was made with barley smoked with peat, hardwood, and bourbon wood.

'This sweet and smoky whiskey is then blended with a Highlands Scotch,' says Kirby. 'The goal with this spirit is a subtle dialogue between two very different smoky notes—the classic peated note from the Scotch, and the upstart sweet smoke of our smoked whiskey. The resulting Discourse Smoked Whiskey is a hit amongst bartenders as it gets the creative cocktail ideas flowing immediately.'

Kirby has mixed Highland Scotch, Canadian rye, and an American whiskey made to a bourbon mash bill. 'The goal was to create whiskey where the sum is better than the parts,' he says proudly. 'This is a lovely whiskey where each of the components can shine, but none overpowers the others.'

The experimentation extends to other spirits, and it should therefore come as no surprise to find chili vodka and oak-aged gin in the range. Kirby says that he encourages everyone involved with the making of the distillery's spirits to take pride in them.

His enthusiasm is infectious. 'This is the real deal,' he says. 'Spirits made with a sense of place and a connection to the people who grew the raw ingredients.'

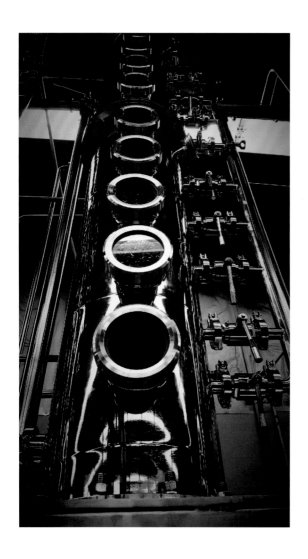

2ND STREET DISTILLING

LOCATION KENNEWICK, WASHINGTON
WHISKEY STYLES SINGLE MALT, RYE
VISITOR FACILITIES TASTING ROOM AND SHOP
OPEN DAILY

One of the most satisfying aspects of American craft distilling is the number of family-run businesses, and distilleries with an energetic and youthful approach to whiskey-making. New distillers across the nation are giving American whiskey a major boost. 2nd Street Distilling is one of the many micro-distilleries where the head distiller is a woman. She's Lora Roser, and she works closely with co-owner Roser Farm to make sure that the distillery gets the finest grains.

In fact, the distillery is co-owned by a group of families, makes a wide range of products, and is another distillery tapping into the Pacific Northwest's rich harvest of natural ingredients for gin, vodka, and liqueurs. All the spirits are produced on three unusual stills. The whiskey, called R J Callaghan, is matured in both American and Hungarian oak.

Reser's Rye has been created in honor of one of the company founder's family, Senator William P Reser, Washington State's first Senator in 1889. 2nd Street Distilling Rye Whiskey is made with 100 per cent Washington rye grain.

BLACKFISH

LOCATION SEATTLE, WASHINGTON **FOUNDED** 2014
WHISKEY STYLES BOURBON, RYE, APPLE PIE
MOONSHINE **VISITOR FACILITIES** TASTINGS AND
TOURS DAILY

Blackfish is a family-run distillery which uses locally harvested produce for what they term a 'harvest-to-glass' operation. In addition to its whiskeys, the distillery makes a broad range of spirits and liqueurs.

'We chose the name "Blackfish" because it captures the adventurous spirit of the Pacific Northwest and the magic we feel as we watch each drop of our spirits emerge from our stills,' says the distillery.

Blackfish bourbon is matured in new medium char American oak barrels and is 90 proof. The distillery's Doc Brewer's Rye whiskey is hard to get hold of. It's made with a recipe of 70 per cent rye and 30 per cent corn and is reputed to go particularly well with vanilla ice cream.

'It has a finish like a Scotch, and has an old soul to match,' says the distillery.

If you're wondering about apple pie moonshine, it's basically vodka instilled with cider and apple pie spices.

2BAR SPIRITS

TATOOSH

LOCATION WASHINGTON **FOUNDED** 2010 **WHISKEY STYLES** BOURBON, MOONSHINE **VISITOR FACILITIES** TOURS ON FRIDAYS AND SATURDAYS

LOCATION SEATTLE, WASHINGTON **FOUNDED** 2009 **WHISKEY STYLES** BOURBON, RYE, SINGLE MALT **VISITOR FACILITIES** NONE

The Kaiser family settled in southern Texas more than a century ago, set up the 2Bar Ranch, and have traded under the 2Bar brand name ever since. 2Bar Spirits was founded in Seattle by Nathan Kaiser in 2010, though the official opening wasn't until 2012. It is a grain-to-glass operation, and with a small team the emphasis is on high quality.

2Bar Spirits is one of many American craft distilleries with a female head distiller, and Maddie Kelly is challenging old conventions head on, making a fine classical butterscotch-tinged bourbon. From 2018, all the distillery's bourbon will be aged for more than two years, and with an age statement.

As for the moonshine, Nathan hints that the Kaiser family might have been familiar with un-aged corn whiskey back in the day. In the same way as the bourbon, all the ingredients are from the American Northwest. Occasional special bottlings are released, but they are highly popular and extremely hard to get hold of.

Tatoosh Distillery was created by friends Joe Eliason and Troy Turner to restore a whiskey-making tradition stretching back 100 years. Troy is of Scottish–Irish descent, and his relatives settled in Louisiana, where his great-grandfather made moonshine through the Prohibition years. He was eventually forced to leave by the authorities, and headed north to Washington State, where he continued to make whiskey.

So Troy grew up with whiskey, and it was perhaps just a matter of time before he started making it himself.

'I grew up with moonshine like an Italian family would have wine on the table,' he recalls. 'We always had some homemade spirit.'

Today Tatoosh makes a distinctive and enjoyable single malt whiskey matured in French oak casks; a bourbon that has a light and citrusy nose and a rugged, woody, and earthy taste; and a rye made with a selection of rye grains and matured in new American oak casks.

WESTLAND

LOCATION SEATTLE, WASHINGTON **FOUNDED** 2010
WHISKEY STYLES SINGLE MALT **VISITOR FACILITIES**
A 90-MINUTE TOUR CAN BE BOOKED ONLINE
IN ADVANCE; THE CANTILEVER ROOM OFFERS
TASTINGS, COCKTAIL FLIGHTS, AND LIGHT BITES

American single malt whiskey is set to become one of the defining trends in world whiskey in the coming years.

But it's still very early days. Most American malt efforts are still very young, and it will be years before we see how the better ones mature with age. It may be we will witness regional differences across the country. After all, if whisky can be influenced by region in a country as small as Scotland, how great will the differences be in the United States, given the distance between Alaska and Texas? Will an American blended whiskey category emerge? Or an entirely new category of whiskey based on an American model? Exciting times indeed.

Certainly Westland is likely to be in the vanguard of any movement. This distillery has achieved masses in its first decade, having attracted the interest of an international drinks company. And that should come as no surprise to anyone who has tasted any of its core range, or its special releases. There can be no doubt that we are seeing the birth of an exciting new style of single malt whiskey.

'A new category of single malt is taking root, one that offers us the chance to make a mark in the world of whiskey,' says the distillery. 'It must be led by our own ideas, done on our own terms, and realized through our own hard work. We have the ingredients here to inspire us to pursue our own unique American single malt to rival the finest whiskies in the world. With each expression we work to create something that both honors the traditions of distilling that we admire, and adds something worthwhile at the same time. Something new and distinctly American.'

The distillery's three core bottlings are influenced by Scotland. Rich and full in flavor, they hold up well against Scotland's single malts. But they are distinctly different too.

They are:

• American Oak: a single malt using Washington State barley matured for 24 months in new American oak;

• Sherry Wood: matured in high-quality ex-Pedro Ximenez and Oloroso casks; and

• Peated, which uses heavily peated barley and is matured in first fill and new American oak casks.

The regional taste issue is already being explored at Westland. Peat is made up of the remains of local flora and fauna that have been compressed over centuries in the ground to form a coal-like, slow-burning fuel. Westland uses local peat, made up of vegetation that has little or nothing in common with the plants, bushes, and trees of Scotland. As a result, the peat affects the barley during the drying process in a different way.

The distillery also makes whiskey matured in Garry Oak oak casks, called Garryana. This oak is unique to Washington and very rare—consequently, a part of the distillery's job as it expands is to find a sustainable source of it. Not an easy task, but further proof that the team at Westland will leave no log unturned in its pursuit of making the finest whiskey.

Westland is situated in the downtown SoDo district of Seattle, and is the country's biggest single malt distillery. It offers space for private events, including weddings, and argues that its unique olde worlde rustic architecture and impressive exposed beams make it a special place for function.

WOODINVILLE

LOCATION WOODINVILLE, WASHINGTON
FOUNDED 2010 **WHISKEY STYLES** BOURBON, RYE,
STRAIGHT AMERICAN WHISKEY **VISITOR FACILITIES**
THE TASTING ROOM IS OPEN DAILY, AND THE
DISTILLERY OFFERS COMPLIMENTARY TOURS ON
FRIDAYS, SATURDAYS, AND SUNDAYS

One of the unsung heroes of American craft distilling is David Pickerell, who was master distiller at Maker's Mark for 14 years, and currently teaches, guides, and advises distilleries across the country. Pickerell is an expert on grain types and wood maturation, and without exception the distilleries he works with are among the country's best. He is a friend and mentor to the men behind Woodinville Distillery, so expect quality whiskey.

The distillery was founded in 2010 by two friends, Orlin Sorensen and Brett Carlile, and is currently producing seven barrels of whiskey a day. They make rye and bourbon, matured in oak that has been seasoned outdoors for two years. The product is a rarity in that it is made with 100 per cent rye. But Woodinville's most fascinating whiskey is the one it calls Straight American Whiskey, which is made from a mixture of rye and corn grains.

WALLA WALLA

LOCATION WALLA WALLA, WASHINGTON
FOUNDED 2007 **WHISKEY STYLES** LIGHT WHISKEY,
BLENDED WHISKEY **VISITOR FACILITIES** VISITS BY
APPOINTMENT

Walla Walla's aim is to combine Old World traditions with New World techniques and cutting-edge technology. It takes its name from a word in the Sahaptin Indian language meaning 'place of many waters.' It is these clean glacial streams flowing down from the Blue Mountains that not only enhance the natural beauty of the region but also provide meltwater irrigation for thousands of acres of grapes, orchards, and fields of grain.

The distillery is environmentally sensitive, and its makers have designed and constructed a range of highly efficient stills made entirely from salvaged, repurposed stainless steel. It has also worked to develop innovative, efficient new vacuum-distillation technologies in its attempts to address some of the world's current environmental and social challenges.

Walla Walla Whiskey is a blended liquor made up of barrel-aged straight whiskeys. The distillery also sells a Light Whiskey, which is a white whiskey with an earthy and sweet corn taste and a smooth finish.

III (THREE) SPIRITS

LOCATION TALENT, OREGON **WHISKEY STYLES**
SINGLE MALT, HYBRID THREE GRAIN **VISITOR**
FACILITIES VISITS BY APPOINTMENT

III Spirits is a small distillery located on a farm in South Oregon. The facility and equipment were purpose-built by the distillery owners, Todd Kemp and Alex Turner. Whiskeys are made by hand on a very small scale. Todd has brewing and distilling experience stretching back to the 1980s; Alex is a marine engineer with a love of science, mechanics, tinkering, and problem-solving.

The influence of Scotland is more obvious than at many other micro-distilleries. Both owners have spent time in Scotland, and Todd in particular visited many of the country's most famous distilleries.

They distill two whiskeys that nod to Scotland. One is an interpretation of a Highland single malt whiskey, aged for one year in small American oak barrels, and then finished in French oak Oregon syrah barrels. The other is an Islay-style peated whisky. Made from heavily peated malt from Scotland, the spirit spends between six months and a year in many different small American oak barrels, some new and some first fill ex-corn and rye whiskey barrels.

The distillery's most unusual whiskey is Jefferson Gold, which is 30 per cent corn, 30 per cent rye, and 40 per cent single malt whiskey. Most of the whiskey is matured for a year, although some of the spirit is younger. Then it is finished in a 135-liter (30-gallon) French medium toast wine barrel.

BULL RUN
DISTILLING CO.

LOCATION PORTLAND, OREGON **FOUNDED** 2010
WHISKEY STYLES BOURBON, AMERICAN
WHISKEY, SINGLE MALT **VISITOR FACILITIES**
THE TASTING ROOM IS OPEN FROM WEDNESDAY
TO SUNDAY

Bull Run Distilling Company was set up in 2010 by Lee Medoff. He was born and raised in Oregon and started his professional life as a brewer. He moved on to wine-making, and eventually became a distiller in 1998. He set up House Spirits Distillery in 2004, making the award-winning Aviation Gin. Finally the lure of making dark spirits, and in particular an Oregon single malt whiskey, resulted in him setting up Bull Run.

What sets his distillery apart is the way it combines some of the techniques of the world of brewing with those of distilling. The wash is made at Burnside Brewery and fermented at the distillery with ale yeast. The result is a high alcohol, dry, beer, which is rich in esters.

'The ester creation is on purpose,' says Lee. 'It concentrates well in the distillate, giving the grainy, cereal-driven spirit with a surprising brandy-like nose. Once in the barrel it disappears, and so we wait until it returns.

'Barrel aging defines and refines the whiskey. We strongly believe that malted barley is uniquely suited to stand up to new oak casks. The intensity of the new oak with its char wrestles with the richness of the malt until a balance is found. The signal for us is the re-emergence of those fruity notes first developed years back in the fermented wash. The result is a whiskey at once familiar yet surprisingly new.'

Bull Run sells whiskey at standard strength of 44.54 per cent (89.08 proof) and cask strength; it also makes bourbon, and an American whiskey.

CLEAR CREEK/ HOOD RIVER

LOCATION PORTLAND, OREGON **FOUNDED** 1985
WHISKEY STYLES SINGLE MALT, HOPPED WHISKEY
VISITOR FACILITIES THE TASTING ROOM IS OPEN
EVERY WEEKDAY AFTERNOON

Clear Creek and Hood River distilling are linked together because, although Clear Creek Distillery was founded in 1985, Hood River Distillers took it over in 2014. Both still have their own websites, but they have much in common with each other and their main whiskey is sold on both sites.

Clear Creek is traditionally best known for its eau-de-vies—clear fruit brandies that have won numerous awards and are widely regarded as some of the finest spirits of their type in the world.

Meanwhile over at Hood River, the distillery bottles a range of whiskeys, including imported Canadian whiskies under the name Pendleton, and a hopped whiskey created in association with the local Double Mountain Brewery.

The whiskey that both distillery websites promote is their most famous: McCarthy's Oregon Single Malt Whiskey. The whiskey is sold internationally, and has received a range of awards and accolades. It is distilled in a Holstein pot still using one-pass distillation. The premium, non-chill-filtered product is then barrel-aged in air-dried Oregon oak barrels. The result is a smooth and very drinkable three-year-old whiskey.

Its future success has seemed assured ever since it achieved a score of 97 and was awarded the Chairman's Trophy for the Best American Single Malt Whiskey at the 2017 Ultimate Beverage Challenge. It also won Gold Medals at both the renowned 2017 San Francisco World Spirits Competition and the 2017 Los Angeles International Spirits Competition.

OREGON SPIRIT DISTILLERS

LOCATION BEND, OREGON **FOUNDED** 2009
WHISKEY STYLES BOURBON, WHEAT, RYE **VISITOR**
FACILITIES A TASTING ROOM AND A LOUNGE NAMED
BARREL THIEF FOR PRIVATE FUNCTIONS AND EVENTS

Although Oregon Spirit Distillers make a range of different spirits, whiskey is key to their operation. The distillery was set up by Brad Irwin, who was passionate about comparing and contrasting different whiskey styles.

The distillery's in Bend, Oregon, for three reasons: firstly, it's Brad's hometown; secondly, because the three basic ingredients of whiskey are not only in plentiful supply in this part of Oregon, but they are also of the finest quality; and thirdly, because the distillery fits right in with a town that is currently thriving on the back of a range of craft businesses.

The distillery's bourbon is made with four grains rather than the standard three, with the corn at the heart of the whiskey joined by malted barley, wheat, and rye. It is aged for four years. The company's wheat whiskey is made with Oregon winter wheat, rye, and barley, and is also matured for four years.

RANSOM

LOCATION SHERIDAN, OREGON **FOUNDED**
1997 **WHISKEY STYLES** STRAIGHT AMERICAN
WHISKEY, HYBRID **VISITOR FACILITIES** A TASTING
ROOM IS OPEN THURSDAYS TO SUNDAYS

Founded by Tad Seestadt, Ransom moved many times before reaching its current location, the 16-hectare (40-acre) organic Ransom Farm. Tad's operation combines old-fashioned production methods with innovative whiskey-making. All spirits are made on an alembic French pot still, and all cuts are made manually by taste and smell. But there is nothing traditional about the distillery's use of mash bills and casks.

Two of Ransom's whiskeys stand out. The first, named Emerald, is the distillery's attempt to recreate the taste of 19th-century Irish whiskey. It is widely believed that Irish whiskey in the 1800s would have tasted nothing like it does today. Trouble is, there is none of it left to find out. But in 1865 a British excise agent wrote down the mash bill for an Irish whiskey, and it was discovered by acclaimed writer, archivist, and cocktail expert David Wondrich, who passed it on to Ransom. Spirit made to the recipe of the original mash bill is matured in American and French oak, making a highly aromatic whiskey.

The other star product, named Rye, Barley, Wheat Whiskey, is made with six grain components and matured in used 227 liter (60-gallon) toasted French oak barrels that previously contained pinot noir. The cask adds richness and depth to the whiskey while leaving the grainy notes in place, making for a complex and rewarding premium spirit.

ROGUE SPIRITS

LOCATION NEWPORT, OREGON **FOUNDED** 1998
WHISKEY STYLES SINGLE MALT, RYE, FLAVORED,
HYBRID **VISITOR FACILITIES** A TASTING ROOM IS
OPEN MONDAYS TO SUNDAYS

Rogue describes itself as a small revolution, and that's bang on. It began with a group of friends with a desire to run a brew pub and make great beer. A pub was duly opened with a brewery in the basement. Expansion thereafter was rapid. A fortuitous encounter with Mohava Niemi, founder of Mo's Restaurants, led to a new and bigger brew pub in Newport.

Rogue, with its relaxed, amicable, and positive approach to brewing, and its distinctive red star and stylish bottles, was at the forefront of the craft brewing revolution that hit America in the 1990s, and has rightly grown into a substantial and respected business.

When the craft distilling craze swept through America, it was no surprise that Rogue decided to seek a piece of the action—and its whiskeys reflect its beers. In fact, its most famous whiskey, a single malt named Dead Guy Whiskey, is made with the same three malts as its award-winning Dead Guy Ale, which is inspired by the style of a German maibock.

This distillery has plenty of exciting products, but nothing as far out as Rogue Chipotle Whiskey.

'It begins in the dirt at Rogue Farms in Independence, Oregon, where we plant, grow, and harvest our jalapeño peppers,' says the distillery. 'We then take them to our distillery, where they are dried and smoked over cherry and alder wood. This turns our farm fresh jalapeños into the sweet, smoky, and spicy chipotle peppers we use three ways in our Chipotle Whiskey. Rogue Chipotle Whiskey is brewed, distilled, and barrel-aged with our chipotle peppers for three times the flavor—and a touch more heat.'

The resulting drink is palate-challenging but generally regarded as a taste well worth acquiring.

AMADOR WHISKEY CO.

LOCATION ST HELENA, CALIFORNIA **FOUNDED** 2012
WHISKEY STYLES BOURBON, HOPPED WHISKEY

The foundation date here is a little misleading because the Amador Whiskey Company is owned by Trinchero Family Estates, a Napa Valley company which owns vineyards and has more than 45 wine and spirits brands. The business was established more than 70 years ago by an Italian immigrant, but spirits were added only in 2012. The people behind Amador are totally transparent about their Double Barrel Bourbon, publicly declaring that they buy in Kentucky bourbon and then finish it in their own wine barrels. The company's Ten Barrels release is altogether more exciting. Crafted by Charbay's master distillers Miles and Marko Karakasevic, it is a blend of 60 per cent straight malt whiskey and 40 per cent hop-flavored whiskey distilled from a craft IPA beer. Both components were aged separately for more than two years in French oak wine barrels before being married together. The blend is then put in to the Estate's Chardonnay barrels for another two years before being bottled.

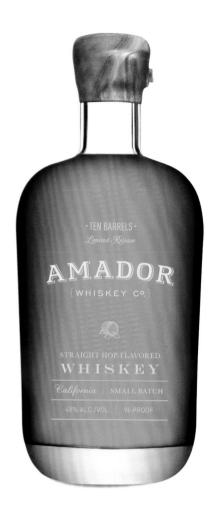

ASCENDANT SPIRITS

LOCATION BUELLTON, CALIFORNIA **FOUNDED** 2013 **WHISKEY STYLES** BOURBON, CORN, MOONSHINE **VISITOR FACILITIES** TOURS AND TASTINGS ARE AVAILABLE

'Before I was 30, I'd never made spirits,' says Ascendant's founder, Steve Gertman. 'I made television shows. I made some money. I met celebrities. But I wanted to make something that mattered. So I quit. I always loved the way whiskey brought people together. I loved the tradition. I loved the craft. I dreamt of becoming a master distiller. So I became a student. And flying to my first whiskey-making class, sitting in between the life I left and the one I raced toward, I felt like anything was possible.'

This is the essence of craft distilling. Although Ascendant Spirits is in a region where wine-making is the norm, the warm climate is ideal for the production of spirits, too. Gertman 's flagship bourbon has a high rye content, and each small batch is made from eight hand-chosen barrels, each aged for more than five years. The distillery also makes one bourbon that is wheated and another that is finished in port barrels.

CUTWATER SPIRITS

LOCATION SAN DIEGO, CALIFORNIA **FOUNDED** 2007
WHISKEY STYLES SINGLE MALT, BOURBON
VISITOR FACILITIES TOURS AND TASTINGS AVAILABLE

They're an ambitious bunch at Cutwater, and keen to go on a journey of discovery as they look for exciting ways of making top-quality spirits. They started off as an offshoot of Ballast Point Brewing, but are now a separate company. In 2016, they started work on a much bigger distillery—4,645 sq m (50,000 sq f)—and in the following year they opened a restaurant and tasting room, where they indulge their passion for cocktails. The distillery makes a range of spirits, including a single malt whiskey and a bourbon. The two have much in common: they both make use of the finest ingredients; they are both distilled in small batches; they are both matured in heavily charred barrels; and they are both bottled under the Devil's Share moniker at a strength of 46 per cent ABV. The distillery holds a series of events throughout the year, and is gaining a strong reputation for its drinks and restaurant food: both its whiskeys have won top awards at America's leading spirits competitions.

DORWOOD DISTILLERY

LOCATION BUELLTON, CALIFORNIA **FOUNDED** 2012 **WHISKEY STYLES** MALT WHISKEY **VISITOR FACILITIES** DORWOOD CAN BE HIRED FOR PRIVATE EVENTS

DorWood is ran by Jeff and Jay Lockwood. Jeff and partner Joanne Lockwood originally lived in Santa Barbara and worked as real estate developers for 25 years. They then retired and for 10 years owned and operated the Cavalli Farms and Vineyard, running an equine business and making small-batch wines for their exclusive wine club. Jay gave up a 38-year career in Custom Home Industry to become head distiller of DorWood Distillery. The new venture stemmed from a conversation between the brothers about how hard it was, despite the growing craft spirits industry, to get hand-made, small-batch spirits. The brothers' approach to distilling is the same as to wine-making, using as many local ingredients as possible, and aiming to be a complete grain-to-glass operation. They describe their White Hawk as whiskey even though it is un-aged, but what makes it different from other white dog spirits is the fact that it is made with malted barley, and the barley is smoked with mesquite rather than with peat.

DO GOOD DISTILLERY

LOCATION MODESTO, CALIFORNIA **FOUNDED** 2013
WHISKEY STYLES BOURBON, SINGLE MALT, RYE,
HYBRID **VISITOR FACILITIES** THE DISTILLERY OFFERS
TOURS AND TASTINGS, AND HOLDS A RANGE OF
EVENTS

The name alludes to Benjamin Franklin's maxim, 'You do well by doing good.' That's the motto that founder Jim Harrelson lived by until his death, aged 38 years, from a heart attack in July 2017. His widow Liz said he never set himself a goal that he didn't accomplish. He was a keen runner, a standout baseball pitcher, and an avid home brewer. Before he began distilling, he spent 14 years at the Stanislaus County Sheriff's Department, serving as a member of the bomb squad and as a training officer. Jim died while doing what he loved. He was president of the California Artisanal Distillers Guild and helped to lobby successfully to change the law and allow small-batch distillers to sell their products on their properties. Do Good makes a hop-flavored whiskey, and whiskeys made with barley smoked over beech and cherrywood, as well as over peat.

GREENBAR DISTILLERY

LOCATION LOS ANGELES, CALIFORNIA
FOUNDED 2004 **WHISKEY STYLES** SINGLE
MALT WHISKEY **VISITOR FACILITIES**
TOURS AND TASTINGS PLUS COCKTAIL-
MAKING LESSONS

Greenbar was set up ahead of the current craft distilling boom, and has the distinction of being the first new distillery in Los Angeles since the end of Prohibition in 1933. It offers a wide range of organic spirits, and a fully interactive visitor experience with in-depth tours, a choice of six spirit tasting options, and cocktail evenings when experienced mixologists offer guests expert advice as they prepare their own cocktails. Tasting sessions to seek out new flavors are held regularly.

Greenbar's concoctions include liqueurs, syrups, and bitters. Its organic whiskey is highly unusual. Slow Hand Organic Six Woods Whiskey is the first to be matured in six different kinds of wood—white oak, grape vine, hickory, mulberry, red oak, and maple. The resulting drink is complex. It imparts notes of butterscotch, plum, currant, clove, and black tea. A cask-strength version is also available. And Greenbar plants one tree for every bottle of whiskey sold.

J. RILEY DISTILLERY

LOCATION REDLANDS, CALIFORNIA **FOUNDED** 2015
WHISKEY STYLES WHITE WHISKEY, BOURBON
VISITOR FACILITIES THE TASTING ROOM IS OPEN
WEDNESDAY TO SUNDAY, AND ALSO HOLDS EVENTS

SEVEN STILLS DISTILLERY

LOCATION SAN FRANCISCO, CALIFORNIA
FOUNDED 2013 **WHISKEY STYLES** HOP-BASED
WHISKEYS, HYBRIDS **VISITOR FACILITIES** DAILY
TOURS AND TASTINGS

J. Riley is Jason Riley, who set up his distillery in 2015 with three launch whiskeys. He puts his passion for whiskey-making down to his Irish ancestry and to the fact that two of his ancestors were bootleggers who went to jail. His distillery now makes about 600 bottles of whiskey a week.

California Clear is described as 'original, truly American white whiskey unlike any other.' It is made from a bourbon mash dominated by non-genetically modified organic corn and malted barley. It is matured for 30 days in heavily charred American white oak casks, and then the color is carefully removed, leaving the charred oak flavor in the spirit.

Riley's 1775 whiskey is named for the year in which untrained Americans fought the British as the United States sought independence. Made of corn, rye, and malted barley, it has layers of honeyed raisins, followed by herbaceous tones of anise and peppered cinnamon, with a sweet and spicy finish. Jeremiah Riley Bourbon is described by Jason as 'our finest and proudest American spirit.'

Seven Stills Distillery grew out of a craft brewery operation. It is the creation of Tim Obert and Clint Potter. Their early spirits were distilled at Stillwater Distillery, but Seven Stills came into its own in 2016, when it moved to a central San Francisco site and began producing vodka and whiskey. At the heart of the whiskey is craft beer, and the distillery has experimented with a host of beer styles, including offbeat ones such as peanut butter milk stout, sourdough beer, and coffee porter. The distillery has two ranges of whiskey: the Seven Stills range, comprising seven whiskeys to reflect San Francisco's seven hills; and the Collaboration Series, for which the distillery works with local breweries, using their beers to make the whiskey. To get a sense of the innovation going on here, take the distillery's Frambooze, which sounds amazing. The base framboise was brewed at Libertine Brewing in San Luis Obispo. The sour beer was then trucked to the distillery, where it was aged in new American oak, and then finished in Libertine Framboise barrels with raspberries.

LOST SPIRITS

LOCATION LOS ANGELES, CALIFORNIA
FOUNDED 2010 **WHISKEY STYLES** SINGLE MALT
VISITOR FACILITIES YES BUT ONLY BY APPOINTMENT

Lost Spirits is using science to investigate new flavors, and is pushing out daringly into uncharted territory as it seeks to innovate and change conventional perceptions of what whiskey is. The distillery makes single malt, and has experimented extensively with smoking and peating methods. It has introduced a highly advanced computer system to take over the production process so that the team can focus on experimentation. While it has become fashionable to adopt labor-intensive and traditional methods of production, Lost Spirits has gone totally the other way, harnessing high-tech equipment to help make whiskey. The team even refers to its workplace as 'The Lab.' In 2013 the distillery launched Umami, a single malt whiskey made using brine drawn from the Pacific Ocean. This ingredient imparted a savory taste and complexity not found in other whiskeys. The team found that yeast cells thicken in sea brine fermentations. They also reduce their reproduction levels and live much longer or in some cases become seemingly 'immortal.' The laboratory approach has paid off handsomely, and Lost Spirits has had to move to new premises more than once. It is now in downtown Los Angeles, and boasts advanced technology and cutting-edge distilling techniques.

'Designed with the booze geek in mind, it is highly personal, educational and expressive,' says the distillery. 'Industry guests are allowed in, but by invitation only.'

The distillery's latest creation is made up of Islay peated malt but adapted under its own laboratory conditions. It is radically different from pretty much anything else ever.

'It's a peated malt so controversial we called it Abomination,' says the distillery.

SONOMA COUNTY DISTILLING CO.

LOCATION SONOMA COUNTY, CALIFORNIA
FOUNDED 2010 **WHISKEY STYLES** RYE, BOURBON, WHEAT **VISITOR FACILITIES** SEMINARS AND TOURS

Sonoma County Distilling Co. was founded in 2010 by Adam Spiegel, who was born and raised in San Francisco and who fell in love with Sonoma County on regular visits to the region's beaches, attending concerts and tagging along with his parents at wine-tasting events. He got a passion for distilling from 2008, when he helped out a distilling friend in Santa Rosa and realized what quality could be achieved through micro-distilling. Spiegel was ahead of the craft distilling boom:

'While working with great master distillers and blenders over the years, I've honed my skills to continually raise the bar with each new product and batch,' he says.

'There are no "masters" here. We're just regular people striving every day to better themselves and their craft. I like to say we're making whiskeys in a small way for a big world.'

Sonoma makes standard and cask-strength versions of rye, as well as one with grain smoked over a cherrywood fire. The distillery has three styles of bourbon: one with grain smoked over cherrywood; one high in wheat, making for a softer drink; and one high in rye, for added spiciness. The distillery's 2nd Chance Wheat Whiskey comes in two formats, one matured in ex-bourbon or rye casks, and the other additionally aged in ex-Cognac barrels.

Sonoma is environmentally friendly and energy-efficient. It is a grain-to-glass distillery that tries to source its raw materials locally wherever possible.

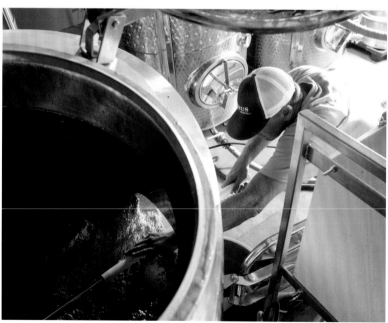

VENUS SPIRITS

LOCATION SANTA CRUZ, CALIFORNIA **FOUNDED** 2013 **WHISKEY STYLES** RYE, BOURBON, SINGLE MALT **VISITOR FACILITIES** TASTINGS AND COCKTAIL SESSIONS ARE HELD ON FRIDAYS, SATURDAYS AND SUNDAYS

American craft distilling is not yet near reaching its peak, and while some predict that distilling will emulate craft brewing and shake out many of its numbers as the market consolidates, it may not happen. There are two crucial differences: one, it takes more money and effort to make whiskey than beer, so investors are more likely to be in for the long haul; and two, the industry is in a state of flux, with many counties and even states still 'dry' but potentially open to change.

According to Sean Venus, founder of Venus Spirits, 'The number of new distilleries will continue to rise around the world, and especially here in the United States, as barriers to entry continue to fall away.'

Venus is currently producing organic, small-batch whiskey and a range of other spirits. Most notable are its three types of Wayward Whiskey, which Sean describes as having 'a 60 per cent rye mash bill, a much lower percentage than a lot of modern ryes. The flavor is balanced out with corn, wheat, and barley, resulting in a spirit that is slightly sweet.'

He continues: 'We are not just trying to replicate traditional American whiskey. Our goal is to push the boundaries and develop new flavors and expressions while highlighting traditional approaches.'

8 FEATHERS DISTILLERY

LOCATION BOISE, IDAHO **FOUNDED** 2013 **WHISKEY STYLES** BOURBON, MOONSHINE, HYBRID **VISITOR FACILITIES** THE DISTILLERY HOSTS TOURS

8 Feathers was founded by two couples with a wealth of different experience that collectively ensures they're covering all bases. Marjie Lowe has a background in events management; Greg Lowe has 30 years' experience in technology; Sandee Price is an expert in marketing and advertising; and Larry Price has a career in sales and sales management behind him. The quartet set up the distillery in 2013 and a year later brought in Rick McKinney, a skilled engineer, to help with distilling.

8 Feathers makes standard whiskeys such as bourbon, but it does more unusual spirits too. Vanilla Bean is just that: a whiskey infused with Madagascan vanilla beans to provide a sweet, creamy, spicy taste. In the past the distillery has also made teff whiskey. Teff is the smallest grain in the world; it originated in North Africa and is now grown in Idaho.

8 Feathers also offers would-be distillers a two-day course in the theory and practice of the art led by the head distiller.

BRANDED HEARTS DISTILLERY

LOCATION RENO, NEVADA **FOUNDED** 2015 **WHISKEY STYLES** BOURBON, WHEAT **VISITOR FACILITIES** THE DISTILLERY OFFERS TOURS AND TASTINGS

Branded Hearts Distillery was founded by Ryan Cherrick and Joshua Nichols when they took a detour from their careers in law enforcement. They set about making rum and whiskey, and were acclaimed for both. They say they are drawn to craft distilling because they are able to involve themselves in all parts of the process, even printing the labels.

'The science behind it is quite romantic,' says Ryan, 'but that's not what the name implies.' He explains that a branded heart refers to the portion of spirit kept during distillation that is aged in charred oak barrels. But it implies something else as well: 'When you walk away from something having had a good experience, it stays with you. You now have a branded heart,' says Josh.

Branded Hearts makes bourbon with oats in its mash bill, and wheat whiskey made with hard red and soft white wheat from Nevada, and bottled at 40 per cent and 59 per cent ABV.

VERDI LOCAL DISTILLERY

LOCATION VERDI, NEVADA **FOUNDED** 2014
WHISKEY STYLES FLAVORED WHISKEYS **VISITOR FACILITIES** YOU WON'T NEED LONG

Verdi Local looks nothing like a distillery. A mile from the California border, it is an unassuming little house between a saloon and a coffee shop. At one time it may also have been the smallest distillery in the world, though a garden shed in Angus, Scotland, and an operation launched in November 2017 in Canada may since have pipped it. Inside are a couple of tiny 117-liter (26-gallon) stills, two fermenters, and a bar. But Verdi Local is important because owners Jeremy and Katey Baumann are well and truly going in their own direction, specializing in flavored whiskeys. Spirits include off-the-wall ideas such as a 33 per cent ABV apple cinnamon whiskey, a garlic-flavored whiskey, a mahogany-flavored whiskey (made in stainless steel tanks with mahogany soaked in the spirit), and a lemon-flavored whiskey. A seasonal whiskey called Headless Horseman released in 2017 combined pumpkin with cinnamon.

HIGH WEST DISTILLERY

LOCATION PARK CITY, UTAH **FOUNDED** 2006
WHISKEY STYLES BOURBON, RYE, SMOKED BOURBON **VISITOR FACILITIES** TOURS, TASTINGS AND WHISKEY EVENTS AT DIFFERENT SITES

High West is one of the great success stories of American craft distilling, and has grown from a local husband-and-wife team operation into an internationally acclaimed whiskey brand currently being made at four separate sites. It was launched by David and Jane Perkins. David is a former biochemist who became aware of the links between his work and the fermenting and distilling process when he visited Maker's Mark distillery in Kentucky. The couple started distilling in Park City in 2007 from an old livery stable and garage, and they also have a saloon there, serving as a gastro-distillery, featuring alpine-inspired western food. In 2015, High West opened a new distillery in Wanship, Utah, which offers educational whiskey tasting, pairings, and tours, and houses a 7,200-liter (1,600-gallon) copper pot still. The whiskeys are outstanding. High West produces bourbon and two styles of rye: Double Rye and Rendezvous Rye. Best of all is Campfire, a peated bourbon, inspired by a dessert of ripe honeydew melon drizzled with peated syrup, tasted at Bruichladdich distillery on Islay.

SUGAR HOUSE DISTILLERY

LOCATION SALT LAKE CITY, UTAH **FOUNDED** 2013
WHISKEY STYLES MALT WHISKEY, BOURBON
VISITOR FACILITIES CONDUCTS TOURS

America's craft distilling industry started as a trickle, then grew rapidly as new distillers showed maturity and responsibility in their working methods, and one state after another relaxed the rules and opened the door for more distillers to follow. But the change wasn't a uniform one, and in Utah would-be distiller James Fowler had to play a long waiting game before he was permitted to start making spirits. But the lengthy wait goes with the territory when it comes to making premium spirits, and since his first vodka rolled off the stills, James has been happy to grow his business one step at a time, increasing capacity as and when it was right to do so.

Sugar House began making whiskey in 2014. It was a malt whiskey, matured in tiny 45-liter (10-gallon) and 67-liter (15-gallon) barrels to maximize the effects of the wood The distillery now makes bourbon using local grains.

ARIZONA DISTILLING CO.

LOCATION RENO, NEVADA **FOUNDED** 2007
WHISKEY STYLES BOURBON, RYE, WHEAT, MALT, MOONSHINE **VISITOR FACILITIES** THE DISTILLERY HAS MOVED TO A NEW SITE AND WILL OFFER TOURS WHEN THE MOVE IS COMPLETED

'First the West, then the World' states the company's website, and the distillery declares that its mission is to take Arizona to the world, one glass at a time. So after ten years the news that all distillery tours were to be cancelled until further notice, as the business sets about moving to a bigger and better location, suggests that the plan for global supremacy is moving in the desired direction.

'We devote ourselves to every spirit with exceptional ingredients and the utmost care,' the team says. 'Ours are the drinks of outlaws, handcrafted spirits that refuse to be denied or forgotten. We're carving our place in history, and we want you to be a part of it.'

That might sound arrogant, but then you take note of the medal haul the distillery has picked up and it all makes sense.

Arizona Distilling Co. makes a fine bourbon and rye, but of special note is its Humphrey's Arizona Malt Whiskey, created in partnership with a prominent local brewery, and its Desert Durum Wheat Whiskey.

HAMILTON DISTILLERS

LOCATION TUCSON, ARIZONA **FOUNDED** 2006 **WHISKEY STYLES** MALT WHISKEY **VISITOR FACILITIES** THE DISTILLERY HOSTS PUBLIC AND PRIVATE TOURS

Some people's journey from one career to the world of micro-distilling can be very strange indeed. In the case of Stephen Paul and his team, the idea came from a chance conversation over a glass of Scotch and a barbecue.

'We were barbecuing with mesquite scraps from our custom furniture company, Arroyo Design,' Stephen says. 'And we had a thought. Why couldn't we malt barley over mesquite instead of peat, for a single malt whiskey with a flavor distinctive to the American Southwest?'

Arroyo Design had started life the same way, taking wood from Arizona and making it into furniture through careful wood selection and attention to detail. So Stephen set about learning how to distill, and experimenting on a small still. And in 2011, with daughter in tow, he graduated to a 180-liter (40-gallon) still, and set up Hamilton Distillers properly. Hamilton moved again in 2014 and now has three malt whiskeys on the market under the name Del Bac, including one that is smoked over Arizona's most predominant mesquite species.

THUMB BUTTE DISTILLERY

LOCATION PRESCOTT, ARIZONA **FOUNDED** 2013 **WHISKEY STYLES** BOURBON, MALT, RYE **VISITOR FACILITIES** THE DISTILLERY HOSTS TOURS AND TASTINGS

It's not often that a distillery makes a virtue of the fact that its spirit is very young, but Thumb Butte Distillery does.

'Our whiskey is less than two years old,' say the distillery's founders, Dana Murdock, James Bacigalupi, and Scott Holderness. 'We use old-world technologies that until recently have fallen into disuse. One such technique is motion/vibration and mimics the old "technology" of putting whiskey in barrels and shipping it from place to place.

'The Japanese have developed many new technologies to create a world-class single malt in a few months. Smaller barrels have a greater liquid-to-wood ratio.'

Thumb Butte makes bourbon and rye, and is experimenting with single malts matured in barrels that previously held the distillery's Bloody Basin Bourbon. The makers explain: 'We have started a program of introducing smoke to our single malt. We started with cherrywood-smoked malted barley as a small percentage of the mash bill. We are planning to employ mesquite and maple in search of the perfect flavor.'

ROUGHSTOCK DISTILLERY

LOCATION BOZEMAN, MONTANA **FOUNDED** 2008
WHISKEY STYLES BOURBON, RYE, CORN, WHEAT,
MALT **VISITOR FACILITIES** THE DISTILLERY
HOSTS TASTINGS

Montana is natural whiskey-making territory, with an ideal climate and an abundance of high-quality water. This distillery is the first legal distillery in the state for more than 100 years. They are very proud of the fact that the entire whiskey-making process is carried out at the distillery using old-fashioned hands-on methods. The malt whiskey here is made in an unusual way. The mash is not drained to form a wash, but instead it is transferred whole into two open-top wooden fermenters, where it remains for 72 hours.

Roughstock makes bourbon, rye, and un-aged corn whiskey. It also makes a special wheat whiskey with local white spring wheat. Once distilled, it is aged in barrels that were used to make malt. After the whiskey is matured, it is finished in a heavily toasted French oak cask for a few months which adds body and complexity on the finish.

STONEHOUSE DISTILLERY

LOCATION WINSTON, MONTANA **FOUNDED** 2014
WHISKEY STYLES BOURBON, WHEAT, RYE, CORN,
SINGLE MALT **VISITOR FACILITIES** TOURS AND
TASTINGS BY APPOINTMENT ONLY

John Grahlert is a retired policeman from Germany; his wife Snezhi is from Bulgaria; they met in the United States. In 2011 they shared a cocktail and were left unimpressed, concluding that they could do better themselves. They both have distilling backgrounds. Snezhi's family recipes for hand-crafting spirits were passed down from one generation to another. John's family was involved in developing clear-grain spirits.

In 2012, they traveled to Europe to explore regional distilling techniques. In Bulgaria, they met monks who shared ancient brandy-making practices. In Germany, they talked with several distillers. In Scotland, they received a week's training at the Glendronach Distillery.

Now they make a range of rums and a range of whiskeys including, somewhat bizarrely, Bon Fire Bourbon, named after the late AC/DC singer Bon Scott, who is pictured on the label.

TRAILHEAD SPIRITS

LOCATION BILLINGS, MONTANA **FOUNDED** 2013
WHISKEY STYLES RYE, WHEAT, FLAVORED
VISITOR FACILITIES THE DISTILLERY HAS A SIZEABLE
TASTING ROOM OPEN SIX DAYS A WEEK

Casey and Steffanie McGowan, both brought up in Montana, believe that owning a distillery was their destiny. Before they realized their dream and overcame bureaucratic red tape to obtain a distilling licence, Casey sold commercial insurance products and ran a local office, and Steffanie worked in real estate. Casey's family has run the farm from which the couple take most of their grain for more than a century, and he also has ancestral links to one of the region's most accomplished moonshine bootleggers.

Trailhead makes a range of spirits including three whiskeys named Highwood. They are a rye, a wheat whiskey made with farm winter wheat, and Highwood Chocolate Flavored Whiskey, made from Montana wheat and specialty malts flavored with dark roasted cocoa nibs and vanilla beans. This opens with a sweetness followed by notes of caramel and toffee before a cocoa finish. The distillery has a large tasting room which the McGowans say has become an iconic downtown destination.

WYOMING WHISKEY

LOCATION KIRBY, WYOMING **FOUNDED** 2009
WHISKEY STYLES BOURBON **VISITOR FACILITIES**
TOURS ARE HELD MONDAY TO FRIDAY

So there you are at work when your employers announce that they want to make bourbon and they want you to help. Problem is, none of you knows how to do it. That's how it was for Wyoming Whiskey cofounder David DeFazio, who had been an attorney at Brad and Kate Mead's firm in 2006 when they had an idea for practicing something other than law.

So what to do? David enlisted the help of consultants before hiring legendary Maker's Mark distiller Steve Nally. Smart move. They were distilling by 2009, and since then some seriously heavyweight whiskey folk have praised it. A lot.

Wyoming makes single-barrel, small-batch, and barrel-strength bourbon, aged for at least five years. It is distilled from 68 per cent corn, 18 per cent wheat, and 14 per cent malted barley. The whiskey is put into the barrel at 55 per cent ABV, and after it has matured it's brought to 88 proof (44 per cent ABV).

BRECKENRIDGE DISTILLERY

LOCATION BRECKEKENRIDGE, COLORADO
FOUNDED 2007 **WHISKEY STYLES** BOURBON,
SPECIAL FINISHES, MALT, SPICED **VISITOR**
FACILITIES TOURS DAILY; VIP TOURS; A
RESTAURANT, AND A BAR

Bryan Nolt made his living as a physician until 2007, when he decided he would like to run a distillery. So he cashed in his life savings, his kids' college fund, and eventually his house to cover monthly payroll and taxes.

'We bootstrapped our way through the early years, loving every minute of it,' he says. 'Today it would be fair to call us a successful distillery. We made it this far by checking our egos at the door, assembling the best cast and crew, and exhibiting the tenacity of a starving honey badger.'

The clutch of awards displayed on the company's website would indicate that the effort has paid off. Today Breckenridge, which lays claim to being the highest distillery in the world, makes a a blended bourbon that contains its own bourbon as well as bourbons from Kentucky, Tennessee, and Indiana. It also makes bourbons finished in port and sherry; whiskey distilled from malt spirit; and a whiskey flavored with winter spices and roots.

DANCING PINES DISTILLERY

LOCATION COLORADO **FOUNDED** 2008
WHISKEY STYLES BOURBON, RYE **VISITOR**
FACILITIES THE DISTILLERY HAS A TASTING ROOM
AT ESTES PARK

The name of the distillery is taken from a moment when founders Kristian and Kimberly Naslund were renovating their mountain cabin and noticed the snow-covered pines outside the window swaying in time to the music they were playing.

'If you are alone in the Colorado wilderness, the trees take on a life of their own,' says Kimberly. 'It doesn't matter if it is summer or winter, they may be weighed down and fat with snow, or fragrant with pine sap. The breeze starts up the valley, and you can hear it travel your way. As it rustles through the pine needles…the trees begin to dance. Once you've experienced this phenomenon, the wilderness will be forever tangled in your heart.'

The Naslunds, and Kristian's father Chris support wildlife charities and pay for each employee to do conservation work for 40 hours a year. The distillery makes bourbon and rye with local organic grains, and a walnut-flavored bourbon liqueur.

FEISTY SPIRITS

LOCATION FORT COLLINS, COLORADO
FOUNDED 2012 **WHISKEY STYLES** BOURBON, RYE,
MALT, HYBRID **VISITOR FACILITIES** FREE DAILY
TOURS ARE HELD, AND THERE ARE BARREL TASTINGS
WITH THE OWNERS

'Feisty' is defined as 'having or showing exuberance and strong determination' and that summarizes the folk behind this distillery rather aptly. It took the founders a long time to come up with their idea for a micro-distillery, but when they did, they set about digging deep into new and exciting areas.

David Monahan and Jamie Gulden knew they wanted to do something different as far back as 2008. They each dreamed of creating a quality product that they enjoyed, running a business their own way, and having a job that didn't feel like a job.

But it took them until early 2012 to launch Feisty Spirits, the first craft distillery in Fort Collins, Colorado. Now they have a

team of spirit-makers who practice hand-crafted, small-batch distilling. They use only natural and organic ingredients, and source locally whenever possible.

They make conventional spirits, but what sets this distillery apart is its use of unusual grains and its desire to showcase its unique features and to develop an adventurous range of new and exciting flavors.

The whiskeys produced by Feisty Spirits fall in to three main categories:

Single-barrel whiskeys: each Feisty Spirits single-barrel whiskey is made with organic grains, and aged in charred American oak barrels. Styles include blue corn bourbon, Better Days bourbon, and rye;

Nectars, or flavored whiskeys: flavors from natural ingredients are infused into smooth and mellow whiskey. These are light whiskeys, made for sipping by themselves or to be used in combination with other ingredients. Flavors include cinnamon oat, blackberry, and vanilla orange;

Elementals (single-grain whiskeys): elementals fall into two types, un-aged and aged. The 'clear' whiskeys include kamut, millet, quinoa, and triticale, and the aged ones include barreled oat, barreled kamut and barreled triticale.

GOLDEN MOON DISTILLERY

LOCATION GOLDEN, COLORADO **FOUNDED** 2008 **WHISKEY STYLES** PORT CASK FINISHED BOURBON AND RYE, SINGLE MALT WHISKEY **VISITOR FACILITIES** THE DISTILLERY HAS A SPEAKEASY-STYLE COCKTAIL BAR AND TASTING ROOM

Golden Moon Distillery, also known as Maison De La Vie, is to spirits distillation what Heston Blumenthal is to cuisine—looking a long way back into history for long-forgotten recipes to resurrect and turn into exciting and modern concoctions.

Stephen Gould and Karen Knight founded the distillery with the specific intention of rediscovering and remaking premium, hand-crafted herbal liquors and liqueurs. Even their more conventional spirits tend to have a twist on them.

'We do so by using the best available herbs, spices, and botanicals, and made with the same type of artisan production processes utilized by distillers making premium products in the mid-to-late 1800s,' they say.

With this in mind, Stephen has put together a highly impressive research library of hundreds of rare books on distillation and related products and processes. Most of the collection dates back to the 1700s but a few go even farther back, to the 1500s.

As head distiller, Stephen puts the drinks together with exacting attention to detail and pure craftsmanship. Distillation is carried out on four antique stills dating back to the early to mid-1900s.

The distillery boasts a single malt whiskey made with Colorado malted barley and matured for a year in new oak casks. Gunfighter double-cask bourbon and double-cask rye are made the same way as each other. They are aged for a minimum of six months in new American oak barrels, and then finished in used French port barrels. They are bottled at 50 per cent ABV.

And Golden Moon is not just about whiskey; it also makes absinthe, gin, grappa, apple jack, and specialty liquors including crème de violette.

One of the highlights here is the speakeasy lounge with its extensive list of cocktails made with the distillery's spirits.

LEOPOLD BROS

LOCATION DENVER, COLORADO **FOUNDED 2001**
WHISKEY STYLES GRAIN WHISKEY, FLAVORED
WHISKEYS **VISITOR FACILITIES** TOURS; TASTING
ROOM OPEN WEDNESDAY TO SATURDAY

Todd and Scott Leopold pooled their resources and opened a brewery in Ann Arbor, Michigan in 1999. Specializing in eco-friendly beer production, the enterprise was a great success, so the brothers branched out into distilling. Their first spirits were made in 2001, and seven years later they moved the whole operation to their home state of Colorado.

Leopold Bros produces a large range of whiskeys, gins, vodka, liqueurs, fernet, absinthe, and aperitivo. Everything—from milling and mashing to bottling by hand—is carried out at the distillery.

Its small-batch whiskey is made with a cold fermentation of rye and corn, a slow process that ensures a softer whiskey, and is barreled at a low 49 per cent ABV (98 proof). This was apparently the strength used before Prohibition. The brothers also produce a fruity and floral Maryland-style rye, and whiskeys flavored with apple, peach, cherry, and blackberry.

SYNTAX PRECISION SPIRITS

LOCATION GREELEY, COLORADO **FOUNDED** 2010
WHISKEY STYLES BOURBON **VISITOR FACILITIES**
THE DISTILLERY OFFERS TOURS AND HOSPITALITY
FACILITIES, HOLDS TASTINGS, AND HOSTS PARTIES
AND EVENTS

Syntax Precision Spirits owner and head distiller Heather Bean was a busy woman for the three years up to the fall of 2018. She has more than 25 years of mechanical, chemical, and software engineering experience, so she was able to design and build Syntax's production line and, as demand has grown in recent years, she has continued to expand it to meet demand.

Now that the distillery has moved into bigger premises, the scale of engineering has got all that much larger. Syntax remains in its native town, Greeley, Colorado, which was voted as having the best water in the country by the American Water Works Association in 2017.

Syntax's straight bourbon is a pure grain-to-glass product, made using only Colorado products and aged for at least two years in 240-liter (53-gallon) barrels.

Syntax offers its services to outside distillers, and will make spirit to a bespoke recipe or to one of its own, providing help and advice to them as they do so.

WOOD'S HIGH MOUNTAIN DISTILLERY

LOCATION SALIDA, COLORADO **FOUNDED** 2012
WHISKEY STYLES RYE, SINGLE MALT **VISITOR FACILITIES** DAILY TOURS AND TASTINGS

PT and Lee Wood had long dreamed of opening a distillery, but it took a big piece of luck and a big dose of going back to the future before their ambition became a reality. A friend introduced the brothers to 'Ashley,' an antique German pot still built around the 1880s. It had been brought to the United States in 1960 but had been idle for 50 years. The Woods jumped at the chance to start doing what they had always wanted to do. It took them several years of gathering equipment and know-how, and searching for a suitable base for their activities, before they settled on their present location in historic downtown Salida, Colorado.

Here the brothers now make an extensive range of spirits and liqueurs, but by far their most important products are two distinctive whiskeys, which they sell through their own tasting room, and at selected outlets in Colorado, and some places in Europe.

Tenderfoot Malt Whiskey is made with a range of different malts—two-row malt, chocolate malt, cherrywood malt, malted wheat, and malted rye. It is bottled at 90 proof (45 per cent ABV). It is a big malt whiskey with rye spice, leather, chocolate, fruit, oak, vanilla, and a hint of sweet and smoke.

Alpine Rye Whiskey is made from 73 per cent malted rye, 13.5 per cent chocolate, and 13.5 per cent cherywood smoked malt. The brothers describe it as a 'truly unique rye whiskey with smoke, dark chocolate, rye spice, cherries, sweet malt, pipe tobacco, oak, and toffee.'

Woods High Mountain's tasting room is open most days, and tours are possible throughout the day by arrangement, but the distillery prefers visitors to come in at 4pm.

SANTA FE SPIRITS

LOCATION SANTA FE, NEW MEXICO **FOUNDED** 2008
WHISKEY STYLES SINGLE MALT, UNAGED MALT
VISITOR FACILITIES THE DISTILLERY OFFERS TOURS
AND TASTINGS, AND CHOCOLATE PAIRING AND
COCKTAIL CLASSES

The journey of Santa Fe Spirits founder and distiller Colin Keegan is a strange but inspiring one, and a convincing demonstration of the principle that, with the right desire and motivation, anyone can change direction in life and succeed in distilling.

Colin is from Newcastle in northeast England, and he made his living from designing luxury homes at the premium end of the property market. 'At one point he designed a home in a four-acre [1.6-hectare] apple orchard, but the client pulled out of the purchase, so he ended up building the home for himself,' says Adam Vincent, marketing manager of the distillery.

'Then one year there was a bumper crop, and he ended up with 500 gallons [2,250 liters] of cider, more than any person can reasonably consume. Someone suggested he distill it, so he made a small still, and made brandy.'

Then came the huge economic crash of 2008; there was a major downturn in the property market, and Colin was left without work. So he took the bull by the horns, enrolled on a distillation course, and turned to distilling full time, making apple brandy and an un-aged malt whiskey spirit that he called Silver Coyote.

The distillery's flagship product is Colkegan Single Malt Whiskey, which is smoky like Scotch, but distinctively American. This is because a portion of the grain is smoked over mesquite wood, and some of the spirit is aged in new American oak. Aging takes place at a high altitude, leading to high levels of evaporation but a speedy maturation.

The result is a whiskey that has a sweet, mild, and meaty smoke taste.

PROOF ARTISAN DISTILLERS

LOCATION FARGO, NORTH DAKOTA **FOUNDED** 2015 **WHISKEY STYLES** AMERICAN MALT WHISKEY, FLAVORED WHISKEY, BOURBON **VISITOR FACILITIES** OPEN WEDNESDAY TO SATURDAY EVENINGS FOR FOOD, INCLUDING AMERICAN-STYLE TAPAS

Joel Kath's passion for spirits ensured that when he had the opportunity of owning and running a distillery, he hit the ground running. He wanted to combine his love for quality spirits drinks with a social atmosphere and the chance to enjoy wholesome food. His offering in some ways is pretty conventional—gin, vodka, bourbon American whiskey. But he's also prepared to tinker at the edges, and his range includes Old Tom, a sweeter style of gin, and a gin aged in whiskey barrels. The tasting room here is home to a number of mixologists capable of turning spirits into innovative and exciting cocktails, and the distillery holds events and is available for hire. Certainly Proof Artisan Distillers has caught the imagination of the local North Dakota community. More than 400 outlets stock the distillery's spirits, and Joel says proudly that visitors to the state will find the distillery's spirits in nearly all bars, restaurants, and liquor stores across North Dakota and the lake country of Minnesota.

Proof Artisan Distillers cheekily calls its American malt whiskey Glen Fargo. Perhaps it may be wise not to tell the Scotch Whisky Association.

BRICKWAY BREWERY AND DISTILLERY

LOCATION OMAHA, NEBRASKA **FOUNDED** 2013
WHISKEY STYLES AMERICAN SINGLE MALT, BOURBON,
WHITE WHISKEY, FLAVORED WHISKEYS   **VISITOR**
FACILITIES THE DISTILLERY OFFERS TOURS, HOLDS
EVENTS AND TASTINGS, AND IS AVAILABLE FOR HIRE

Brickway team members describe what they do as 'living headfirst,' and this is what happens when you put craft beer and spirit nerds alongside an ex-policeman, an ex-marine, and a former chef. The brewery and distillery are situated in the heart of the Old Market district, and the team, headed by Zac Triemart, has produced an impressive range of spirits and beers. Brickway puts a fun face on a serious business, with stills made by Forsyths of Scotland. There's lots going on at the distillery. Hoppy hour is held Thursday to Sunday.

CUT SPIKE DISTILLERY

LOCATION LA VISTA, NEBRASKA **FOUNDED** 2008
WHISKEY STYLES SINGLE MALT WHISKEY **VISITOR**
FACILITIES THE DISTILLERY HAS A TASTING ROOM
AND OFFERS TOURS FROM WEDNESDAY TO SATURDAY

This distillery takes its name from the hand-forged spikes that were once used to dig railroad tracks by hand. The distillery has links with the Lucky Bucket Brewing Co., and both brewery and distillery keep everything simple, focusing on high quality for a small number of brands, and packaging them stylishly. The distillery's single malt whiskey is aged for two years in American oak barrels, a solid period of time for an American single malt that has been awarded double gold at the San Francisco World Spirits Competition.

UNION HORSE DISTILLING CO.

LOCATION LENEXA, KANSAS **FOUNDED** 2010
WHISKEY STYLES BOURBON, RYE, WHITE WHISKEY
VISITOR FACILITIES THE DISTILLERY OFFERS TOURS
AND PUTS ON EVENTS THROUGHOUT THE YEAR

Delve into the website of the Union Horse Distilling Company, and eventually you'll come across a blog posting entitled 'Barrels: Our Unsung Heroes.' What follows is one of the most thorough, clearly explained, and informative guides to every aspect of the role of oak barrels in the whiskey-making process, from the trees they are made from to the moment the used barrels are transported across the world to be used by someone else for something else.

This tells you almost all you need to know about the high seriousness with which master distiller and cofounder Patrick Garcia and his team approach the creation of their spirits. There are other clues, too. For instance, the distillery's straight rye is a 100 per cent rye, a particularly difficult spirit to distill. The bourbon is made using just corn and rye, another difficult feat to carry off. And while some craft distillers are bottling their spirits at just a few months old, Union Horse always ages for more than two years so that its spirits can be termed 'straight whiskeys'—in some cases the whiskey is up to five years old. The distillery boasts three event rooms and can cater for up to 350 guests.

ANDALUSIA WHISKEY CO.

LOCATION BLANCO, TEXAS **FOUNDED** 2016
WHISKEY STYLES SINGLE MALT WHISKEY, WHITE
WHISKEY **VISITOR FACILITIES** THE DISTILLERY
HOLDS TOURS AND TASTINGS, AND PUTS ON
EVENTS THROUGH THE YEAR

The Andalusia Whiskey Company is the product of a coming together of two like-minded craft beer lovers with distinct and in-depth skills. Tommy Erwin, a microbiologist, and Ty Phelps, the lead brewer, struck up a strong friendship, and when the Texan authorities changed the laws to allow a flexible approach to distilling, the duo took a leap of faith and opened up a whiskey distillery. And not just opened it. They and a friend built it from scratch, and without proper plans. Then they set about creating challenging whiskeys. That takes plenty of guts, but with their combined backgrounds in brewing, chemistry, biology, culinary arts, and restaurant management, they gave themselves the best possible chance, and their expertise has paid handsome dividends.

The name of the operation is derived from the fact that the distillery is built on land that was once known as Andalusia Ranches, and the region of Texas in which they are operating looks like the Andalusian region of Spain. You need plenty of water to make whiskey, and water is scarce in Texas, so the distillery has a 212,000-liter (56,000-gallon) rainwater collection tank.

The Andalusia Whiskey Company looks to Scotland for inspiration, and makes a peated style of whiskey called Revenant Oak. It also makes Stryker, which brings a Texan twist to whiskey. Rather than burning peat, Stryker is mashed from malted barley that has been smoked in the Texas barbecue tradition: with oak, mesquite, and applewood.

FIRESTONE & ROBERTSON

LOCATION FORT WORTH, TEXAS **FOUNDED** 2011
WHISKEY STYLES BLENDED WHISKEY, BOURBON
VISITOR FACILITIES THE DISTILLERY'S WHISKEY RANCH
IS OPEN TUESDAY TO FRIDAY AND THE DISTILLERY IS
PLANNING TO OFFER TOURS

'We're against mass production, shortcuts, and prohibitions.
We love everything about the world of whiskey: the history,
the people, the techniques, the art, the science, the
equipment, and the satisfaction of sharing an incredible
bottle with friends.'

These are the opening words of the mission statement
by Leonard Firestone and Troy Robertson, who cofounded
the Firestone & Robertson Distilling Company, the first craft
bourbon and whiskey distillery in North Texas. The words
stand out because, while every craft distiller talks about the
desire to make premium spirits for discerning drinkers, the
exuberance and enthusiasm of this duo come shining through
their every word and deed.

The two friends had both independently harbored dreams
of becoming distillers, but neither knew that the other one
was also keen. That was until they both made appointments
to visit the same craft distillery a week apart from each other,
and the owner told Troy that another Forth Worth guy had
recently been in touch. It was a total surprise when it turned
out to be Leonard.

The rest is history. The two of them built a distillery in an
old Prohibition-era warehouse just south of downtown Fort
Worth. They have since opened a second venue at the Glen
Garden Country Club and Golf Course. Called The Whiskey
Ranch, it provides ample proof that this is a big, consumer-
friendly operation. Both the main whiskeys are very well made
and highly enjoyable. Firestone & Robertson is very much a
distillery to watch: it's on the move, upward and outward.

BALCONES

LOCATION WACO, TEXAS **FOUNDED** 2009 **WHISKEY STYLES** BOURBON, SINGLE MALT, SMOKED HYBRID WHISKEY **VISITOR FACILITIES** THE DISTILLERY HAS A SHOP, OFFERS TOURS THURSDAYS, FRIDAYS, AND SATURDAYS, AND HOLDS TASTINGS

Texas distiller Balcones is at the forefront of America's new whiskey movement, and has played a pioneering role in establishing the credibility and market presence of US single malt. But while the company has been an inspiration to many, and has achieved massive success worldwide, its journey into uncharted territory has not been without incident, and its pitfalls and mistakes will have served as a warning to others embarking on the same path.

The business was founded by enigmatic whiskey-maker Chip Tate, who built the distillery, defined its objectives, and achieved success as an international ambassador, bullishly taking his products to Europe. But rapid expansion required weighty decisions about investment, staffing, and management, and when he fell out with his investors in quite dramatic fashion he was ousted from his own distillery. That acrimonious dispute still reverberates a few years on. Chip's role in the success of Balcones has been airbrushed out of the company's history.

After this big fallout, Chip kept a low profile for some time. Some people thought that he was doomed commercially without the Balcones infrastructure, but it turned out that he was playing a long game, gradually building a whole new distillery from the ground up. And while he could have dabbled and produced small-batch whiskey years ago, he has slowly and painstakingly built a factory capable of returning him to the forefront of American distilling.

Opened in 2018, his Tate & Co. Distillery has two 13,500-liter (3,566-gallon) wash stills, each with an innovative direct firing system, and four 4,000-liter (1,056-gallon) steam-heated stills. 'We are set up to be able to work with a number of different ingredients,' says Chip. 'But the focus will be on whiskeys. Our mash house is about three metric tonnes [3.3 tons] capacity.'

Meanwhile Balcones has continued to produce fine and groundbreaking whiskey. Its output falls into two distinct and distinctive camps. Firstly, there is a range of whiskeys based on the core ingredient of blue corn. Baby Blue was the country's first legal Texas whiskey, and it was followed by a family whose members include: True Blue; True Blue 100; the award-winning charcoal-driven Brimstone; and, most recently, Texas Blue Corn Bourbon.

Brimstone is an exciting and very different whiskey, but what set Balcones apart was the second part of its offering: American single malt whiskey. No. 1 Texas Single Malt was one of the first 'new wave' American single malt whiskeys, and since its launch there have been a number of special releases and cask-strength offerings. None of them tastes anything like Scottish single malt, and the combination of a Texan climate and the fact that they are matured in virgin oak means that they are intense, malty whiskeys but with unmistakable bourbon-like qualities.

Balcones has continued to grow, and has now moved into a new distillery in Waco.

'Long-term we hope to solidify supply of our core range, and continue the process of exploration, which is really what keeps us engaged day-in and day-out,' says distillery ambassador and brand manager Winston Edwards.

'Hopefully our recent expansion will allow us to address supply issues, and get more whiskey in the hands of folks who love what we make, and allow us the flexibility and capacity to keep doing new product development as we look for the next gem.'

IRONROOT REPUBLIC

LOCATION DENISON, TEXAS **FOUNDED** 2013
WHISKEY STYLES BOURBON, MOONSHINE **VISITOR
FACILITIES** TOURS ARE HELD EVERY SATURDAY
AND THE BAR AND LOUNGE ARE OPEN SATURDAY
AFTERNOONS AND EVENINGS

You might not immediately associate one of America's most macho states with the stately grace of one of Britain's finest wine merchants, but there is a link, and it's a significant one.

The wine merchant is Berry Bros & Rudd, a charming slice of history located among the cigar retailers and restaurants of the Mayfair district of London. And amazingly, when Texas declared its independence in 1836, it was above Berry Bros that it set up what was effectively its embassy in Britain. Nine years later, Texas became the 28th State of the Union, and the London mission was closed. The Texan delegation departed the capital leaving a £160 rent bill outstanding.

Berry Bros also has a fine range of spirits, and its whisky-maker Doug McIvor is one of the most respected blenders in the business. When the company decided to mark the Texan–London link, it was to Ironroot Republic that Doug turned.

He worked with the owners, the Likarish Brothers, to create a special Texas Legation Bourbon Whiskey, which is made up of three different batches of the distillery's bourbon. It's a lively, bold, and tasty bourbon packed with fruit, toffee, honey, and distinctive vanilla notes.

For brothers Robert and Jonathan Likarish, their journey up the whiskey ladder has been rapid. Robert is a graduate of Austin College and St. Louis University Law School. After completing his degrees, he realized that his passion was not for law, and he turned to distilling instead. He has studied under some of the best-known craft distillers in the United States, including Hubert Germain-Robin, Don Poffenroth, and Chip Tate.

Jonathan Likarish is now the head distiller at Ironroot. He studied industrial engineering at Texas Tech in Lubbock, and biomedical engineering in St Louis. Both he and his brother learned their trade in public, with ordinary early efforts giving way to a range of distinctive and stylish whiskeys. These days their whiskeys, which come in weighty and impactful bottles in keeping with the popular image of Texas, are big and bold in flavor, and full of character.

'One of the most wonderful things about being a craft distiller is to play with tradition and innovate,' says Robert. 'Whether that's with oak types, specialty toast and char levels, different heirloom corns, or yeasts, pushing yourself to try something new is integral to what we do on a daily basis at the Ironroot Distillery.'

JEM BEVERAGE

LOCATION PILOT POINT, TEXAS **FOUNDED** 2012
WHISKEY STYLES RYE, BOURBON FINISHED IN PINOT
NOIR CASKS, CANADIAN-STYLE WHISKEY **VISITOR**
FACILITIES THERE ARE A COUPLE OF TOUR OPTIONS,
WHICH ARE HELD ON FRIDAYS AND SATURDAYS;
THE NEW DISTILLERY BOASTS A STAGE AND A PATIO
AREA FOR EVENTS

If any local resident tells you that this distillery is pants, they're not being rude. Jem Beverage Company moved its operation to a large site at Pilot Point. Before long the owners and distillery founders realized that residents referred to it as the old panty factory. That's because it once belonged to renowned women's clothing manufacturer Russell Newman Inc. The factory was at the center of the local community, and everyone either worked there or knew someone who did. Vodka is the main spirit from this distillery, but the new site's added equipment includes an artistically fashioned pot still, and this will open up additional whiskey-making opportunities. At the moment, the distillery makes three products: a bourbon matured in virgin oak casks and finished in Napa Valley pinot noir casks; a 90 per cent rye whiskey matured in virgin oak casks and finished in the distillery's Red River bourbon casks; and a Canadian-style whiskey. Each of these spirits is made with a characteristically Texan flourish.

WITHERSPOON DISTILLERY

LOCATION LEWISVILLE, TEXAS **FOUNDED** 2011
WHISKEY STYLES BOURBON, BOURBON FINISHES,
WHITE DOG, SINGLE MALT **VISITOR FACILITIES**
TOURS AND TASTINGS ARE HELD ON FRIDAYS AND
SATURDAYS, AND THERE ARE EVENTS MOST FRIDAY
AND SATURDAY EVENINGS

Quentin D Witherspoon has lived quite a life, and his route to owning his own distillery is anything but conventional. The fifth generation Lewisville local joined the US Marines and traveled the world. It was while he was in Central Africa, where access to beverages was limited, that he started distilling. He returned to live in Charleston, South Carolina, where he immersed himself in the world of moonshining. Then he took another left turn and headed for Puerto Rico with his master distiller to learn rum-making. Rum isn't easy to produce, but to this day the distillery makes successful versions of it. It's not all about bourbon and single malt, however: Witherspoon's love of moonshine is represented by White Dog, while a strictly limited double cask project sees bourbon finished in sherry and port casks.

YELLOW ROSE DISTILLING

LOCATION HOUSTON, TEXAS **FOUNDED** 2010
WHISKEY STYLES BOURBON, SINGLE MALT, RYE, BLENDED, AMERICAN WHISKEY, FLAVORED WHISKEY
VISITOR FACILITIES TOURS ARE HELD EVERY FRIDAY AND SATURDAY NIGHT, AND THE BAR IS OPEN TOO

There are few more resonant legends in Texas than that of the Yellow Rose, the byname of Emily D West, aka Emily Morgan, who helped General Sam Houston to defeat the Mexican army at the Battle of San Jacinto in 1836, and thus paved the way for the foundation of the Republic of Texas.

If you take on that sort of iconic name you'd better be able to step up to the plate when it comes to your whiskeys. Thankfully, this distillery does. Yellow Rose is a result of one of those evenings among friends when you throw in an idea and run with it. The idea of a distillery stemmed from 2010, and by 2012 whiskey was being produced there. The distillery has excelled, picking up several awards as it has gone along, and it is now part of an impressive Texas distilling scene. Yellow Rose makes a range of different whiskeys, including a blend that the distillery claims has a fuller flavor than a Canadian whisky, and an American whiskey that is reputedly sweeter than the spirits from the North. If you're going on a tour, the distillery folk suggest that you pitch up early and buy a cocktail to take with you around the premises.

11 WELLS

LOCATION ST PAUL, MINNESOTA **FOUNDED** 2013
WHISKEY STYLES WHEAT, RYE AND WHITE WHISKEY
VISITOR FACILITIES THE DISTILLERY HOSTS EVENTS
INCLUDING DISTILLERY TOURS

11 Wells was set up by Bob McManus and Lee Egbert, who combined their differing views on how a distillery should work, and learned their art by visiting no fewer than 40 distilleries. Their current operation is part of a regeneration of the Payne Avenue corridor of St Paul, and occupies a site near the Flat Earth Brewery that was once occupied by the blacksmith and millwright of the Hamms Brewery. It really does sit above 11 wells, too. The distillery is proud to be part of a citywide movement, and is thus happy to recognize neighboring bars and to promote their drinks. 11 Wells itself makes a wheat whiskey using local wheat. It has a prototype series for its rye and bourbon whiskeys. Production details such as charring levels, yeast type, and composition of mashbills are included on the label alongside the information that normally appears about a brand, and the distillery encourages public feedback to help the makers develop the whiskeys.

BENT BREWSTILLERY

LOCATION ROSEVILLE, MISSOURI **FOUNDED** 2007
WHISKEY STYLES HOPPED WHISKEY **VISITOR FACILITIES** THE DISTILLERY HOLDS REGULAR EVENTS

There are more than 1,200 craft distilleries in America. Bent Brewstillery isn't the biggest or best of them, but it's included here for two reasons: one, because it epitomizes how a craft distillery can grow organically; and two, because it is bending beers and spirits into new shapes, mainly through trial and error. The company website has a frame-by-frame guide to how Bartley Blume received a home-brew kit from partner Brenda, and slowly and surely grew a hobby into a business that now makes a range of exciting-sounding spirits as well as beers, and holds events including barbecue and chili nights. The whiskey here is made from the brewery's beer, so it is hopped. Double IPA-Skey is an exSPIRITmental whiskey (they like inventing words here) matured in American and French oak casks and bottled with a hop cone for extra bitterness. Everything about this brewery and distillery is distinctive and fun. There's a chili Superbowl on Superbowl weekend, and on other weekends visits by food trucks to cater for parties.

PANTHER DISTILLERY

LOCATION OSAKIS, MINNESOTA **FOUNDED** 2011 **WHISKEY STYLES** AMERICAN WHISKEY, BOURBON, FLAVORED WHISKEYS **VISITOR FACILITIES** TOURS ARE HELD DAILY, BUT YOU CAN ALSO JOIN THE 'SKAL' WINE, BEER AND LIQUOR TRAIL

Minnesota is particularly rich in raw ingredients perfect for making quality spirits, so the creation of a craft distillery here was inevitable. Large lakes, corn, red wheat, and red rye are abundant throughout the state. Panther was founded in 2011 by Adrian Panther, who set out to bring fine spirits to the region. To help him to do so, he teamed up with the most talented individual he knew, Brett Grainger. Brett had learned the art of distilling from some of the most respected distillers in the United States. Panther makes two whiskeys, aged for two and four years in charred American oak casks, and its bourbon is matured for three years.

CEDAR RIDGE DISTILLERY

LOCATION SWISHER, IOWA **FOUNDED** 2005 **WHISKEY STYLES** SINGLE MALT, WHITE, RYE, BOURBON, WHEAT **VISITOR FACILITIES** TOURS ARE HELD AT WEEKENDS, AND THE DISTILLERY HAS AN INFORMAL PIZZA AND DINING MENU

Cedar Ridge is a vineyard set up by Jeff and Laurie Quint in 2005, but if anyone doubted its credentials as a whiskey-making distillery, the issue was laid to rest in 2017 when the American Distilling Institute chose it as its Distillery of the Year. Iowa is famed for its corn, which it exports to many distilleries in Kentucky. Cedar Ridge makes a range of whiskeys, but of special note are its single malts, and the experimental nature of some of its bottlings. For instance, Barrel 34 (Maple Brown Porter), a collaboration with Lion Bridge Brewing Co., is malt whiskey matured in Maple Brown Porter casks. Maple Brown Porter was originally aged in Cedar Ridge ex-bourbon barrels.

MISSISSIPPI RIVER DISTILLING CO.

LOCATION LE CLAIRE, IOWA **FOUNDED** 2010
WHISKEY STYLES BOURBON, RYE, FLAVORED
WHISKEYS **VISITOR FACILITIES** FREE PUBLIC TOURS
DAILY; PRIVATE TOURS AND EVENTS FOR UP TO
50 PEOPLE; OPEN HOUSE SOCIALS ON THE FIRST
FRIDAY OF EVERY MONTH

Mississippi River Distilling was set up by brothers Ryan and Garrett Burchett, who gave up other careers to learn the craft of whiskey-making.

Ryan had worked as a television meteorologist in the Quad Cities, and has worked in other Iowa communities, including Mason City, Des Moines, and Cedar Rapids along with Lafayette, Louisiana. Garrett left his job as a transportation planner in Dallas, Texas, to move back to Iowa and work full time at the distillery. Their father and uncles worked tirelessly running a construction companion in Iowa for more than 40 years, so the two brothers have grown up with a busy work ethic, and today you'll find them serving as distillers, bartenders, tour guides, cash register attendants, salesmen, and more. Both are trained in the art of distillation, with classwork completed in Chicago, Michigan, and Germany. They look forward to educating people about the ins and outs of distillation, as well as the art of tasting during Mississippi River Distilling Company tours. In addition to a standard core range of whiskeys, the distillery has a range of 'Still Crazy' whiskeys. These include Cody Road Double Barrel Whiskey, which is matured for two years in newly charred oak barrels, and is then finished in barrels used to age a local winery's sweet dessert wine.

SQUARE ONE DISTILLERY

LOCATION SQUARE ONE BREWERY **FOUNDED** 2006
WHISKEY STYLES AMERICAN WHISKEY, BOURBON,
HOP WHISKEY **VISITOR FACILITIES** THE DISTILLERY
HAS A RESTAURANT AND FUNCTION ROOM, AND
HOLDS EVENTS SUCH AS MACARONI MONDAYS AND
HAPPY HOUR EVENINGS

From the street, Square One looks like a conventional restaurant, and that's basically what it is. But when the current business was established in 2006 it also found a home for a micro-brewing operation.

The building in which the restaurant, the brewery, and now the distillery operate has a long history as a tavern stretching back to the 19th century. In the 1900s it was bought by Anheuser-Busch, who turned it into a tied house, in the days before the company dominated the world with its Budweiser beer brand. The building was badly damaged by fire in 2004, but that gave restaurant lessee Steve Neukomm the opportunity to turn the space into a revamped restaurant with a craft brewery.

The distillery occupies a compact site, and produces a range of spirits, including cucumber and jalapeño vodkas. Its whiskeys include: J. J. Neukomm, a single malt made with 25 per cent cherrywood smoked barley; Vermont Night, a maple-flavored whiskey infused with fresh citrus, winter spices, and vanilla beans sweetened with Vermont maple syrup; and a hop-flavored whiskey called Hopskey.

WOOD HAT SPIRITS

LOCATION NEW FLORENCE, MISSOURI **FOUNDED** 2010 **WHISKEY STYLES** BOURBON, CORN WHISKEY **VISITOR FACILITIES** TOURS ARE HELD FROM THURSDAY TO MONDAY; BIG GROUPS CAN BE ACCOMMODATED

You know you've come of age when the pilot episode of a new national television series is dedicated to your business. That is what has happened to Gary Hinegarder and his Wood Hat distillery.

TasteMAKERS launched in the Fall of 2017 to 'explore the maker movement, covering artisan producers across the country who are making a lasting impact on today's American food culture.'

'Meet cheese makers, butchers, chocolatiers, bakers, and even oyster farmers,' says presenter and producer Cat Neville. And, it would seem, whiskey-makers, because Wood Hat featured in the pilot episode.

Gary looks every bit the moonshine distiller, with bushy gray beard, glasses, and symbolic wooden hat, but he's serious and painstaking about the whiskeys he makes. Wood Hat Spirits is the first craft distillery in Montgomery County, Missouri, and its wood-fired still is believed to be the only one of its type in the United States. Wood Hat makes an extensive range of whiskeys, liqueurs, and cordials, and sources all its raw ingredients locally.

The distillery's bourbons include: Bourbon Rubenesque, which is distilled on a pot still and matured for ten months before being bottled as a single-barrel whiskey; Brew Barrel Bourbon, which is aged in barrels that have been lent to local micro-brewers to age beer in; and Double Wood, which is Bourbon Rubenesque finished in charred pecan barrels.

StilL 630

LOCATION ST LOUIS, MISSOURI **FOUNDED** 2012
WHISKEY STYLES HOPPED WHISKEY, BOURBON, RYE
VISITOR FACILITIES OWNER DAVID WEGLARZ
CONDUCTS TOURS AND TASTINGS AT WEEKENDS
WHEN HE IS AVAILABLE

No, that's not a misprint. StilL 630 really is written that way. It's certainly different, and for owner David Weglarz that's the whole point.

'I believe that life should be filled with passion and intensity,' he says. 'That it is absolutely vital to live life to its fullest. That's not only how I've lived my life, but it's also how I run StilL 630.

'I've always wanted my life to be spectacular. I want StilL 630 to be different, not just an assembly line churning out product.'

The distillery is located in a former fast-food restaurant in downtown St Louis. It was founded in 2012, and David is a self-taught distiller prepared to dabble in a wide range of spirits as well as whiskey.

The distillery's initial flagship spirit is Rally Point Single Barrel Straight Rye, which in 2016 was named Best Rye Whiskey in America under Two Years Old by the American Distilling Institute. The distillery also produces a range of special spirits under the title of the Brewery Collaboration Series.

'We have been working with great local breweries to take a delicious and interesting beer of theirs, distill it into a whiskey, and age it,' says David. 'We then release it alongside the same beer which the brewery has been aging in our used Rally Point Rye Whiskey barrels. This line has some really different and incredible spirits.'

One of the distillery's most unusual and memorable spirits, though, is S. S. Sorghum Whiskey, which is created with 100-per-cent-local sorghum syrup and boasts wonderful sorghum, fig, and spice notes that make it almost a hybrid rum-whiskey in taste.

RESTLESS SPIRITS

LOCATION NORTH KANSAS CITY, MISSOURI
FOUNDED 2015 **WHISKEY STYLES** SINGLE MALT
WHISKEY, BLENDED **VISITOR FACILITIES** TOURS ARE
CONDUCTED MONDAY TO SATURDAY AFTERNOONS

Restless Spirits was founded and is still owned by Mike and Benay Shannon, who wear their Irish heritage as a badge of honor. The link stretches back to the mid-1800s, when Mike's great-great-grandfather left his Irish home and immigrated to the United States. The family settled in Kansas City, Missouri, and became 'Rabbits' (supporters of their kinsman, local political boss Joseph Shannon, against Thomas J. Pendergast's 'Goats'). When the Shannons were establishing Restless, they consistently used the symbol of the rabbit on all of the distillery's spirit labels and marketing materials.

The Irish link carries through to the distillery's spirits, too. Pádraig's Rebellion Poitín, for instance, is named after Irish poet and rebel leader Pádraig Pearse, who was executed in 1916 for his part in that year's Easter Rising against the British. The distillery's Builders Botanical Gin is named for the Irish carpenters who helped to construct the shops, offices, and houses in Kansas City.

There is also a strong Irish tone to the liquor itself. Sons of Erin 15-year single malt whiskey is a limited edition import from Dundalk, Ireland. ('Erin' is an affectionate and somewhat romantic, poetical alternative name for Ireland.) For this product, Mike and Benay traveled back to the old country and there hand-selected a small number of barrels with the help of Irish whiskey heavyweight John Teeling.

Restless also produces GullyTown single malt whiskey, which it claims is the first American single malt whiskey, 100 per cent mashed, distilled, and aged in Kansas City. (Gully Town was the original nickname for Kansas City before it officially became a city in 1853.)

ROCK TOWN DISTILLERY

LOCATION LITTLE ROCK, ARKANSAS **FOUNDED** 2010 **WHISKEY STYLES** BOURBON, FLAVORED BOURBON, RYE, WHITE WHISKEY **VISITOR FACILITIES** THE DISTILLERY HOSTS PRIVATE TOURS AND TASTINGS BY APPOINTMENT

In 2015, acclaimed whisky writer Jim Murray chose Rock Town Distillery's single-barrel bourbon as his craft whiskey of the year, describing it as 'unquestionably one of the great micro-distillery bourbons of all time.' Not bad for a distillery that had then been in existence for only five years. The business was founded by Phil Brandon, a sixth-generation Arkansan, who set out to make bourbon from the abundance of resources available to him in what is known as 'the Natural State.'

Phil is always on the lookout for something unusual, and the single barrel bourbon is just one of his variants; among his others are a four-grain and a hickory-smoked wheat whiskey.

DOOR COUNTY DISTILLERY

LOCATION STURGEON BAY, CARLSVILLE **FOUNDED** 2011 **WHISKEY STYLES** SINGLE MALT, BOURBON, RYE **VISITOR FACILITIES** THE DISTILLERY HAS A TASTING ROOM, A RETAIL AREA, AND A COCKTAIL BAR, AND IS OPEN DAILY

Door County Distillery was established in 2011 at the Door County Winery, which was opened in 1974. Current owners the Pollman family took over in 1984 and built up visitor and tasting facilities for wine enthusiasts. When the opportunity to add a distillery presented itself in 2011, the owners took it. The distillery makes a range of spirits, and its single malt whiskey is made with wash brought in from a local brewery. It is matured for one year. The distillery also uses Door County ingredients to produce a bourbon and a rye; among its other products is a cherry-flavored moonshine.

GREAT LAKES DISTILLERY

LOCATION MILWAUKEE, WISCONSIN **FOUNDED** 2005 **WHISKEY STYLES** AMERICAN BLENDED WHISKEY, BOURBON, RYE **VISITOR FACILITIES** REGULAR TASTINGS AND TOURS ARE HELD AND CAN BE BOOKED ONLINE, THOUGH THERE ARE SOME WALK-UP TICKETS

There is considerable debate about whether craft distillers are a force for good when it comes to whiskey. At their best, they are taking spirits to new audiences and educating them, and that's the case here. On its website, Great Lakes goes to great lengths to explain chill filtering, and why cloudy whiskey is a good thing. The distillery makes a wide range of spirits, among them Kinnickinnic whiskey, a blended whiskey which includes malt and rye whiskey from Great Lakes, and bourbon from another top American distillery.

INFINITY BEVERAGES

LOCATION EAU CLAIRE, WISCONSIN **FOUNDED** 2010 **WHISKEY STYLES** SINGLE MALT, HOP-BASED WHISKEYS, EXPERIMENTAL WHISKEYS **VISITOR FACILITIES** TASTINGS AND TOURS ARE HELD DAILY; THERE IS A TASTING ROOM, AND THE MEZZANINE CAN BE HIRED FOR PRIVATE EVENTS

While many people turn to craft distilling on a whim, Matthew Rick made a long-term conscious decision to learn how to make wine and distill, then drew up a business plan and set about building a company. He started infusing spirits in 2004. The result is Infinity Beverages. The distillery makes whiskey from doppelbock beer and chocolate oatmeal stout, but the most exciting spirits are the experimental apple malt whiskey and a single malt whiskey aged five times in virgin American oak.

LO ARTISAN DISTILLERY

LOCATION STURGEON BAY, WISCONSIN **FOUNDED** 2011 **WHISKEY STYLES** RICE WHISKEY **VISITOR FACILITIES** THE DISTILLERY HAS A SHOP AND TASTING FACILITIES

There is an argument that this place doesn't warrant inclusion in this book, but it is here because it shows how far the boundaries are being stretched by craft distilling. Lo Artisan Distillery is a family-run, artisan distillery that manufactures and bottles what it calls Yerlo X Rice Whiskey. You can't make whiskey with rice, so we're crossing a line here. The 'X' is because the distillery says it is aimed at a new generation of young whiskey drinkers. The mash is fermented for six months before being distilled. Then it is aged in new American oak charred barrels for four months. Finally it is filtered and bottled at 90 proof.

QUINCY STREET DISTILLERY

LOCATION RIVERSIDE, ILLINOIS **FOUNDED** N/A **WHISKEY STYLES** BOURBON, RYE, CORN, MOONSHINE **VISITOR FACILITIES** TOURS AND TASTINGS TAKE PLACE ON FRIDAYS, SATURDAYS, AND SUNDAYS

The Quincy Street Distillery is sited in a historic building that is also home to a shop and a speakeasy cocktail bar. It is the brainchild of Derrick Mancini, who uses double-distillation in a pot still, the method of distilling typically used to produce spirits such as cognac, Irish and Scotch malt and single-pot still whiskeys. He explains his purpose thus: 'We want a more grain-intense flavor profile that's closer to what you would have found in the early 19th century.'

Quincy Street makes a rye and bourbon, and a single-barrel bourbon named Laughton Bros.

BLAUM BROS. DISTILLING CO.

LOCATION GALENA, ILLINOIS **FOUNDED** 2013
WHISKEY STYLES BOURBON, MOONSHINE
VISITOR FACILITIES TOURS ARE HELD
EVERY DAY

On the distillery's website, a quote accompanies a picture of the two sibling founders: 'The brothers' grandfather did not distill moonshine for Al Capone, they don't have a secret family recipe, and they were not the first distillery since Prohibition to do this or that.' They make various spirits, including bourbon and moonshine, but they're going for the long haul maturation-wise, so they have brought in selected casks of quality bourbon and blended it. This will eventually be replaced by their own bourbon. Their Lead Mine Moonshine is distilled from corn, rye, and barley, and filled directly into the mason jar at 100 proof. Their Hellfyre spirit has jalapeños, habaneros, and pepper.

CHICAGO DISTILLING CO.

LOCATION CHICAGO ILLINOIS **FOUNDED** 2010
WHISKEY STYLES BOURBON, HOPPED AMERICAN
SINGLE MALT, WHITE WHISKEY **VISITOR FACILITIES**
TOURS AND TASTING ARE CONDUCTED DAILY

Founded in 2010, the Chicago Distilling Company is owned and operated by the DiPrizio family. Using organic grains, they are attempting to continue a Chicago distilling history which goes back several generations.

Their whiskeys are made from stout, Belgian dark ale, dark wheat beer, and a smoky single malt not unlike a Scottish Islay whisky. The distillery's bourbon is called Blind Tiger, which recalls the days when speakeasies beat Prohibition by taking payment from visitors to see a blind tiger or a blind pig. When the promised animal failed to materialize, the customers were compensated with a free—and therefore legal—drink.

FOX RIVER DISTILLING CO.

LOCATION GENEVA, ILLINOIS **FOUNDED** 2014
WHISKEY STYLES SMALL BATCH WHISKEY, BOURBON,
MOONSHINE **VISITOR FACILITIES** THERE ARE TOURS
AND TASTINGS ON FRIDAYS AND SATURDAYS; AN
OPEN HOUSE EVENING IS HELD ON FRIDAYS, WITH
LOCAL RESTAURANTS PROVIDING POP-UP FOOD

Fox River is inspired by the rich history of distilling in America before Prohibition all but destroyed it. The original distillery here was closed in this way. Now, says the company, craft distillers are bringing that heritage back: 'This is the way you should be buying your distilled spirits, from someone you know, rather than mass-produced from a foreign land.'

The distillery's Bennett Mill Bourbon is named after an old grist mill that supplied the pre-1920 operation.

FEW SPIRITS

LOCATION EVANSTON, CHICAGO, ILLINOIS
FOUNDED 2011 **WHISKEY STYLES** BOURBON, RYE,
SINGLE MALT **VISITOR FACILITIES** THE DISTILLERY
OFFERS REGULAR TOURS, HOSTS EVENTS, AND CAN
BE BOOKED FOR PRIVATE TOURS

Buying local produce and producing something that has distinct links with the region it comes from is a recurring theme for micro-distillers, and FEW Spirits is no exception, even though it's hidden away in an urban location. The distillery even grows its own hops for use in its award-winning gin.

'FEW is all about local,' says national public relations manager Jason Hope. 'All the grain—corn, wheat, rye, and barley—used in our products is grown in the Midwest, and some other ingredients are sourced from even closer: I planted Cascade hop vines at the distillery, which we use in FEW American Gin. If we can't grow it ourselves, we buy it locally, and if we can't buy it locally, we buy it from friends. Our entire philosophy is based on the fact that we're small. We make in a month what a brand like Jack Daniel's spills on the floor every day. All of our products are unique in one way or another, from the unusual yeasts that ferment our bourbon and rye to the unusual botanicals that go into our gins.'

The policy has certainly paid off, and while the distillery may be small, there's more than a hint of thinking local but acting global. FEW Spirits has not been shy about targeting overseas markets, and its spirits have found their way into retail outlets and bar shelves across the world.

FEW is located 19km (12 miles) north of downtown Chicago in Evanston—the home of the Temperance Movement, and a dry city for almost a century. In dire need of liquor laws that weren't penned the same year as the invention of the Band-Aid, FEW's master distiller overturned old prohibition laws to become the first distiller of grain spirits within the Evanston city limits.

Since then, the distillery has boomed, first by creating support locally and then by extending farther afield.

The secret of the distiller's success, says Jason, has been to stay in control of the whole whiskey-making process. Every part of it—fermentation, distillation, aging, bottling, and labeling—is carried out at the distillery, which nestles in a suburban alleyway. The whiskeys have been tweaked to make them distinctive.

The distillery makes a bourbon using a high rye mash bill to give the whiskey extra spice and kick, and a rye whiskey made with a French wine yeast to give it extra fruitiness.

But possibly FEW's most distinctive whiskey is its single malt, which has a distinctive smoky flavor with some vanilla, spice, and chocolate notes. Some of the barley used in its production is dried over cherry wood, setting it way apart from whiskey made in Scotland.

The distillery is very much at the heart of the community, offering a range of events, including cocktail classes and vinyl spinning and cocktail sipping evenings.

KOVAL
DISTILLERY

LOCATION CHICAGO, ILLINOIS **FOUNDED** 2008
WHISKEY STYLES BOURBON, MILLET, OAT, HYBRID
VISITOR FACILITIES TOURS AND TASTINGS ARE HELD
FOUR DAYS A WEEK, WITH PRIVATE TOURS FOR BIG
PARTIES; THE DISTILLERY ALSO HOSTS WHISKEY
WORKSHOPS AND COCKTAIL CLASSES

When Koval opened in 2008, it was the first distillery to have been established legally in Chicago since the mid-1800s. Subsequently it has acquired an unparalleled reputation for high-class organic spirits by creating its own new, signature style—using only the 'heart' cut of the distillate. The aim has been to produce a brighter, cleaner style of whiskey.

The distillery was founded by husband-and-wife team Robert and Sonat Birnecker, who gave up their former academic careers to fulfill their ambition of bringing the distilling traditions of Robert's Austrian family to America. In making this decision, they vowed to make organic spirits from scratch (avoiding the common industry practice of purchasing and bottling pre-made spirits) in an effort to change the way people understand whiskey.

The name Koval means 'blacksmith' in numerous Eastern European languages, but the word in Yiddish also refers to a metaphorical black sheep, or someone who forges ahead or does something new or out of the ordinary.

'Sonat's great-grandfather earned "Koval" as his nickname when, at the ripe old age of 17, he surprised his family and emigrated from Vienna to Chicago in the early 1900s to start a business,' says Robert.

Coincidentally, the surname of Robert's grandfather (at whose side Robert learned the art of distilling) is Schmid—German for 'smith.' Sonat and Robert chose the name Koval to honor both men—and to reflect their own extraordinary decision to leave their careers to make some of the most unusual whiskey in America.

Success has seen major expansion in recent years. The owners of Koval Distillery cemented their future in the Ravenswood district of Chicago by purchasing the building in which they had previously been leasing space. They plan to take over the entire building and thus quadruple their working area.

With its planned expansion, Koval will increase annual production from 315,000 liters (70,000 gallons) to 450,000 liters (100,000 gallons). As recently as 2011 it was distilling just 67,500 liters (15,000 gallons).

Koval makes a line of unique, single-barrel whiskeys using a combination of alternative and traditional grains. On the more traditional side of things, it produces a 100 per cent rye whiskey, and a white rye.

But its bourbon is distinctive and different. It contains 51 per cent corn grain, as all bourbons must, but unlike most bourbons there is only one other grain, and that grain is millet.

'Out of the bottle, this duet opens with notes of mango chutney, while the millet renders a soft whisper of vanilla throughout,' says the distillery. 'Then harmonizing, the grains sing with the sweetness of apricot custard. This pair finishes with peppery caramel, a diminuendo into a wisp of clove-spiked tobacco lingering on the tongue.'

Koval also produces the only American whiskey made entirely of millet, and other whiskeys in the distillery's product line include Four Grain (oat, rye, wheat, and malted barley), and 100 per cent oat and 100 per cent white rye whiskeys.

It also makes limited edition, single-barrel, single-grain organic whiskeys aged in a 135-liter (30-gallon) toasted barrel. All limited edition whiskeys are aged between two and four years, and the light color is indicative of aging in a toasted, as opposed to a charred, barrel.

COPPERCRAFT DISTILLERY

LOCATION HOLLAND, MICHIGAN **FOUNDED** 2012
WHISKEY STYLES RYE, BOURBON, BLENDED BOURBON
VISITOR FACILITIES TWO BARS AND RESTAURANTS

Coppercraft owner Walter Catton makes a range of products including applejack, rum, and flavored vodka using a stainless steel mash tun and two stills. He also has two restaurant and bar outlets in Holland and nearby Saugatuck. The whiskey from the distillery includes: a rye whiskey made of 95 per cent rye and 5 per cent malted barley; a single-barrel aged bourbon; and a blended bourbon comprising 20 per cent ten-year-old bourbon and 80 per cent four-year-old bourbon.

TWO JAMES SPIRITS

LOCATION DETROIT, MICHIGAN **FOUNDED** 2012
WHISKEY STYLES RYE, BOURBON, SMOKED BOURBON, HYBRID WHISKEY **VISITOR FACILITIES** TASTING ROOM IS OPEN FROM NOON EVERY DAY, PRE-BOOKED TOURS ARE HELD ON FRIDAYS, SATURDAYS, AND SUNDAYS

This distillery is named for James Bailey and James Landrum, close relatives of cofounders Peter Bailey and David Landrum, who revere them as 'two great men who, through hard work, perseverance, and passion for life, left lasting impressions on those they loved and the communities in which they lived.'

The whiskeys from Two James are excitingly offbeat. Johnny Smoking Gun whiskey—70 per cent corn and 30 per cent rye—is intended to be matched with the rich pork and fish broths of Japanese cuisine. Grass Widow bourbon has a high rye content and is finished in Madeira casks. J. Riddle Peated Bourbon nods to Scottish single malt by using 79 per cent Michigan corn and 21 per cent peated British barley.

DETROIT CITY DISTILLERY

LOCATION DETROIT, MICHIGAN **FOUNDED** 2014
WHISKEY STYLES AMERICAN WHISKEY, BOURBON,
RYE **VISITOR FACILITIES** THE DISTILLERY HAS A
TASTING ROOM AND HOLDS TOURS AND TASTINGS
AT ITS WHISKEY FACTORY

The plans for Detroit City Distillery were hatched during a bachelor party weekend at a remote log cabin. The wedding never happened, but the distillery did. In fact, the original distillery has been expanded to a second site, and one dripping in history. The building used to house the Goebel Brewing Company in the 1930s, which was set up to compete with Stroh's, the dominant local brewer. That clearly failed because Stroh's bought the building and turned it into an ice cream parlor. The distillery now produces a 97 per cent rye to an old recipe, and its Butcher's Cut Bourbon is named to commemorate master distiller John P Jerome's grandfather, who worked as a a butcher next door to what is now the Detroit City Distillery, but was once a slaughterhouse.

GRAND TRAVERSE DISTILLERY

LOCATION TRAVERSE CITY, MICHIGAN
FOUNDED 2006 **WHISKEY STYLES** AMERICAN
WHISKEY, BOURBON, RYE, SMOKY RYE
VISITOR FACILITIES TOURS AND TASTINGS
ARE HELD REGULARLY

When Kent Rabish was a boy, he and his siblings found an old still hidden at the back of a barn on the family farm. It turns out that it belonged to his grandfather, who made spirits on it from excess grain. Kent re-established the distilling link in the early part of the new millennium, playing a pioneering role in kick-starting the craft distilling movement in Michigan. His son Landis has now joined him, working as head distiller, and the family team is continuing to make hand-crafted spirits. Its range of whiskeys includes Islay Rye, a whiskey made with 80 per cent locally sourced rye and 20 per cent smoked barley. The distillery is firmly established in Michigan, and has won a number of awards for its spirits, which include a range of flavored products.

JOURNEYMAN DISTILLERY

LOCATION THREE OAKS, MICHIGAN **FOUNDED** 2010
WHISKEY STYLES BOURBON, RYE, WHEAT, SINGLE
MALT, HYBRID **VISITOR FACILITIES** THE DISTILLERY
OFFERS REGULAR TOURS, HOSTS EVENTS, AND HAS
BOTTLING PARTIES

Journeyman founder and owner Bill Welter's journey to running his own distillery has roots stretching back to the start of the millennium.

In 2000, he traveled to Scotland to learn more about golf. While there he met Greg Ramsey, the master barman at the Road Hole Bar at St Andrew's, and the two became firm friends. Greg is Tasmanian, and has a love of the drinks industry as well as the world of golf. Today, he is the owner of the New Zealand Whisky Company. But during the intervening years he invited Bill to Tasmania, where Bill worked in various distilleries, developed a passion for distilling, worked briefly in the hospitality business, and finally took the giant step of building his own distillery.

He settled on a site in Three Oaks, Michigan, that used to house the E K Warren Historic Featherbone Factory. The eponymous Warren, a staunch prohibitionist, founded the building in 1883 as a buggy whip and corsets factory.

'He revolutionized the manufacturing of corsets with the use of the softer featherbone, over the stiffer whalebone for corsets in the late-19th century,' says Bill. 'E K Warren's success reached worldwide attention, putting Three Oaks, Michigan on the map.'

The distillery opened in 2010, at the very beginning of the micro-distilling boom. Today Journeyman makes a range of whiskeys, all of them organic. The names of some are linked to the old factory: Buggy Whip Wheat Whiskey, Featherbone Bourbon Whiskey, Last Feather Rye Whiskey. Silver Cross Whiskey—equal parts rye, wheat, corn, and malted barley—is named after a medal awarded during the early days of the British Open Golf tournament.

But Journeyman is taking its grain spirits into whole new areas with innovative whiskeys including Kissing Cousins, which is the distillery's regular Featherbone Bourbon finished in Wyncroft Winery cabernet barrels. Three Oaks is a 100 per cent malted barley aged in used Featherbone Bourbon barrels for 18 months, then moved into used Road's End Rum barrels for 15 months. And finally it is finished for three months in used port wine barrels.

The distillery has looked backward with its whiskeys as well as forward. Not A King, for instance, was a replication of George Washington's original rye whiskey recipe, with the distillery's own twist.

'Our aim in making whiskey is to make the highest-quality product available,' says Bill. 'All of our whiskeys, with the exception of Kissing Cousins, are certified organic and kosher. Using locally harvested grains we have sustainability in mind, and want to support other local, small, family-owned businesses. We are using modern-day distillation equipment and techniques with old-world methods and recipes.'

The distillery is keen to share its history, so it hosts a range of evenings, from open-mic nights and craft markets to Sunday brunches, and its tours tell the story of the factory stretching back to the 1800s.

Is the link with Greg Ramsey and the Southern Hemisphere still in place? It would seem so: you'll find New Zealand whisky for sale in the online shop.

LONG ROAD DISTILLERS

LOCATION GRAND RAPIDS, MICHIGAN **FOUNDED** 2015 **WHISKEY STYLES** WHEAT, SINGLE MALT, BOURBON **VISITOR FACILITIES** THE DISTILLERY HAS A RESTAURANT AND A COCKTAIL BAR; THERE ARE REGULAR TOURS WITH GUIDED TASTINGS

It's early days for founders Kyle Van Strein and Jon O'Connor, but they have already caught the eye of critics across America, and those of their spirits that do not need lengthy maturation are picking up numerous accolades: their aquavit is particularly celebrated. Whiskeys—wheat, bourbon, and malt—have thus far been made in limited editions. The single malt is one to watch. It's made to an Irish-style recipe of malted and unmalted barley. The bourbon is made to four different mash bills, suggesting that the team is will experiment in the future.

MAMMOTH DISTILLERY

LOCATION TORCH LAKE, MICHIGAN **FOUNDED** 2013 **WHISKEY STYLES** WHISKEY, BOURBON, RYE **VISITOR FACILITIES** TASTING ROOM AND VISITOR CENTER WITH FOOD AND A SHARED EXPERIENCE WITH FRESH COAST CHOCOLATES, WHICH IS HOUSED IN THE SAME SPACE

This distillery has two sites: at Central Lake is a community project with a family atmosphere; at Traverse City a cocktail bar is sited next to Fresh Coast Chocolates, and the two businesses work together. It's early days for whiskey here, so the distillery brings in five-year-old whiskey from Kentucky, and finishes it in once-used Grand Cru Merlot barrels. For its Woolly Bourbon, Mammoth makes aggressive tail cuts to optimize the aging process. The spirit is matured in 22.5-liter (5-gallon) and 135-liter (30-gallon) barrels.

NEW HOLLAND

LOCATION HOLLAND, MICHIGAN **FOUNDED** 2005 **WHISKEY STYLES** BOURBON, RYE, SINGLE MALT **VISITOR FACILITIES** LOTS TO DO HERE: DISTILLERY, BREWERY, COOL RESTAURANT, AND PUB; TOURS ON SATURDAYS

New Holland is a mini-hospitality business. In addition to the distillery, there is the original brewery, a pub, and Knickerbocker, a stylish restaurant with some of the most mouthwatering dishes you'll ever come across. Some smoked garlic sausage with brown mustard and sauerkraut, anyone? Warm smoked whitebait with breadcrumbs and matzo crackers?

All in all, this is some operation, and the drinks don't let the side down either. New Holland is one of the bigger players in the craft distilling movement, and one of the oldest. The brewery was established in 1996, but the company moved to its current premises in 2005, and it was then that the owners began micro-distilling. More recently the premises were substantially expanded. Every one of New Holland's whiskeys is of interest. Its Beer Barrel Bourbon and Rye are finished in the brewery's Dragon's Milk stout; Zeppelin Bend is one of the finest examples of an American single malt whiskey. Best of all, Zeppelin Bend Reserve is a single malt matured for four years in new American oak before being finished in sherry casks from the Bodega Alvear in Córdoba, Spain.

New Holland products can be enjoyed at Knickerbocker and also in the Pub on 8th at 66 East 8th Street, Holland.

12.05 DISTILLERY

LOCATION INDIANAPOLIS, INDIANA **FOUNDED** 2014 **WHISKEY STYLES** CORN, WHEAT, RYE, HOPPED WHISKEY **VISITOR FACILITIES** TOURS AND TASTINGS ARE HELD FROM THURSDAY TO SUNDAY FOR A SMALL CHARGE, REDEEMABLE ON PURCHASES

Indiana has played a key role in the development of the craft distilling movement in America. One of the main US corn producers, the Midwestern state transports its grain to distilleries across America and ships it to international markets overseas. Unsurprisingly therefore, 12.05 uses corn in its whiskey-making process, but there's much more to this distillery than that. The name comes from the date on which Prohibition was repealed, December 5, 1933: Christmas that year must have really been something.

12.05 was originally set up by Teresa Webster, and was operated by Brad Colver and Nolan Hudson, who purchased it in 2017.

The whiskeys from the distillery are well constructed and have interesting backstories. Four Finger Rye Whiskey is aged for as long as necessary, at least a year, and is deliberately less spicy than many ryes, with a mash bill of just 55 per cent rye.

The name of White on The Line Wheat Whiskey refers to the habit of bootleggers during Prohibition of hanging white washing on the line when it was safe for people to come and collect their illegal liquor.

If you want innovative and trendy, look no farther than The Barreled Reporter, which is distilled from Flat 12 Pogue's Run Porter, and is believed to be the only whiskey matured from a sour beer.

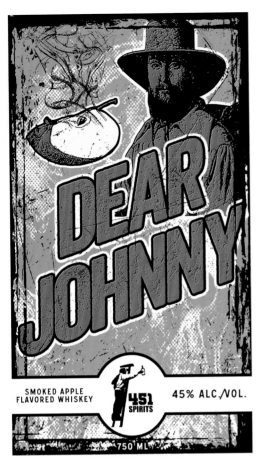

451 SPIRITS

LOCATION COLUMBUS OHIO **FOUNDED** 2001
WHISKEY STYLES HYBRID WHISKEY, SMOKED
WHISKEY **VISITOR FACILITIES** THE DISTILLERY
HOSTS TOURS THURSDAY, FRIDAY AND SATURDAY

Are the people behind 451 Spirits the most eccentric/most innovative (scratch as you see fit) in the whole of America?

'A big part of our mission here at 451 Spirits is to push the boundaries of what is possible in the world of distilling,' says the team. 'Art, science, and madness converge here in the form of small-run, limited releases. Friends, the animals are running the zoo and nothing is too far out there for us to not consider.'

So far, so wacky, but is 451 all words, no action? Let us briefly examine the evidence. Exhibit one: Pizza Pie'Chuga

II, which is inspired by a relatively obscure spirit produced in southern Mexico.

'We decided to put our own twist on it, and partnered with one of our favorite pizza-makers,' says the distillery. The result is white whiskey infused with sun-dried tomato, garlic, basil, pepperoni, and whole slices of pizza bread, before being re-distilled.

The distillery's mainstream whiskey isn't this left-field—yet—but certainly there is a lot going on here. Bone Shaker whiskey is made from an unusual mash bill of almost equal parts of barley, rye, and oats, and enhanced by the addition of roasted and chocolate malt. It is distilled in a pot still, and matured using a solera system.

Dear Johnny smoked whiskey is made in a similar way to Bone Shaker, but it takes its own road with the smoking process. Incredibly, 451 cold-smokes apples for 24 hours, then soaks them in the whiskey spirit for the same length of time before the spirit is distilled again. The result is intensely smoky with a hint of the apple added. This is one to watch.

ERNEST SCARANO DISTILLERY

LOCATION FREMONT, OHIO **FOUNDED** 2010
WHISKEY STYLES AGED RYE **VISITOR FACILITIES** THE
DISTILLERY HOSTS TOURS BY APPOINTMENT

Ernest Scarano is one of the many craft distillers who have challenged prohibitive legislation. He fought successfully against a bizarre and petty law that denied a licencing certificate to any distillery in a county with a population of less than 800,000. His distillery makes only 450 liters (100 gallons) of spirit a year: small batches of Old Homicide, aged for four years with barrel proof strength of 70 per cent ABV; Widmer Winter Rye; and Whiskey Dick (65 per cent ABV), mellowed in sugar maple charcoal, finished in a hickory barrel.

NORTHSIDE DISTILLING CO.

LOCATION CINCINNATI, OHIO **FOUNDED** 2015
WHISKEY STYLES BOURBON, CORN WHISKEY,
MOONSHINE **VISITOR FACILITIES** TOURS BY
APPOINTMENT; THE DISTILLERY HAS A BAR AT 922
RACE STREET

For years Chris Leonidas and Josh Koch dabbled together making beer and wine in their own kitchens. One day their business got so big that their wives wanted them out of the house. They moved as quickly as distillation laws allowed, and as soon as they were permitted to open a bar, they moved to a downtown site from where they now provide a complete production, bar, and visitor package. The distillery's first product was a meticulously planned corn whiskey, 83 per cent corn and 17 per cent malted barley, distilled twice and suitable for aging. Its first bourbon, aged in very small barrels, was released in November 2017.

MIDDLE WEST SPIRITS

LOCATION COLUMBUS OHIO **FOUNDED** 2008
WHISKEY STYLES BOURBON, VARIOUS RYES **VISITOR**
FACILITIES TOURS BY APPOINTMENT ARE HELD
DAILY FOR A SMALL FEE

Brady Konya and Ryan Lang founded Middle West Spirits in 2008, and opened the distillery for commercial production two years later. But from the outset the distillery was about more than just making fine whiskey. With backgrounds in marketing and manufacturing, the partners wanted to focus particularly on championing Ohio's world-class agriculture, small business innovation, and culinary inspiration in order to champion the state as an artisan producer of spirits and other food products. Local ingredients are important to this distillery, and the likes of red wheat and pumpernickel rye find their way into several of its recipes.

Middle West is a 1,486-sq-m (16,000-sq-ft) open-air distillery which serves as a showcase for the company's spirits, a spirits shop, an educational venue, and a tasting room.

In distillation terms, there are all sorts of clever twists and turns. The distillery's bourbon and wheat whiskey, for instance, are finished in sherry casks; and its Michelone Reserve Bourbon is a flavor-forward blend of sweet yellow corn, soft red winter wheat, dark pumpernickel rye, and two-row barley. Most exciting of all is the groundbreaking OYO Dark Pumpernickel Rye Whiskey, which is America's first straight rye whiskey made from nearly 100 per cent rye pumpernickel flour, and aged for more than four years.

THE OAK N' HARBOR DISTILLERY

LOCATION OAK HARBOR, OHIO **FOUNDED** 2014
WHISKEY STYLES CORN, BOURBON, MOONSHINE
VISITOR FACILITIES SHORT TOURS ARE HELD ON
WEDNESDAYS AND SATURDAYS

Joe Helle did a lot in his first 30 years: he was, among other things, a boat dock attendant, a pizza-maker, a taco cook, a private chef, an infantry sergeant, a paramedic, a police officer, and mayor of Oak Harbor. He is a pretty determined guy, having faced a long struggle to get a distilling licence, and been prepared to tell the duty and excise people exactly what he thought of their bureaucracy. While waiting for the green light on his proposals, he learned how to distill and prepared his distillery, so that when he finally got his permit he was good to go the very next day. Joe now distills rum— no easy job—and makes moonshine, a corn whiskey, and a limited edition bourbon.

RED EAGLE DISTILLERY

LOCATION GENEVER, OHIO **FOUNDED** 2012 **WHISKEY STYLES** BOURBON, RYE **VISITOR FACILITIES** THE DISTILLERY IS OPEN DAILY AND HOSTS EVENTS AND DINNERS

The Red Eagle Distillery is located in a region that has long been known for the production of alcoholic drinks. There are stories of farms distilling spirits throughout Prohibition, and wine-making here stretches back for more than a century. One of the aims of the distillery's owners was to preserve the tradition by providing spirits unique to the region. The area is also rich in the grains required to make spirits. Red Eagle is situated in a barn originally built in the 1800s. The distillery is already making two- and three-year-old bourbon and rye, with plans for older versions as the whiskey matures. It supports the craft trade by putting local beer and cider on tap in its bar.

SEVEN BROTHERS DISTILLING CO.

LOCATION CLEVELAND, OHIO **FOUNDED** 2011
WHISKEY STYLES HICKORY-SMOKED WHISKY
VISITOR FACILITIES THE DISTILLERY HOLDS
EVENTS AT LOCAL RESTAURANTS AND BARS IN THE
CLEVELAND AREA

It is frequently observed that the youngest sibling in any large family seems to be the most competitive, and certainly that is the case with Kevin Suttman. The youngest of seven brothers and one sister, he was determined to outshine the others at beer-making. Somewhere along the line, he decided to change the game and turned his attention to distilling. Most amazingly of all, he designed and built an innovative and original distilling system. By reducing pressure through a vacuum system he could lower the boiling point of water, and by doing so, goes the theory, more flavors are left in the liquid, making for tastier and bolder spirits.

The Seven Brothers distillery makes a number of spirits, including one that infuses espresso coffee into the spirit. Its whisky—note the spelling here—is made from Ohio-grown, soft, red winter wheat and yellow corn, and the spirit is instilled with the flavor of locally harvested, kiln-dried, toasted, and smoked hickory in its vacuum still.

WOODSTONE CREEK

LOCATION CINCINNATI, OHIO **FOUNDED** 1999
WHISKEY STYLES FIVE-GRAIN BOURBON, SINGLE
MALT **VISITOR FACILITIES** THE DISTILLERY'S TASTING
ROOM IS OPEN FOR TASTINGS ON SATURDAYS

There's micro and there's micro. And Woodstone Creek is Micro with a big M. In fact, with just 100 to 200 cases a year in total for all its products, it is home to some of the rarest spirits in the world. And not just spirits, either. Everything it makes is bottled as single-barrel whiskey—there is no blending here—and each annual release is genuinely unique. The distillery was shut for a year (2013–14) as it sought a new location, but has now reopened in the thriving village community of St Bernard. It makes a five-grain bourbon and peated and unpeated single malt whiskeys. The master distiller is also a wine-maker, a certified brewmaster, and a mead mazer. Apart from him, there are no other employees, and no automated equipment, no computers, and no bottling line—if this operation were any more compact, it might be invisible to the naked eye.

ANGEL'S ENVY

LOCATION LOUISVILLE, KENTUCKY **FOUNDED** 2006
WHISKEY STYLES BOURBONS FINISHED IN PORT
AND RUM CASKS **VISITOR FACILITIES** TOURS ARE
HELD MOST DAYS BY APPOINTMENT ONLY

Angel's Envy is the distillery where the generations meet, and the new of craft distilling comes up against traditional Kentucky whiskey-making. The name derives from the idea that its products are even better than the 5 per cent that evaporates during barrel aging ('the angel's share').

It's situated around the corner from Whiskey Row in downtown Louisville, and while many craft distilleries are small farmyard operations, this isn't one of them. It occupies a large warehouse space, is furnished with state-of-the-art distilling equipment, and even boasts a spirit safe that is shaped like the company's logo. It's highly impressive.

The company was originally set up by the legendary Lincoln Henderson, who was master distiller at Woodford Reserve and part of a golden era of great distillers, along with his son Wes. Lincoln started working on a new genre of American spirit, taking quality bourbon and finishing it in port casks. Bourbon cannot be made in used casks, so Angel's Envy is a hybrid whiskey spirit, but an extremely good one.

The whiskey is typically aged between four and six years in new, charred 250-liter (53-gallon) American white oak barrels.

The bourbon is now double matured—aged in two different types of barrels. It spends up to six additional months in 270-liter (60-gallon) port barrels. Finally, it is blended into

batches of 8 to 12 barrels at a time. It is a smooth, nuanced, and refined bourbon, and the whiskey is given added depth and fruitiness from its time in ex-ruby port casks.

Lincoln passed away in 2013, and since then Wes's sons Kyle and Andrew have joined the business. Angel's Envy has been highly successful, eventually attracting a takeover by international drinks company Bacardi, who take a hands-off approach to the distillery.

The distillery makes other styles of whiskey. Angel's Envy Rye is made with 95 per cent rye and 5 per cent malted barley. It is aged for at least six years in new American charred oak barrels, and then finished in Caribbean rum casks.

Angel's Envy Cask Strength is aged for up to seven years and was named 'best spirit in the world' by revered whiskey writer Paul Pacult in 2013.

The distillery goes from strength to strength, and Wes Henderson says that he and his sons have every intention of carrying on where his father left off.

'Dad left so many unique ideas, recipes, and samples of various ideas and trials that we have a lot to choose from when the time comes,' says Wes Henderson. 'And his innovative spirit is alive in both Kyle and I. We are already working hard on a few new ideas.'

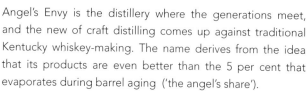

REVERE TRADITION EMBRACE PROGRESS

ANGELS ENVY

BARREL HOUSE DISTILLING CO.

LOCATION LEXINGTON, KENTUCKY **FOUNDED** 2006
WHISKEY STYLES BOURBON, MOONSHINE
VISITOR FACILITIES TOURS AND TASTINGS
ARE HELD FROM WEDNESDAY TO SUNDAY; THE
DISTILLERY ALSO HAS A TASTING OUTLET CALLED
THE ELKHORN TAVERN

Kentucky is, of course, the beating heart of America's whiskey industry, and for some time the craft distilling movement was seen as a challenge to the state's old order. That is an incorrect analysis for two reasons: one, because many of the distilleries associated with the craft distilling movement had been around for some years before they became well known; and two, because new distilleries have been springing up in Kentucky as well as in many less traditional whiskey states.

Barrel House Distilling Co. is owned and operated by Jeff Wiseman and Pete Wright, and is located in the barreling house of the historic Pepper Distillery. The company now makes a barrel proof bourbon; a moonshine named Devil John in honor of Devil John Wright, a lawman and moonshiner from eastern Kentucky in the late 19th and early 20th centuries; and a dark moonshine, which is made to the same recipe as Devil John, but aged for ten months in once-used charred barrels.

LIMESTONE BRANCH DISTILLERY

LOCATION LEBANON, KENTUCKY **FOUNDED** 2012
WHISKEY STYLES BOURBON AND HYBRID WHISKEYS
VISITOR FACILITIES LIMESTONE BRANCH IS PART OF
THE KENTUCKY BOURBON TRAIL AND HOSTS TOURS
AND TASTINGS EVERY DAY

There are two famous names in Kentucky: Boon, as in Daniel; and Beam, as in Jim. The latter is, of course, closely linked to whiskey distilling. Steve and Paul Beam, the driving forces behind Limestone Branch, are on a mission to re-establish a link between their ancestors of 200 years ago and their branch of the Beam family today. Their distillery occupies a site in Lebanon, not far from Maker's Mark, close to where their forebears had their distillery. It's an area rich in grain and with a plentiful supply of water, and the brothers operate a small 675-liter (150-gallon) copper still capable of making spirits one barrel at a time.

The distillery makes a two-year-old straight rye whiskey, and is developing a bourbon but has so far bottled bourbons selected by the brothers from elsewhere and blended at the distillery before bottling at 52.5 per cent ABV, 105 proof.

MICHTER'S DISTILLERY

LOCATION LOUISVILLE, KENTUCKY **FOUNDED** 2014
WHISKEY STYLES SINGLE-BARREL RYE, SMALL-
BATCH AND SINGLE-BARREL BOURBON, UNBLENDED
AMERICAN WHISKEY **VISITOR FACILITIES** THE
MICHTER'S BUILDING ON WHISKEY ROW IS A
COMPLETE VISITOR EXPERIENCE AND RETAIL OUTLET

In 2018, Michter's opened its state-of-the-art visitor experience in Louisville's Whiskey Row, joining several other distillers and liquor companies in making Kentucky's biggest city a deserved focal point for American whiskey. This development marks a remarkable turnaround for Michter's, which is one of American whiskey's most iconic names.

The current company might only be a few years old, but it has a history stretching back to a time before Kentucky even existed as a state. In fact Michter's is linked to America's first distilling company, established by John Shenk, a Swiss Mennonite farmer who settled his family in Pennsylvania's Blue Mountain Valley in the 1700s. With his farm producing an abundance of crops, in 1753 Shenk decided to build a small distillery to convert his excess rye into whiskey. Eventually this little distillery, with its hand-hammered stills, would come to produce what would someday be known as the famous Michter's whiskey.

The distillery was closed throughout the Prohibition period, and although it subsequently reopened, it faced a series of crises and changed hands many times. It was finally closed down in 1990, and the distilling equipment was stripped away.

The modern-day story of Michter's starts in the 1990s with the intervention of industry heavyweights Joseph J Magliocco and Richard 'Dick' Newman, who started production of whiskey in the Louisville suburb of Shively.

Michter's makes a range of high-quality bourbons and ryes, including a 20-year-old, made up of the very best barrels selected by the master distiller. It's very hard to mature bourbon to such an age.

KENTUCKY PEERLESS DISTILLING CO.

LOCATION LOUISVILLE, KENTUCKY **FOUNDED** 2015 **WHISKEY STYLES** RYE, BOURBON **VISITOR FACILITIES** TOURS ARE HELD THROUGHOUT THE YEAR, BUT ARE LESS FREQUENT IN WINTER

It takes a brave man to set up a distillery right in the heart of Whiskey Row in Louisville, the largest city in the bourbon state of Kentucky, and then set about making a spirit that flies in the face of convention and deviates from the spirit made in the state's dozen or so other distilleries.

Spend any time with Corky Taylor and you realize that he's only too willing to blaze a trail for Kentucky Peerless Distilling Co. He is proud of a strong ancestry that links his family directly with Henry Kraver, the entrepreneur who set up the Worsham Distilling Company in the 1880s. The business made peerless bourbon and changed its name to Peerless in the early 1900s.

Five generations later, Corky and his son are at the helm of a new version of Peerless, but the links with the past are strongly maintained. The distillery visitor center offers a pictorial history, and Corky points proudly to the distillery's Distillery Spirits Plant (DSP) number.

'The original Kentucky Peerless Distilling was Distilled Spirits Plant number 50,' he says. 'Today, we are privileged to have that same number. The newly assigned DSP numbers are in the 20,000s. We are happy to say DSP-KY-50 is our own.'

Downtown Louisville is special because, although many of its businesses have closed, the original building façades have been preserved, so when it came to looking for a site for the distillery, Corky was able to choose a 115-year-old building close to Whiskey Row.

The Peerless distillery is now one of the most automated distilleries around. All under one roof, the select Kentucky Peerless grains are milled, cooked, fermented, double-distilled, and barreled as bourbon and rye whiskey.

Traditional enough spirits, then, but that isn't the whole story. Peerless has eschewed the sour mash process used in bourbon-making. This is the process by which the dregs of the previous production run—a mixture of water and spent grains (with all their sugars removed, hence sour) and known as backset—are added in to the start of the next run. This is done because the backset controls the bacteria in the next fermentation, and that in turn helps to ensure consistency in the new spirit.

Peerless instead produces spirit in sterilized conditions, and believes that this will result in a better and unique bourbon when it is eventually bottled in 2019.

There is another difference, too, between the method here and conventional practice. The Peerless distillers take the view that adding water to the finished spirit just before casking is a clumsy way of bringing it down to bottling strength. So they add water at the start of the maturation process, putting the spirit in the barrel at a strength in the mid-50s ABV, which is significantly less than the standard casking strength.

No doubt other distillers are watching Peerless with a mixture of curiosity and bemusement, but that's what craft distilling should be all about. And when the rye was released in 2017, the price may have caused mumblings, but the quality of the whiskey didn't. It is fabulous, as good as anything produced anywhere in the world. Kentucky Peerless is back with a bang.

Head distiller Caleb Kilburn, an amiable and enthusiastic man who can dazzle you with his technical knowledge, sums it up perfectly: 'We're making whiskey in downtown Louisville and it's great,' he says. 'We're living the dream.'

WILLETT DISTILLERY

LOCATION BARDSTOWN, KENTUCKY **FOUNDED** 2012 **WHISKEY STYLES** BOURBON, RYE **VISITOR FACILITIES** THE DISTILLERY WELCOMES VISITORS FOR TOURS YEAR-ROUND

Although the new Willett Distillery started producing spirit for the first time in 2012, Willett as a business has a history stretching back much farther. Indeed, a Willett Distillery was opened in 1937. The original distillery is long gone, but a whiskey business has continued in Bardstown, the pretty Kentucky town known as the capital of bourbon. Members of the Kulsveen family have run Willett since the 1960s. In recent years, it has effectively operated as an independent bottler, buying in spirits and blending them to create its core range of whiskeys. Some time ago, and well before the current craft distilling boom, the decision was made to build a new distillery, but in order to avoid borrowing large sums of money the family decided to build it themselves, as and when finance was available to move the project forward. That process was completed in 2012, and the year before that Warehouse A was restored—the very warehouse into which Aloysius Lambert Thompson Willett, known as Thompson Willett, put the very first cask in 1937.

Today the distillery continues to sell its Small Batch Boutique Bourbon Collection, which comprises Rowan's Creek, Noah's Mill, Kentucky Vintage, and Pure Kentucky.

And Willett has added to a range of whiskeys that now includes Willett Family Estate Bottled Bourbon and Rye Whiskey, and a 'new' version of the traditional Willett whiskey, Old Bardstown.

PRICHARD'S

LOCATION KELSO AND NASHVILLE, TENNESSEE
FOUNDED 1999 **WHISKEY STYLES** RYE, MALT
BOURBON, FLAVORED BOURBON, SINGLE MALT
VISITOR FACILITIES BOTH SITES CONDUCT TOURS
AND TASTINGS

Whiskey and rum were originally made here in the 1820s by Benjamin Prichard and then by his son, Enoch. The Prichard family was known to make the best whiskey in the area way before it was legal to do so. When descendant Phil Prichard opened Prichard's Distillery in Kelso in 1999, he restored a lost art form. Both rum and whiskey are key to the company now.

Prichard's still has the distillery in Kelso, and now also has a distillery at Fontanel, a 75-hectare (186-acre) property formerly owned by country star Barbara Mandrell. Here the production facility includes an alembic copper still custom-designed by Vendome Copper and Brassworks in the style of cognac-makers in France. The tasting center is in a log cabin next door.

The distillery's Tennessee whiskey is the only one to be allowed to use that name without including the charcoal mellowing method known as the Lincoln County process in its production. Among the company's offerings is a chocolate-infused bourbon made in partnership with Nashville-based chocolatier Olive & Sinclair.

CHATTANOOGA WHISKEY CO.

LOCATION CHATTANOOGA, TENNESSEE **FOUNDED**
2015 **WHISKEY STYLES** BLENDED, BOURBON
VISITOR FACILITIES TOURS AND TASTING ARE HELD
DAILY, A COCKTAIL LOUNGE IS OPEN THURSDAY TO
SATURDAY EVENINGS

This micro-distillery is making the first legal whiskey in the town for more than 100 years. At its peak, Market Street, where it is located, had 20 distilleries. Known as the Tennessee Stillhouse, the company's distillery is described as an experimental distillery, and although the company is still very young, the distillers are open to new ideas.

'It's part experiment and innovation lab, part museum and all good,' says the company. 'It's a place to showcase the craft process and the whiskey tradition we come from, while also allowing us to get creative with techniques and to showcase our current products.'

The distillery currently makes bourbons at 45 per cent ABV (90 proof) and 56.8 per cent ABV (113 proof). The still is known affectionately as 'Doc.'

CORSAIR

LOCATION NASHVILLE, TENNESSEE **FOUNDED** 2008
WHISKEY STYLES SINGLE MALT, RYE, OAT, QUINOA,
AMERICAN WHISKEY **VISITOR FACILITIES** ALL THREE
COMPANY SITES OFFER TOURS AND TASTINGS

Craft distilleries come in all sizes, but Corsair is a shining example of just what can be achieved if you get everything in order, and the spirits, imagery, and marketing hit the button. Although the company has ended up in the Tennessee section of this book because that's where it principally operates from, its first distillery, which it still operates, was at Bowling Green, Kentucky. That's because when the company was launched, Tennessee's laws prevented it from distilling in the state. Once distilling began, though, success followed, and law changes meant that Corsair could expand by returning to its native state. It now operates two additional distilleries in Nashville: the more recent one houses a modern still and visitor facilities that include a matching copper libation and tasting bar; the older one has a brewery and distillery, and offers tastings of experimental whiskeys and unique beers. The company also makes other spirits, including gin and absinthe.

The distillery was set up by childhood friends Darek Bell and Andrew Webber who began home-brewing beer and wine in Darek and Amy Lee Bell's garage. At one point and for reasons known only to them, they were working on a biodiesel plant when they hit a problem. Andrew made an offhand comment about it being easier to make whiskey, and so they decided to give it a try. To their surprise, they found out that it was.

The duo decided not to limit themselves to any particular style of whiskey, and they have now tried many varieties. Not all of them have been a huge success, but overall Corsair has become synonymous with groundbreaking and experimental whiskeys, including one made with oats (not easy: the sticky mix can clog up the system) and another made with the super health food quinoa (if you're going to sell whiskey in California or San Francisco quinoa is a must, Darek once explained).

The whiskeys are all packaged in cool black and white Rat Pack-cum-gangster-style packaging. They have playful names such as Ryemageddon and Oatrage, and are marketed under the collective descriptor 'Booze for Badasses.'

At any given time there are several core releases and a regularly changing collection of special releases. Past bottlings have included Buck Yeah, made with buckwheat and Victory malt; Galaxy, which is a single malt whiskey flavored with hops; Citra Double IPA, a malt whiskey flavored with citra hops; and Nashville, a distinctively American cherrywood-smoked bourbon.

Corsair has been picking up awards consistently ever since its first whiskeys were launched.

JOHN EMERALD DISTILLING CO.

LOCATION OPELIKA, ALABAMA **FOUNDED** 2015
WHISKEY STYLES SINGLE MALT WHISKEY **VISITOR FACILITIES** THE DISTILLERY OFFERS TOURS BY APPOINTMENT

John Sharp and his son Jimmy left a lucrative specialty plaster business (creating interior decorative plaster for Louis Vuitton stores all over the world) to open this micro-distillery.

The reason was simple. When Jimmy's wife gave birth to a daughter, neither dad nor granddad could face the prospect of missing the little girl growing up. They toyed with the idea of making beer, but decided to go for spirits instead.

They went about the task properly. They went to whiskey school in Breckenridge, Colorado, and to rum school in Loveland, Colorado, and they attended a technical distilling course at the Siebel Institute in Chicago. Jimmy also completed an internship at the Scottish malt distillery Springbank in Campbeltown.

All the training gave them the confidence to start producing two of the hardest spirits of all to distill—rum and single malt whiskey.

Both the distillery, which covers 743-sq-m (8,000-sq-ft), and the single malt are named after one of their relatives, John Emerald Sharp, who 'lived a life to be proud of, a life of integrity and honor, with love for God, his fellow man, and his family.'

Their single malt is made with barley that has been smoked with peach and pecan wood. It is the first whiskey to be produced legally in Alabama for more than 100 years.

WIDOW JANE DISTILLERY

LOCATION BROOKLYN, NEW YORK **FOUNDED** 2014
WHISKEY STYLES BOURBON, AGED RYE MASH
VISITOR FACILITIES CHOCOLATE AND WHISKEY. WHAT A COMBINATION

Widow Jane Distillery was founded by Daniel Preston and named after the Widow Jane Mine, from which came much of the rock used to build the city of New York.

The distillery is making and laying down whiskey, but its releases to date have been brought in from a distillery in Kentucky. The offerings include: a ten-year-old bourbon; a rye mash matured in American wood and applewood casks; and, most intriguingly, Widow Jane Dregs. When the company empties casks for bottling it leaves the last inch of spirit because it is full of charcoal and sediment. But the distillers found that once the sediment had been filtered out, a gutsy and bold whiskey was left, so it bottles it for those who like something more fiery than the regular spirit.

COOPERSTOWN DISTILLERY

LOCATION COOPERSTOWN, NEW YORK **FOUNDED** 2013 **WHISKEY STYLES** BOURBON, AMERICAN WHISKEY, BLENDED, FLAVOURED WHISKEY **VISITOR FACILITIES** TOURS ON SATURDAY AFTERNOONS YEAR ROUND; EXTRA TOURS IN THE SUMMER

Founded and still owned by Gene Marra, Cooperstown is a farm distillery in the upstate New York village of the same name. It is located close to the National Baseball Hall of Fame, and the baseball theme is used extensively in the distillery's products. Some of the whiskeys come in baseball-shaped glass decanters, and its bourbons include Beanball (a baseball term for a dangerous pitch thrown by frustrated pitchers to scare batters off the plate) and Spitball, a cinnamon whiskey named for a ball illegally tampered with.

Cooperstown makes bourbons, American whiskeys, flavored whiskeys, and a white whiskey. Some of its whiskeys are blended and additionally distilled at Cooperstown, but are bought in as bourbon from Indiana.

CATSKILL DISTILLING CO.

LOCATION BETHEL, NEW YORK **FOUNDED** 2010
WHISKEY STYLES BOURBON, RYE, WHEAT, HYBRID,
WHITE **VISITOR FACILITIES** TOURS AND TASTINGS
DAILY; PRIVATE TOURS CAN BE ARRANGED

Catskill is a farm distillery a stone's throw away from the site where the legendary Woodstock Festival was held. Proprietors Monte and Stacy Sachs also own the adjacent hostelry, The Dancing Cat Saloon, which sells Catskill spirits as well as high-quality craft beer and quality food. Dr Monte Sachs learned to distill while at veterinary college in Italy. There he met an 80-year-old named Bernardini, who taught him how to make grappa. Monte now makes this spirit at Catskill.

The Sachs are serious about their spirits business. They commissioned German still-makers Christian and Jacob Carl to create the bespoke copper stills that are today visible behind the glass wall of the distillery's tasting room; and they used the late, great Lincoln Henderson as a consultant. Lincoln spent many years as commercial distiller at Brown Forman, playing a key role in the development of Jack Daniel's and Woodford Reserve.

The themes of history, art, music, and community are important not only to the distillery but also to The Dancing Cat Saloon and The Stray Cat Gallery, which opened across the street in the spring of 2013. The art deco bar at the distillery comes from the 1939 World's Fair in Flushing. The music of the concerts at Bethel Woods Center for the Arts, located on the Woodstock site, is echoed in weekly performances at the distillery. The artwork created by Stray Cat artists is displayed on the walls of The Dancing Cat.

Throughout the year the distillery hosts a range of events, from musical concerts to cocktail competitions, and the aim of its owners is to create a strong feel for the community.

Catskill works closely with local farmers to source grains and fruit for its products. Water is taken from the Catskill Mountains.

The distillery's whiskey offering includes the following: Most Righteous Bourbon, created by Monte Sachs and Lincoln Henderson, and featuring a mash bill of 70 per cent corn, 20 per cent rye, and 10 per cent malted barley; Catskill and Defiant straight ryes; Fearless wheat whiskey; and 'the One and Only' Buckwheat, made with 80 per cent buckwheat, which is a pulse and not a grain, meaning that it is strictly not a whiskey at all.

DARK ISLAND SPIRITS

LOCATION ALEXANDRIA BAY, NEW YORK
FOUNDED 2012 **WHISKEY STYLES** BOURBON,
WHEAT, HYBRID, FLAVORED **VISITOR
FACILITIES** FREE TOURS ARE AVAILABLE
ON REQUEST

Between New York and Canada, to the east of Lake Ontario and near the mouth of the St Lawrence River, is a waterway full of small islands. It was on some of these during Prohibition that illicit distillers worked, and revelers came by motorboat and island-hopped from one party to the next. It is these partygoers and bootleggers that Dark Island Spirits honors with its products. This distillery isn't conventional. Having observed that casks spending months on trains or in the hull of a ship matured better than those that remained always in a single place, because the spirit in the casks was constantly moving, the owners of Dark Island designed a machine to mature their spirits through a process that uses a muscial accompaniment, which creates liquid waves that force the spirit into the wood, thus aiding maturation. Among the Dark Island whiskeys are a bourbon matured to R & B, and Snow Wheat Whiskey, matured to the sounds of Christmas carols.

DENNING'S POINT

LOCATION BEACON, NEW YORK **FOUNDED** 2014
WHISKEY STYLES BOURBON, AMERICAN CORN
WHISKEY **VISITOR FACILITIES** TOURS ARE CONDUCTED
ON SATURDAY AND SUNDAY FOR A SMALL FEE

Denning's Point Distillery is the result of a collision of two worlds. Cofounders Karl Johnson and Susan Keramedjian have very different backgrounds and experiences, but pooling their respective talents has created a distillery that is more than the sum of its parts.

Karl grew up on a large farm in Minnesota, studied under his father, a plant geneticist and agronomist who bred barley for malt. Karl later worked in chemical engineering, distilling rocket fuel components. Meanwhile Susan spent many years in corporate marketing and design in New York City. Together they are now creating and promoting spirits that include a straight bourbon bottled at 50 per cent ABV (100 proof) and a smooth American whiskey made from corn mash and bottled at 52 per cent ABV (104 proof). These spirits are distilled on a bespoke hybrid still that features both a pot and a column.

HILLROCK ESTATE DISTILLERY

LOCATION ANCRAM, NEW YORK **FOUNDED** 2011
WHISKEY STYLES SINGLE MALT, WOOD-FINISHED
RYE **VISITOR FACILITIES** THE DISTILLERY HAS A BAR
AND TASTING ROOM; TOURS CAN BE ARRANGED BY
APPOINTMENT

Once upon a time, the State of New York produced more than half the country's barley and rye, and hundreds of distillers produced whiskey and gin. Prohibition ended that, but the Hudson Valley remains a fine place to make whiskey and distilling is now making a comeback. Hillrock Estate Distillery occupies an 1806 Georgian house built by a successful grain merchant and Revolutionary War captain. It has been meticulously restored to its original beauty, and overlooks the distillery's own barley fields and the distant Berkshire Mountains.

The distillery itself, the malt house, and the granary and barrel houses are located at the center of the estate surrounded by rolling grain fields.

Hillrock has custom-made copper distillation equipment. The copper pot still, mash tun, and spirit receiver were handmade by American craftsmen to the distillery's specifications. Housed in a traditional barn, the equipment provides extraordinary control over the character and quality of each individual small batch of spirit.

The owner of the distillery is Jeffrey Baker, and he has brought in former Maker's Mark distiller and American whiskey heavyweight Dave Pickerell to oversee distilling and production. The result is a number of top-quality whiskeys. These include a bourbon made using a solera system, in which new whiskey is added to the top of the barrel as matured whiskey is removed from the bottom to be bottled.

LONG ISLAND SPIRITS

O'BEGLEY

LOCATION BAITING HOLLOW, NEW YORK **FOUNDED** 2007 **WHISKEY STYLES** BOURBON, RYE, AMERICAN SINGLE MALT **VISITOR FACILITIES** THE DISTILLERY HAS A TASTING ROOM WHICH IS OPEN DAILY

LOCATION DUNDEE, NEW YORK **FOUNDED** 2011 **WHISKEY STYLES** POTEEN, IRISH-STYLE WHISKEY **VISITOR FACILITIES** THE DISTILLERY HAS A TASTING ROOM AND HOLDS TASTING EVENTS

This is the first craft distillery to be newly established on Long Island since the 1800s. In view of the fact that it is surrounded by 2,000 hectares (5,000 acres) of potato farms, it is perhaps unsurprising that its principal product is LiV Vodka. The distillery is also in the heart of an acclaimed wine region; the surrounding countryside is picturesque, and hence a popular stage on many tourist itineraries.

Long Island Spirits is housed in an old barn that was originally built in the 1900s but later fell badly into disrepair. The owners spent all of 2007 retrofitting and modernizing the interior of the barn as a state-of-the-art craft distillery. The distillery now mashes, ferments, distills, and bottles all its spirits on site.

The whiskeys currently produced at Long Island Spirits include Rough Rider Happy Warrior, which is a cask-strength bourbon aged in 250-liter (55-gallon) new American oak barrels for a minimum of four years. The base ingredients are then mingled in a small batch with older bourbon, and after that a second maturation takes place for a further three to six months in French former Merlot and Chardonnay oak casks that have been washed in aged brandy.

The distillery's Rough Rider Bull Moose is a rye that spends time maturing in three different, specially selected casks. First the rye is put into New American oak casks; it is then transferred into casks that had previously held bourbon; finally it is matured in a cask that previously contained the distillery's Pine Barrens Single Malt Whiskey.

O'Begley distillery makes Irish-style spirits, and the Irish link is a direct and strong one. The whiskey here is named Old Kilfountan after the farm in County Kerry, Ireland, that some members of the family behind the distillery have worked continuously since the 1880s.

'Today it is a dairy farm, where the traditions of agriculture and hard labor remain unchanged,' says the family. 'Most distilleries are built by businessmen and financiers. For us it was a different story.'

The O'Begley distillery was built from scratch over a three-year period. Most of the equipment was salvaged from shuttered factories. Motors and switches were pulled from outdated manufacturing operations in Rochester and Buffalo; pumps were purchased from the liquidated inventory of food processing plants, and the stills were built from old pharmaceutical reactors, modified and repurposed specifically for the production of whiskey.

Grain is locally grown, and each batch is crafted from grain milling to bottling at the distillery.

The distillery's poitin is effectively a white whiskey. It is made up of 75 per cent unmated barley, 20 per cent malted barley, and 5 per cent oats, all gently fermented by a beer-style ale yeast before distillation.

Old Kilfountan is a pot still whiskey, triple distilled in the Irish tradition. It is made from a fermented mash of locally grown barley, malted barley, and oats. Aged in reused bourbon casks, it has distinctive spice notes and a delicate texture.

UPSTATE DISTILLING CO.

LOCATION SARATOGA SPRINGS **FOUNDED** 2016 **WHISKEY STYLES** BOURBON, RYE **VISITOR FACILITIES** TASTING ROOM OPEN AT WEEKENDS YEAR-ROUND

The Upstate Distilling Co. officially opened its doors for the first time only at the back end of 2016, so it is still too early to make a definitive judgment about the quality of its products and its market potential. Nevertheless, founder and owner Ryen VanHall has high hopes for his bourbon and rye whiskeys, which are maturing in the barrel at his Saratoga Springs distillery.

Upstate is sited in a former bicycle factory that shut down in 2013. The large manufacturing floor provides sufficient room for a complete micro-distillery as well as ample storage space for American and Romanian oak whiskey barrels. There is also an area for bottling the spirits when they are ready.

So far the releases have been limited. Ryen's Rye is a cask-strength whiskey; Saratoga Springs is a whiskey made up of three grain spirits in almost equal proportions; and Winner's Circle is a white whiskey named with reference to the horse racing at nearby Saratoga Race Track.

VAN BRUNT STILLHOUSE

LOCATION BROOKLYN, NEW YORK **FOUNDED** 2012 **WHISKEY STYLES** BOURBON, RYE, AMERICAN WHISKEY, SINGLE MALT **VISITOR FACILITIES** TASTING ROOM OPEN THURSDAY TO SUNDAY; TOURS AND COCKTAILS

Van Brunt Stillhouse is inspired by the pioneering spirit of Cornelius Van Brunt, a farmer in the Dutch colony of Breukelen, and the distillery was founded by husband-and-wife team Daric Schlesselman and Sarah Ludington, who share a love of craft and who source all their ingredients from New York State.

Van Brunt Stillhouse American Whiskey is a four-grain whiskey made primarily from malted barley and wheat, with a little bit of corn and a touch of rye. Van Brunt Stillhouse Single Malt Whiskey is made with 100 per cent malted barley. The whiskey is matured for nine months in small, new barrels.

The distillery's moonshine is made not from the usual corn but from un-aged malt whiskey: 100 per cent New York State malted six-row barley.

TUTHILLTOWN SPIRITS

LOCATION GARDINER, NEW YORK **FOUNDED** 2005
WHISKEY STYLES BOURBON, RYE, CORN, BABY
BOURBON, SINGLE MALT **VISITOR FACILITIES** THE
VISITOR CENTER IS OPEN DAILY; TOURS ARE HELD
AT WEEKENDS, ALSO A TAVERN, A RESTAURANT,
AND A SHOP

There is an argument that Tuthilltown should not be in this book because the distillery is now owned by Scottish distilling company William Grant & Sons. But William Grant is a family company, Tuthilltown is a trailblazing company, and the distillery provides a great example of how craft distilling can grow from modest roots to be a significant player in the world of whiskey, so it makes the cut.

Tuthilltown was set up in 2005 and became the first new distillery in New York since Prohibition. Before that there had been up to 1,000 farm distilleries in the state. For 220 years Tuthilltown Gristmill, a landmark which is listed on the National Register of Historic Places, used water power to grind local grains into flour for brewing and distilling. It was fitting, then, that when distillery founders Ralph Erenzo and Brian Lee looked to set up a micro-distillery, they set to converting one of the mill granaries on the site. Two and a half years later, Tuthilltown Spirits produced its first batches of vodka from scraps they collected at a local apple-slicing plant.

The distillers also turned their hands to a range of whiskeys, and with smart packaging they were soon grabbing the attention of the slick and fashionable Manhattan crowd.

Today, Tuthilltown Spirits distills the highly awarded and internationally acclaimed Hudson Whiskey line. The company employs more than 50 staff.

WHISTLEPIG

LOCATION SHOREHAM, VERMONT **FOUNDED** 2008
WHISKEY STYLES RYE **VISITOR FACILITIES** N/A

In the often crazy world of craft distilling, there is no whiskey company quite like WhistlePig. It is a soap opera all of its own, complete with a larger-than-life character center stage.

Raj Bhakta has run for national office as a Republican, starred in Donald Trump's television show *The Apprentice*, earned a reputation as a ladies' man, and made bow ties an American fashion item. He has also fought a very public fight with two of his executive board members to keep control of a company he founded, which operates off his farm using materials he has grown, and which has proved massively successful under his stewardship. A back shed distillery operated by a retired school teacher, WhistlePig most certainly is not.

Controversy has followed Bhakta ever since he first set up his whiskey company on a farm he bought in Vermont in 2007. His first battle was to establish that whiskey could be considered a farm product, and therefore covered by agricultural laws and not more probative and expensive industrial ones. And he courted further controversy when he was accused of lack of transparency by buying his first whiskey stocks from Canada, maturing and improving them in America, and not defining them as Canadian.

But it would be a huge mistake to dismiss WhistlePig as some form of fake operation and not to credit Bhakta and his team for producing some amazing rye whiskey.

At the heart of the operation is the former Maker's Mark distiller and ubiquitous whiskey consultant Dave Pickerell, who has done wonders with rye stock that was originally brought in from elsewhere, but is now being produced on a Pickerell-designed pot still which is housed in a 150-year-old barn on the farm site.

WhistlePig is all about rye, which the team says produces the best whiskey in the world.

'As rye contains less sugar than any other grain, it is a challenge to produce, requiring aging longer than other whiskeys to attain a desired smoothness,' says Bhakta. 'But when handled properly, there is no comparison: the brat rye whiskey, once tamed, emerges from many years in the barrel with the power of a linebacker and the grace of a ballerina.'

WhistlePig pursues a policy of 'triple terroir,' which means that it now uses rye grown on the farm, water from its well, and casks made from oak grown on the estate.

'Vermont is about as far north as oak trees can grow,' says Pickerell. 'The shorter growing seasons lead to oak trees with the most growth rings. When aging whiskey encounters a growth ring in a barrel it imparts flavor, so our custom Vermont oak barrels bring tremendous depth to our whiskeys.'

Most of the ryes produced so far by WhistlePig have been bought in, and they cover a range of ages and styles. But the farm influence is starting to make itself known. The oldest rye, at 15 years old, is finished in Vermont oak, and the non-age statement rye Farmstock is a mix of young rye made on the farm mixed with some 5-, 6- and 12-year-old rye.

All whiskeys from this company are very good, but the star of the show is The Boss Hog IV The Black Prince. It's called that because that was the nickname of Edward of Woodstock, an English prince who terrorized the French: Boss Hog is matured in French Armagnac casks.

NEW ENGLAND SWEETWATER

LOCATION WINCHESTER, NEW HAMPSHIRE
FOUNDED N/A **WHISKEY STYLES** SINGLE MALT,
BOURBON, MOONSHINE **VISITOR FACILITIES**
TASTING ROOM; SATURDAY AFTERNOON TOURS FOR
FEE REDEEMABLE AGAINST PURCHASE OF A BOTTLE

Sweetwater is a farm and distillery business. The farm occupies 20 hectares (50 acres) on which chickens are raised and heirloom cider apples, grapes, blueberries, and juniper berries are grown. The distillery is based in nearby Winchester. It makes a range of spirits, including an aged moonshine and a bourbon. Perhaps its best is its Clark & Chesterfield American Single Malt Whiskey, which is double-distilled, matured in ex-bourbon barrels from FEW Spirits, and produced using a solera system. The distillery releases 70–120 bottles per month, with the remainder held back for longer maturation.

LIQUID RIOT BOTTLING CO.

LOCATION PORTLAND, MAINE **FOUNDED** N/A
WHISKEY STYLES RYE, BOURBON, OAT, SINGLE
MALT **VISITOR FACILITIES** THE DISTILLERY
HOLDS EVENTS AND THE SPIRITS CAN BE TASTED
IN THE 'RESTO-BAR'

Liquid Riot Bottling Company was established on the waterfront in Portland's Old Port, just a few blocks from City Hall and the location of the Portland rum riot, in homage to those who fought for their beverage of choice. It consists of a brewery, distillery, and what it describes as a resto-bar, which is an informal dining area with quality craft beer on tap, and an appealing choice of menu items, made mainly with locally sourced seasonal products. Its spirit offering includes bier schnapps, an agave spirit, and Fernet Michaud, which is a bitter spirit from the Italian amaro family.

MAINE CRAFT DISTILLING

LOCATION PORTLAND, MAINE **FOUNDED** 2012
WHISKEY STYLES MOONSHINE, BARLEY SPIRIT,
SINGLE MALT WHISKEY **VISITOR FACILITIES**
THE TASTING ROOM IS OPEN DAILY; TOURS ARE
CONDUCTED THURSDAY TO SUNDAY

Portland has long been a hub for the craft brewing movement, so it should come as no surprise that its craft distilleries tend to be on the creative and innovative side. Maine Craft Distilling uses local land, field, and forest to make its spirits, and it has thought carefully about what it makes, and given it a distinctive twist. Most unusually, Maine Craft Distilling makes a gin-like spirit using carrots. Its Black Cap, named after the Maine State bird, is a triple-distilled barley spirit filtered through maple charcoal; its Blueshine is barley spirit with Maine blueberries and maple syrup added; and its single malt whiskey is called Fifty Stone because it is said that you need 50 stones (318kg) of barley to make a barrel of whiskey. It is smoked with Maine peat and locally sourced seaweed.

SPLIT ROCK DISTILLING

LOCATION BRISTOL, MAINE **FOUNDED** 2014
WHISKEY STYLES BOURBON, WHITE WHISKEY
VISITOR FACILITIES THE DISTILLERY OFFERS
TOURS, TASTINGS AND HIKING TRAILS

When Split Rock Distilling founders Topher Mallory and Matt Page finally opened the doors of their fully organic distillery, it marked the end of two years' intensive effort.

'We spent evenings and weekends building a distillery and tasting room by hand in an old barn on historic Route One,' they say. 'We sourced organic grains and fruits from the fields of farmers we count as friends. We demanded organic sugars, and drew waters so pure locals still harvest winter ice.'

The distillery is named for the dirt track that links the homes of the founders. The two friends proudly claim that this is the only shortcut they've ever taken in the creation of their products. They make gin and vodka, as well as a white whiskey and bourbon. The last named, in particular, is just as Topher and Matt describe it:

'Split rocks, whether worn by water, cracked by fire, or prized apart by a mason with wedges, open to reveal an unexpected smoothness within. Every bottle of Split Rock Organic Bourbon does the same.'

BERKSHIRE MOUNTAIN

LOCATION SHEFFIELD, MASSACHUSETTS **FOUNDED** 2007 **WHISKEY STYLES** BOURBON, CORN **VISITOR FACILITIES** SENSORY NOSING AND TASTING TOURS MOST DAYS; CHARGES APPLY

Berkshire founder, owner, and distiller Chris Weld has had a long career in medicine, obtaining a master's degree in emergency medicine and spending 20 years as a physician's assistant in one of the busiest emergency rooms in the San Francisco Bay area. But he has also had a long-held interest in distilling—he tried to make a still for a school project until his mum found out that to do so was illegal—and when the family decided to move back to the East Coast for a more relaxed life, distilling became a viable option. Chris bought a neglected apple farm, spent three years getting the orchards to bear fruit again, and then decided to make apple brandy. The farm is home to granite-based springwater, which is ideal for making bourbon and corn whiskey. Berkshire Mountain Bourbon has won several awards, including a gold medal from Jim Murray's *Whisky Bible*.

BOSTON HARBOR DISTILLERY

LOCATION BOSTON, MASSACHUSETTS **FOUNDED** 2012 **WHISKEY STYLES** RYE, HOPPED WHISKEY **VISITOR FACILITIES** REGULAR TOURS, TASTINGS, AND COCKTAILS ON FRIDAY AND SATURDAY AFTERNOONS

Boston is a proud city soaked in history, and it would be hard to think of a location more at the heart of it than the harborside. That's where you'll find the Boston Harbor Distillery. It was founded by Rhonda Kallman, who had been at the forefront of the craft brewing movement, but after 25 years was looking for a new challenge and identified whiskey as 'clearly the next emerging category.'

It took two years of searching before she found the perfect site at The Port on Boston Harbor. Built in 1859, it is one of the last remaining mill buildings in the area. It had been seriously neglected, and took more than a year to renovate.

Rhonda recruited whiskey-making genius Dr Jim Swan to perfect her grain spirit offerings, and today the distillery produces a number of grain spirits made with various Samuel Adams beers under the name Spirit of Boston.

TRIPLE EIGHT DISTILLERY

LOCATION NANTUCKET, MASSACHUSETTS FOUNDED
2000 WHISKEY STYLES SINGLE MALT, BOURBON
VISITOR FACILITIES DISTILLERY, BREWERY, AND
VINEYARDS ARE OPEN ALL YEAR AND TOURS OF ALL
THREE ARE CONDUCTED, WITH TOURS RESTRICTED IN
WINTER; THERE IS A CHARGE, BUT YOU GET TO TASTE
TWO BEERS, TWO WINES, AND TWO SPIRITS

Nantucket is an island about 48 km (30 miles) south of Cape Cod, and it is home to this highly successful business, which is made up of a vineyard established in 1981, a brewery called Cisco Brewers, which was set up in 1995, and a distillery called Triple Eight Distillery, which, when opened in 1997, was ahead of the craft movement by some years.

'We are just about the coolest place on planet Earth,' says the distillery. 'Having never personally traveled to other parts of the galaxy, we can't quite say "in all the Milky Way," but we're pretty confident that we would make the top 10.'

That's some boast, but certainly the drink products coming from here—especially Triple Eight, named after the pure water source used to make the spirits—have well and truly put Nantucket on the map.

Few micro-distilleries have won as many international awards as Triple Eight. It is most famous for The Notch, or Not Scotch, which has won countless awards since it was introduced in 2008. It was created in 2000 by founder and original Triple Eight distiller Dean Long, who called in George McClements, former production manager at Islay's Bowmore Distillery, to advise on technique for batch distillation. The Notch Single Malt Whisky was eventually released on August 8, 2008. It is not Scotch, but it is a rich, fruity delight that holds its own with Scotland's finest.

LITCHFIELD DISTILLERY

LOCATION LITCHFIELD, CONNECTICUT **FOUNDED** 2014 **WHISKEY STYLES** BOURBON **VISITOR FACILITIES** TOURS AND TASTINGS ON AFTERNOONS FROM WEDNESDAY TO SUNDAY

Team members at Litchfield Distillery call themselves 'batchers' in honor of the early farmers of Northwest Connecticut.

'This is a region that became known for its ample yield of wheat, corn, and barley. Coaxing these crops from the rocky terrain took a certain type of grit and determination. Today, we take the best our local famers have to offer, and distill fine craft spirits, one batch at a time. They do the growing. We do the batching.'

Located in northwest Connecticut, the distillery was founded by brothers David and Jack Baker, along with their head distiller, James McCoy. The Bakers grew up in the water bottling business. The family company had been bringing the high-quality Connecticut water called Crystal Rock to consumers for more than three generations. That sort of quality water is ideal for making spirits.

Litchfield makes a bourbon, a bourbon matured in two types of barrel, and a number of flavored bourbons.

SONS OF LIBERTY

LOCATION SOUTH KINGSTOWN, RHODE ISLAND
FOUNDED 2010 **WHISKEY STYLES** BOURBON,
PEATED BOURBON, SINGLE MALT, FLAVORED
VISITOR FACILITIES TASTING ROOM WITH WHISKEY
OR BEER FLIGHTS IS OPEN THURSDAY TO SUNDAY;
DISTILLERY TOURS ON SATURDAY AFTERNOONS

The coolly named Sons of Liberty distillery has a very clear idea of what it wants to be and what it wants to do. Founded and owned by Mike Reppucci, the distillery was created 'to revolutionize and redefine American whiskey.' There is no doubt that it is part of the movement doing exactly that.

'We started with a couple of questions,' says Mike. 'Why is no one distilling single malt whiskeys from the beers we love? And why are there so many seasonal beers, but no seasonal whiskeys? With a spirit for innovation, we set out to create a line of whiskeys the world had never seen.'

Sons of Liberty answers these questions with two styles of whiskey. The first is its single malt range. Rather than take a beer and distil it, the distillers are taking the malts associated with different beer styles, such as the dark malts that normally feature in stout, or the Belgian-style malts and yeasts used in the production of Belgian ale, to produce whiskeys heavily influenced by craft brewing techniques. The whiskeys have revolutionary-inspired names such as Battle Cry and Uprising.

The seasonal products include a whiskey infused with the juice of thousands of apples (ideal for evenings in the fall); a honey and chamomile whiskey that offers warmth in winter; and a pumpkin and spice version that is perfect for celebrating the harvest.

BIG SPRING SPIRITS

LOCATION BELLAFONTE, PENNSYLVANIA **FOUNDED** 2014 **WHISKEY STYLES** RYE, AMERICAN WHISKEY, WHITE WHISKEY **VISITOR FACILITIES** THE DISTILLERY IS OPEN MOST DAYS FOR FOOD AND DRINK, AND HOSTS A NUMBER OF LIVE MUSIC EVENTS

From the very earliest days of American distilling, whiskey was made with rye, and one of its heartlands was Pennsylvania. German and Dutch farmers settled there, and progressed from making rye schnapps to making a rye whiskey.

With rye currently in vogue, it's great to see the state awash with new distillers resurrecting the old whiskey styles. Big Spring was set up by the unlikely combination of cell and molecular biologist Kevin Lloyd, who gave up his own business for Big Spring Spirits, and interior designer Paul Cipar. The distillery makes a 100 per cent rye, bottled at a weighty 49.3 per cent ABV (98.6 proof). The distillery also makes what it describes as a 'bourbon-style' whiskey that has a bourbon mash bill of 65 per cent corn, 34 per cent wheat, and 1 per cent rye. It is bottled at 53.85 per cent ABV (107.7).

BLUEBIRD DISTILLING

LOCATION PHOENIXVILLE, PENNSYLVANIA **FOUNDED** 2015 **WHISKEY STYLES** BOURBON, RYE, WHITE WHISKEY, SINGLE MALT **VISITOR FACILITIES** THE DISTILLERY HAS A TASTING ROOM AND INTRODUCED TOURS IN 2018

Bluebird founder and owner Jared Adkins says that this distillery is an accumulation of years of hard work and love of spirits. After he graduated, he started work in engineering and corporate manufacturing, but his heart wasn't in industry. So when he read that Pennsylvania State distilling laws were to be relaxed, he set about learning about spirits, going on courses and visiting as many distilleries as he could. With the help of his father and a good friend, he converted a disused building into today's distillery. The bourbon made here uses four grains in its mash bill, and, unusually, Bluebird makes a wheat whiskey using 100 per cent wheat as well as a 100 per cent rye—both styles require exceptional levels of skill to distil properly. Bluebird pairs with local Phoenixville businesses for events such as food and spirits pairings.

DISOBEDIENT SPIRITS

LOCATION HOMER CITY, PENNSYLVANIA **FOUNDED** 2014 **WHISKEY STYLES** BOURBON, RYE, CORN AND HYBRID WHISKEY **VISITOR FACILITIES** THE DISTILLERY HAS A BAR, RACK HOUSE, AND IS OPEN WEDNESDAY TO SUNDAY; IT IS AVAILABLE TO HIRE

Pennsylvania relaxed its licencing laws in 2012 just as Bob Begg was retiring after 28 years of teaching. At the same time he was approached by his colleague Bob Sechrist, who had made wine for years, and from their meeting the idea for Disobedient was born.

The distillery is located in the hills of Western Pennsylvania, and the name is a nod to the fact that it was nearby that 13 struggling farmers decided to take a stand against what they saw as oppression and unjustified taxes. What followed was the Whiskey Rebellion of 1794.

'Our heroes are people who speak out against injustice and oppression even when such actions are unpopular,' say the founders. 'We celebrate freedom, we honor justice, and invite you to join our cause with a good stiff drink.'

Disobedient Spirits makes a range of spirits, including a rye whiskey.

MANATAWNY
STILL WORKS

LOCATION POTTSTOWN, PENNSYLVANIA **FOUNDED**
2013 **WHISKEY STYLES** AMERICAN WHISKEY,
UN-AGED WHISKEY **VISITOR FACILITIES**
CONDUCTED TOURS AT WEEKENDS INCLUDE
TASTINGS AND ONE OF THE DISTILLERY'S
SIGNATURE COCKTAILS

Pennsylvania is steeped in history, and many parts of it have strong links to the founding of the United States, the American Revolution, the Civil War, and industrialization. Manatawny is a 29-km (18-mile) tributary of the mighty Schuylkill River that cuts through the countryside and has become home to a winery, a brewery, and now a distillery. The name comes from the Lenape Indian *Man'en'tau'wata'wik*, meaning 'the place we meet to drink,' which is totally appropriate to what is happening there now. Manatawny Still Works named some of its early spirits after historical characters who played a part in the development of the region—John Potts, for example, the English Quaker who founded Pottstown.

Manatawny's principal product is an American whiskey called Keystone, which is dominated by malt but also includes wheat, oats, and rye, and is matured for between 12 and 36 months.

NEW LIBERTY

LOCATION PHILADELPHIA, PENNSYLVANIA
FOUNDED 2014 **WHISKEY STYLES** BOURBON, CORN,
MALT, AMERICAN, WHITE **VISITOR FACILITIES** TOURS
AND TASTINGS ON SATURDAYS; THERE IS A CHARGE
FOR EACH

What sets New Liberty apart from many of its competitors is that it has a range of heritage whiskeys that resurrect the memory of long-lost distilleries. Its Melky Miller whiskey, for instance, is named after Miller Rye Whiskey, which was produced at the M J Miller & Sons Distillery just outside the village of Accident, Maryland, until Prohibition. The passage of the Volstead Act in 1919 brought the family business to an end. The distillery itself was closed and left to decay.

The ruins of the abandoned distillery stood for decades until destroyed by fires in the 1970s and 1990s. New Liberty's whiskey isn't a rye, it's 100 per cent corn, but it has a fine backstory. Other whiskeys in the range are Old Maryland and Melvale, both made with mashes of two grains, split 51 to 49 per cent. The Dutch malt whiskey is named in honor of the early pioneers who traveled to America from Germany.

WIGLE WHISKEY DISTILLERY

LOCATION PITTSBURGH, PENNSYLVANIA **FOUNDED**
2011 **WHISKEY STYLES** RYE, BOURBON, WHEAT, AND
ORGANIC MALT **VISITOR FACILITIES** THE DISTILLERY
HAS THREE SITES TO TASTE AND TOUR, WHERE YOU
CAN MAKE YOUR OWN COCKTAILS AND ENJOY EVENTS

Pittsburgh Distilling Co. is the parent company for Wigle— pronounced 'wiggle'—Whiskey. Throughout the 1700s and 1800s, Western Pennsylvania was the center of American whiskey production. Wigle is named after one of the pioneering Pennsylvania distillers. In the 1790s, Phillip Wigle defended his right to distill in a tussle with a tax collector. He was eventually sentenced by George Washington to hang for treason, but was pardoned and continued to make whiskey.

The Wigle Whiskey Distillery opened to the public in 2012, and now makes scores of different award-winning spirits. Among these are several versions of rye, including the quirky Wry Rusky, inspired by a local brewery's Black in the USSR, a Russian imperial stout. Rye and five malts are used for a spirit that is matured in charred oak barrels for 18 months to make a 'spicy, roasty, toasty, boozy, and bold' whiskey.

MINGO CREEK CRAFT DISTILLERS

LOCATION WASHINGTON COUNTY, PENNSYLVANIA
FOUNDED 2016 **WHISKEY STYLES** BOURBON,
CORN, RYE **VISITOR FACILITIES** THE DISTILLERY
CONDUCTS A PAID-FOR TOUR ON SATURDAYS, AND
STAGES MURDER MYSTERY DINNERS AND OTHER
OCCASIONAL EVENTS

Mingo Creek Craft Distillers is confusingly known alternatively as Liberty Pole, and its email address is taken from the latter. So, in order to clarify and prevent misunderstandings, Mingo Creek Craft styles itself 'the purveyor of Liberty Pole Spirits.'

No US state has so many distilleries as proud of their history, their rebelliousness, and their regional culture, as Pennsylvania. The Whiskey Tax introduced by George Washington's government in 1791 was viewed by many people as out of touch with practical reality. Pennsylvania farmers had struggled to survive off the land, and relied on whiskey sales from their grains, using the spirit as a currency. So when Washington decided to tax whiskey to pay off his war debts, there was uproar.

Mingo Creek is where the impoverished local farmers met secretly and vowed not to pay the tax. They were the first men to oppose an act of the new government, and they vowed to stick together. They called themselves the Mingo Creek Society, and as a symbol of their unity they planted liberty poles throughout the county.

The distillery's Bassett Town Rye is made up of four grains and has a relatively low rye content. Its most unusual whiskey is a peated bourbon made with just 59 per cent peated malt and 41 per cent unpeated malt. It is a tribute to the rebellious farmers, many of whom were of Scottish and Irish descent. All Mingo Creek whiskey labels bear a picture of a liberty pole.

COOPER RIVER DISTILLERS

LOCATION CAMDEN, NEW JERSEY FOUNDED
2014 WHISKEY STYLES RYE, EXPERIMENTAL BEER
WHISKEYS VISITOR FACILITIES TOURS, TASTINGS,
AND COCKTAILS EVERY FRIDAY EVENING AND
THROUGHOUT SATURDAY

Cooper River is an ambitious and innovative distillery that launched with a series of rums before turning its attention to an exciting line of one-off, never-to-be-repeated, experimental whiskeys. Its approach to distilling is straightforward and easy to summarize: keep it simple, and be unfailingly honest about what is going on. It is proud to style itself 'the first legal distillery in Camden, NJ, ever!'

Founder and chief distiller James Yoakum was born in Hopkinsville, Kentucky (which he accurately describes as 'a tobacco town through and through'), went to university in Philadelphia, and later worked in real estate. Meanwhile, he developed an interest in craft brewing and then in distilling.

His distillery's unique selling point is the series of blink-and-you'll-miss-them, one-off whiskeys made from a diverse range of beers brewed by local breweries. These include unusual styles such as porter and sour beer, some of which are produced in editions of fewer than 100 bottles.

Cooper River's rye has a traditional mash bill of 63 per cent rye, 23 per cent corn, and 14 per cent barley, and it is matured for just over a year in small, 67.5-liter (15-gallon) new oak barrels.

The distiller launched its first bourbon in 2017, using New Jersey corn and rye. It was distilled in the traditional way on a pot still, rather than by the more widely employed commercial column still method.

The distillery offers tours and tastings, and holds events from time to time. Somewhat bizarrely, however, New Jersey laws do not allow Cooper River to provide alcohol on these occasions, although the distillery says that it is happy for visitors to bring their own food.

OLD LINE

LOCATION BALTIMORE, MARYLAND **FOUNDED** 2017
WHISKEY STYLES SINGLE MALT **VISITOR FACILITIES**
TOURS ARE CONDUCTED ON SATURDAY AFTERNOONS,
OR DURING THE WEEK BY APPOINTMENT; THE
DISTILLERY HOLDS REGULAR EVENTS

It took a chance meeting in Seattle for the seeds of Old Line to be sown. Its creation has ensured that an established whiskey brand has secured a bright and exciting future. Mark McLaughlin and Arch Watkins, ex-Navy fliers with a lifelong love of whiskey, met Bob Stilnovich, who had founded Golden Distillery and had secured success with his American single malt, but was ready to retire. Mark and Arch spent all day six days a week learning how to distill from Bob, and when they were ready they opened their own distillery. They work closely with Middle West Spirits, and in addition to the flagship American single malt they have done limited runs of peated whiskey and a cask-strength version. The distillery's single malt has a taste which includes maple, vanilla, and a hint of apple.

TWIN VALLEY DISTILLERS

LOCATION ROCKVILLE, MARYLAND **FOUNDED** 2014
WHISKEY STYLES BOURBON, AMERICAN WHISKEY,
FOUR GRAIN **VISITOR FACILITIES** FREE TASTINGS
ARE HELD TUESDAY TO FRIDAY, TOURS MAY BE
BOOKED

Twin Valley was founded by Edgardo Zuniga, a chef who became interested in pairing food with suitable alcoholic beverages. Over his career this developed into a fascination, and when he retired from the kitchen he set about making spirits himself. His new business was part of a turnaround for Maryland, as distilling returned to the state which had formerly been a major producer of rye. Consequently it is no surprise that Twin Valley produces a rye, although one that features three additional grains rather than the more conventional two. Among Twin Valley's other products are a young rye, a vodka, and a rum. Edgardo and his team work closely with local farmers, and offers classes in distilling and setting up a micro-distillery.

PAINTED STAVE DISTILLING

LOCATION SMYRNA, DELAWARE **FOUNDED** 2011 **WHISKEY STYLES** RYE, BOURBON **VISITOR FACILITIES** THE DISTILLERY OFFERS TOURS AND IS OPEN THURSDAY AND FRIDAY EVENINGS AND SATURDAY AND SUNDAY AFTERNOONS

If Painted Stave Distilling founders Ron Gomes, Jr, and Mike Rasmussen were to offer a would-be micro-distiller some advice, it would most probably be to involve the authorities as much as possible. They succeeded in setting up a distillery despite hostile local laws, but they had to battle to reach their goal. They were introduced to each other by a mutual friend because they both had an interest in setting up a craft distillery. Although they were approaching the situation from different angles, it quickly became clear that they had broadly similar ideas as to what they wanted to achieve. The trouble was that when they met Delaware legislators they were informed that the State's current legislation would not allow it. At around the same time, the authorities were contacted by Dogfish Head brewery about a craft distillery law that would allow them to expand their current distilling operations in their brew pub. The two companies worked together, alongside the authorities, and with goodwill on both sides a law was passed in April 2012. And not just any law, but one of the most accommodating laws in the whole country.

Now Painted Stave is making a rye whiskey made up of 67 per cent rye, 25 per cent corn, and 8 per cent malted barley, and aged for 10 months, as well as a straight bourbon, and seasonal and experimental whiskeys.

The distillery offers tours at the weekends, and works closely with local companies in Smyrna to ensure that the distillery remains where the owners want it to always be: at the heart of the community.

CATOCTIN CREEK

LOCATION PURCELLVILLE, VIRGINIA **FOUNDED** 2009 **WHISKEY STYLES** RYE **VISITOR FACILITIES** 30-MINUTE TOURS ON THE HOUR EVERY DAY THE DISTILLERY IS OPEN. TASTING FLIGHTS ARE ALSO OFFERED, AND THE DISTILLERY HOSTS EVENTS

When Scott Harris dramatically announced that he wanted to give up a 20-year career as an engineer to open a distillery in 2009, he didn't expect his wife Becky to agree. But she did. She had worked as a chemical engineer before having children, and jumped at the chance to use her skills for making whiskey. Drawing influence from Virginia's history as a state producing rye, the couple created Roundstone Rye, which uses a mash bill of 100 per cent rye. The distillery now makes a range of rye whiskeys.

'Each whiskey is a single-barrel whiskey; therefore, we do not blend across barrels,' says Scott. 'When one barrel develops a richer, more mature flavor, we bottle it separately at a higher proof so as to not disrupt the consistency of the Roundstone Rye flavor.'

The couple have not rested on their laurels, and have been keen to innovate with their whiskeys. They have introduced innovative new products such as Rabble Rouser, designed to show off the whiskey's rye influence, and have been working with Adroit Theory Brewing, a local brewery known for avant-garde and experimental beers.

'We will bring their fearlessness and creativity to the traditional charm of Catoctin Creek to create a truly spectacular malt whiskey,' the couple say. 'The new whiskey has chocolate and caramel notes typical of a porter, with a crisp whiskey finish from the barreling process.'

KO DISTILLING

LOCATION MANASSAS, VIRGINIA **FOUNDED** 2011 **WHISKEY STYLES** BOURBON, RYE, WHEAT, MOONSHINE **VISITOR FACILITIES** THE DISTILLERY OFFERS TOURS FOR A SMALL FEE, AND SPIRITS AND COCKTAIL TASTINGS

The K and the O in the distillery name are Bill Karlson and John O'Mara, who met as classmates and cadet midshipmen at the United States Merchant Marine Academy and have been friends ever since. Although they went their separate ways after graduating, their careers ran in parallel, with both serving in the merchant navy and later in the defense contracting industry. The idea for craft distilling came when they took early retirement, and after starting with gin and a white whiskey they began aging spirit and producing rye, bourbon, and wheat whiskey. It's still very early days for the distillery, however.

RESERVOIR DISTILLERY

LOCATION RICHMOND, VIRGINIA **FOUNDED** 2009
WHISKEY STYLES BOURBON, WHEAT, RYE **VISITOR FACILITIES** TOURS AND TASTINGS ARE HELD ON SATURDAYS

What sets the Reservoir range of whiskeys apart is that all three of them—a bourbon, a rye, and a wheat whiskey—are made with 100 per cent of the dominant grain. That's not easy to do: rye is particularly messy to distill; a small amount of malted barley is normally used to act as a catalyst when fermenting the wash with yeast; and a 100 per cent corn bourbon is very rare indeed. Bourbon differs from corn whiskey because it is matured in charred or toasted new oak barrels. A corn whiskey must be at least 80 per cent corn, but must be matured in uncharred or used barrels. The three whiskeys are then matured in tiny 23-liter (5-gallon) barrels, and the system seems to have worked because all three have picked up gold medals for outstanding achievement.

VIRGINIA DISTILLERY CO.

LOCATION LOVINGSTOWN, VIRGINIA **FOUNDED** 2011
WHISKEY STYLES SINGLE MALT WHISKY, BLENDED MALT WHISKY **VISITOR FACILITIES** THE DISTILLERY HAS A MUSEUM AND CONDUCTS REGULAR TOURS AND TASTINGS ON A DAILY BASIS; THERE IS ALSO A VIP CLUB NAMED COPPER CIRCLE

Virginia Distillery Company was set up by the late Dr George G Moore, an Irishman who had lived in Virginia since the 1970s. Today, George's son Gareth, along with his wife, Maggie, have taken the helm to continue building George's dream.

The distillery spells whiskey without an 'e' and the importance of Scotland to the distillery's whisky-making process is borne out by its tours, which include information about the history of single malt in Scotland.

The company was prepared to wait to launch its first Virginia-distilled American Single Malt Whisky, but in the meantime it released Virginia-Highland Whisky, an aged single malt from Scotland mixed with distillery-produced spirit. The spirit is then finished in a cask that previously contained port. The distillery has also released two limited edition seasonal Virginia-Highland whiskies, one finished in an ex-chardonnay cask for Spring, the other finished in ex-cider casks for Fall.

COPPER FOX

LOCATION SPERRYVILLE AND WILLIAMSBURG, VIRGINIA FOUNDED 2005 WHISKEY STYLES RYE, SINGLE MALT, FLAVORED SINGLE MALT VISITOR FACILITIES FREE TOURS ARE HELD AT BOTH DISTILLERY SITES MOST DAYS; A SMALL FEE IS CHARGED FOR A FOUR-SPIRIT TASTING

Virginia is one of the oldest whiskey-producing areas of America, and it therefore seems fitting that the state should have been ahead of the play when it came to the rebirth of American whiskey. Copper Fox owner and founder Rick Wasmund is something of a distilling legend: his Wasmund's Single Malt Whisky is one of the world's great whiskeys, and his unique approach to whiskey-making has been an inspiration to countless distilling operations across America. If any distilling company deserves to thrive in the current American boom, it's Copper Fox.

Rick's journey into whiskey production started at the turn of the millennium, but it took a trip to Scotland in 2003 and a slew of distillery visits and questioning to get the ball rolling.

'I came away with a great appreciation of the necessary skill, a reinforced conviction, and an offer to intern at Bowmore Distillery on Islay, one of the few distilleries in the world that still malt their own barley,' he recalls. 'Three years later, Copper Fox Whisky was launched into the marketplace.'

Rick learned distilling under the tutelage of Scottish distilling legend Jim McEwan. Perhaps unsurprisingly, then, his Wasmund's Single Malt Whisky has been a success. In 2005, the distillery moved to its first proper site at Sperryvale, and in 2016 a second distillery was opened at Williamsburg.

Rick's experience at Bowmore influenced the method he adopted when he launched his own single malt, but it did not cramp his distinctive style: he devised a unique way of making a whiskey that is like no other single malt in the world. He puts his own twist on the malting process, using applewood and cherrywood to dry the barley—the only distillery in the world to do so. That's not the only thing the distillery does differently. Toasted applewood and cherrywood chips as well as oak are added to the barrel. Maturation takes between 12 and 16 months, although an older version of the whiskey is also available.

Moreover, Copper Fox makes a single malt with barley smoked over peachwood, and its rye is made up of just two grains: two-thirds of it is rye; one-third smoked malted barley.

Copper Fox has thrived during the craft boom, and expanded to cope with increasing demand. The Williamsburg site, opened in 2016, was initially a maturation and bottling site, but Rick is now working on a range of new products there.

BLUE RIDGE DISTILLING CO.

LOCATION BOSTIC, NORTH CAROLINA
FOUNDED 2012 **WHISKEY STYLES** SINGLE MALT
WHISKEY, RYE **VISITOR FACILITIES** TOURS CAN
BE ARRANGED

The Blue Ridge Distilling Company makes the aptly named Defiant Whisky, and it has a mission statement: 'We don't walk down paths, never follow in footsteps, not sorry for writing our own rules, that's the way Defiant was born.'

So why the bullishness? Mainly because the distillery's founder and owner, Tim Ferris, and distillers Eric Meech and Joel Patrino became notorious for turning conventional whiskey-making on its head by dispensing with barrels. They mature their whiskey by placing toasted American oak spirals into containers filled with spirit. They're not the first to use the method, which is frowned upon and outlawed in many territories. The distillery believes that maturation can thus be reduced to 60 days.

The resulting single malt is described as honeyed, with pleasant vanilla and toasted oak notes. A 100 per cent rye whiskey was launched by the company in 2017.

TROY & SONS

LOCATION ASHEVILLE NORTH CAROLINA **FOUNDED**
N/A **WHISKEY STYLES** CORN WHISKEY, AMERICAN
WHISKEY, MOONSHINE **VISITOR FACILITIES**
TOURS AND TASTINGS ARE HELD ALL YEAR-ROUND
(THOUGH LESS IN WINTER) AND THEY ARE FREE

When Troy Ball moved to the Blue Mountains in North Carolina, she quickly learned about the moonshine that was once made extensively throughout the area. She was told that the best 'shine was at home and not being sold down the road. And when she finally tasted some 'kept' moonshine, she was amazed at how smooth and complex it was, and how different it was to the throat-burning white whiskey she had tasted previously.

Troy has glamorous blonde hair, so she named one of her products Blonde Whiskey, which is made with rare heirloom Turkey Red wheat and white corn, an old grain from the 1800s grown on Peaceful Valley Farm in the lowland hills of western North Carolina. Oak Reserve is a corn whiskey matured in ex-bourbon barrels. Troy & Sons also makes what it says is a pure moonshine product named Platinum.

CAROLINA MOON DISTILLERY

LOCATION EDGEFIELD, NORTH CAROLINA
FOUNDED 2013 **WHISKEY STYLES** AMERICAN
WHISKEY, BOURBON, MOONSHINE **VISITOR**
FACILITIES THE DISTILLERY DOES FREE SHORT
TOURS ON A DAILY BASIS

When they say it's all hands to the deck at the Carolina Moon Distillery, they mean it. Master distillers and co-owners David Long and Cal Bowie and their team of two run as pure an example of a micro-distillery as you'll find, their roles including mashers, tasting room clerks, marketing directors, chiefs of operations, bottle labelers, and distillery tour guides.

David and Cal are lifelong residents of Edgefield, and wanted to oversee the production of small-batch spirits. The distillery is so small that the tour takes only ten minutes. Among the spirits the distillery produces is Rabbit Spit moonshine, after the quote by a judge from around 1820: 'Edgefield Whiskey...mean enough to make a rabbit spit in a bulldog's face!' A five-year-old Kentucky whiskey finished at the distillery is called Ole Tom in tribute to the National Wild Turkey Federation in Edgefield.

DARK CORNER

LOCATION GREENVILLE, SOUTH CAROLINA
FOUNDED 2011 **WHISKEY STYLES** MOONSHINE
FLAVORED 'WHISKEYS' **VISITOR FACILITIES** FOR A
SMALL FEE YOU CAN TASTE SIX SPIRITS AND KEEP
YOUR DISTILLERY TASTING GLASS; PRIVATE EVENTS
CAN ALSO BE CATERED FOR

What could be better than tasting whiskey while getting an education? That's what you get with Dark Corner's Carolina Legacy Series. It honors Lewis Redmond, 'an American Robin Hood,' who came from the Dark Corner region of the Carolinas. Each limited edition whiskey is named after a date that commemorates a milestone in his life. 1854, for instance, is a wheat whiskey marking the year he was born, and 1876 was the year he became an outlaw. The full backstory and history are included on the company's website.

Redmond's name hints at the background of the population of Dark Corner, which is in the northeast of the state. The early settlers traveled from Lowland Scotland, Ulster, and northern England, bringing their distilling skills with them.

The distillery's The World's Best Moonshine is a double-distilled corn whiskey, but includes red wheat and barley in its mash bill.

HIGH WIRE DISTILLING CO.

LOCATION CHARLESTON, SOUTH CAROLINA **FOUNDED** 2013 **WHISKEY STYLES** BOURBON, RYE, SORGHUM **VISITOR FACILITIES** TOURS ARE CONDUCTED FROM TUESDAY TO SATURDAY, OR BY APPOINTMENT

Scott Blackwell, who founded High Wire Distilling Co. with his wife Ann Marshall, describes himself as 'a serial entrepreneur,' and before the couple set up the distillery he had founded a natural and organic bakery called the Immaculate Baking Company. After the company was sold to General Mills, the couple worked on a business plan for producing spirits.

'We even consulted with David Pickerell of WhistlePig fame,' says Scott. 'We now produce gins, rums, whiskeys, and vodkas using specialized and premium ingredients.'

High Wire's three whiskeys are bottled under the name New Southern Revival and each has its own quirk: its rye is made up of 75 per cent ancient Italian Abruzzi, an heirloom grain grown in the Carolinas for centuries; its bourbon is made with four grains, including Carolina Gold rice bran; and its third whiskey is made of sorghum grown on a Mennonite farm in Tennessee.

DAWSONVILLE DISTILLERY

LOCATION DAWSONVILLE, GEORGIA **FOUNDED** 2012 **WHISKEY STYLES** CORN WHISKEY, FLAVORED MOONSHINE, MOONSHINE **VISITOR FACILITIES** TOURS OF VARIOUS TYPES

The National Association for Stock Car Auto Racing (NASCAR) is an umbrella organization covering hundreds of racing events. But its roots lie in the moonshine business, and there is a distinctively Southern flavor to it. To this day, most NASCAR teams are based in the South, mainly around Charlotte, North Carolina. The sport has developed from the moonshine days when cars were covered to carry huge moonshine tanks and jazzed up engines so that the driver could outrace the authorities, speeding toward the state line and out of reach of the state's law enforcers. If you've ever seen *The Dukes of Hazzard* you'll get the idea.

Dawsonville Distillery argues that Georgia is the moonshine capital of the world, and is proud of the NASCAR connection, too. It has teamed up with Bill Elliott, Motorsports Hall of Fame Inductee and 16-time winner of NASCAR's Most Popular Driver Award, to produce a range of Moonshine.

R.M. ROSE & CO. DISTILLERS

LOCATION DILLARD, GEORGIA **FOUNDED** 2010 **WHISKEY STYLES** BOURBON, CORN WHISKEY, FLAVORED WHISKEYS **VISITOR FACILITIES** TOURS AND TASTINGS DAILY

R.M. Rose & Co. was originally the name of a distillery company that operated from 1865 until Prohibition in 1920. Founder Rufus Rose was from Connecticut, in the heart of the Union, but during the American Civil War he served as a doctor in the Confederate Army. After the conflict, he saw an opportunity to make high-quality and safe spirits in Atlanta. He built up a successful business, and is thought to have been the first distiller to age the region's corn whiskey in charred oak barrels.

Today, the team behind the recently revived distillery sources its water from a North Georgia mountain stream. It buys the finest corn it can find, and makes its whiskey from wash fermented in open-top cypress tanks and double-distilled in traditional copper pot stills. Eminently palatable, Rose's Georgia Corn Whiskey is bottled at 50 per cent ABV. (100 proof).

KOZUBA & SONS DISTILLERY

LOCATION ST PETERSBURG, FLORIDA **FOUNDED** 2005 **WHISKEY STYLES** RYE, WHITE WHISKEY **VISITOR FACILITIES** TOURS AND TASTINGS BY APPOINTMENT THURSDAY TO SATURDAY

Florida? Whiskey? Really? Yep.

You may already know that Florida's St Petersburg is home to the Salvador Dalí Museum, top-rated restaurants, and beautiful Fort De Soto Park. What you may not know and be surprised to learn is that the city is also home to a whiskey distillery that was founded in Poland in 2005.

Kozumba Zbigniew 'Papa' Kozuba, a biochemist by training, is the company's master distiller. After a successful career at the helm of a laboratory company, Papa retired to the Polish countryside, where he began making cordials. Before long, his sons Matt and Jacob joined the business. After cordials, the company began distilling: first vodka, and then whiskey. Eventually the family decided to move to the United States to become part of the craft distilling movement. Today, the distillery's main product is a rye whiskey distilled on hybrid stills and matured in virgin oak barrels for more than three years.

CHAPTER 4

100 GREAT AMERICAN WHISKEYS YOU SHOULD TRY

It would have been impossible to compile a definitive list of the best of new craft whiskeys, of course, but the whiskeys included in this section give a very good taste of what is happening from Alaska to New Mexico. One word of warning: many of these whiskeys are made in small batches and bars report that they are noting considerable variation in quality from batch to batch. Either because some distillers are lacking in experience, or because they have gone to the time and expense of making the spirit so they are going to sell it whatever, rogue batches do turn up from time to time.

WHISKEYS TO TRY

ANGEL'S ENVY BOURBON FINISHED IN PORT CASKS
46.3% ABV

Angel's Envy was set up by the late former Woodford Reserve master distiller, Lincoln Henderson, and is now run by members of the next two generations of the family. It's a brave move, opening a distillery in the heart of bourbon country and then messing about with tradition. Bourbon can't be matured in casks that have been used for anything else, so this is an ex-bourbon. But it's great. Rich, full-bodied, with toffee, butterscotch, and layers of red and orange fruits.

BALCONES BABY BLUE
46% ABV

Like the other Texan distillers, Balcones is proud of its roots, and it stresses the connection between its whiskeys and the land that spawned them. This is a corn whiskey, made with heirloom blue corn, which means the spirit should be made with at least 80 per cent corn and any maturation must be in used or uncharted barrels. Young this may be, but the color indicates that it has been matured in charred oak. The result is a nutty, oily, and lively young spirit, with feisty spices and a burned popcorn note.

BALCONES BLUE CORN BOURBON
60–65% ABV

This annual release is made in batches and
bottled at barrel strength, which is variable.
It's safe to say, though, that you'll get plenty
of bang for your buck, whichever batch you
find. This is a straight bourbon, which means
that it has spent at least two years in wood—
and it shows. The spice and oak treat you
like a boxer uses a punch bag, and all the
time the biggest bourbon flavors are battling
to make their presence felt. Adding water,
necessary but worthwhile, unlocks flavors of
sweet pink candy and banoffee pie.

BALCONES BRIMSTONE
53% ABV

If Balcones were a rock band, Brimstone
would be the lippy bad boy—a whiskey
equivalent of Nikki Sixx or Gene Simmons.
While its stablemates are all about natural,
clean corn, this is a fire-breathing, smoke-
spitting, heavy grunge corn whiskey. Infused
with the smoke of a scrub oak fire, it mixes
burned steak with church incense, nodding
to some bitter orange marmalade on the
way. Like Sixx and Simmons, you can love it
or hate it, but you can't ignore it. And in the
end, it's a great big dollop of fun.

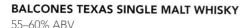

BALCONES TEXAS SINGLE MALT WHISKY
55–60% ABV

Balcones and its whiskeys are everything you might expect them to be—brash, larger than life, and very noisy. The company has grown up in public, and its dirty linen has been well and truly washed. But the distillery came out of the traps at a gallop, and hit the front early. It is making some amazing whiskeys, and this one, bottled in batches and varying in strength, is a bucking bronco of a drink, with plummy fruits, wicked spiciness, and a contradictory tug of vanilla and oakiness. If you can hold on, it's one hell of a ride.

BALCONES TRUE BLUE 100
50% ABV

This is the distillery's True Blue cask-strength whiskey diluted to a more manageable ABV, which Balcones says symbolically represents quality and authenticity. It works well. The added water helps to open out the bourbon, and releases softer, suppler textures. The fruits are easier to enjoy, too. But this is no shrinking violet; it is very much in keeping with the distillery's other robust bottlings. A rich floral and vanilla nose gives way to milk chocolate, hazelnuts, fruit sponge, and marshmallow on the palate.

BALCONES TRUE BLUE CASK STRENGTH
60–65% ABV

If the traditional regions of whiskey are like five giant vessels of liquid, then craft distilling is gleefully splashing around in them, stirring them up and spilling them over the edges so that the liquids become mixed and flow off in new directions. This is a straight corn whisky—note the Scottish spelling—which means that it is an aged corn whiskey. It is oily and dense, but with the addition of water, apricot and peach emerge, with syrup and a mix of macadam nuts and sweet spices. Batches are variable.

CATSKILL FEARLESS WHEAT WHISKEY
42.5% ABV

In her tasting notes, Heather Green of the Flatiron Room in New York describes this whiskey as 'the silky and seductive neighbor you spied on through a window as she slowly peeled off her sundress…a suggestion of her naughtiness as she catches you in a mirror's reflection followed by a tacit agreement between you that it's all perfectly reasonable.' Over the top? Perhaps, but there's no denying that Catskill Fearless is seductive, naughty, and perfectly reasonable. Lots of honey, cream, apple, and pears, too.

CATSKILL STRAIGHT RYE WHISKEY
42.5% ABV

It's fascinating to see how craft distillers are taking rigid categories and mixing them up. Ryes have tended to fall into two camps: the inoffensive and arguably anemic ryes of Canadian whisky, and the spicy ones that have become sought-after in recent years. But this is something else again. Sure, there is spice—lots of it, nutmeg and cinnamon mostly—but this is intertwined with tropical fruits, sweet candy, vanilla, and a new oaky toastiness. This may be the perfect bridge between bourbon and rye.

COPPER FOX PEACHWOOD SINGLE MALT
48% ABV

Copper Fox is most famous for making Wasmund's Single Malt Whiskey, and it is at the forefront of the American single malt whiskey revolution. Rick Wasmund did his homework in Scotland before he started distilling, and it shows. Drying the barley over a peachwood fire has given this whiskey a wispy, smoky twist. There are plenty of dried fruits here, too, as well as orange, spices, and some toasted oak. What makes this a standout malt, though, is its salty and oaky depth.

COPPER FOX RYE WHISKEY
45% ABV

You expect the unusual from Copper Fox, and you won't be disappointed here. It can't be called whiskey in Europe because it is less than three years old, but no matter: this benefits from its youth. It sparkles. A third of the mash bill is made up of hand-malted barley dried in a kiln with applewood and cherrywood smoke. It is double-distilled and matured in bourbon barrels containing new and used applewood and oak chips. The result is a big-flavored fruit and spice treat with soft smoke undertones. Very impressive.

CORSAIR OATRAGE
46% ABV

That these guys mean business is borne out by this seasonal whiskey. Oats are a nightmare to work with, because they expand and clog up the washback. But get it right and you produce a whiskey that is even softer and sweeter than wheat. Corsair uses coffee malts as well as malted oats. The result is much as you'd expect: alcoholic porridge, but it is not oversweet, thanks to some toasty notes, traces of dark chocolate, some bitter coffee, some maltiness, and a trace of earthiness. Bland it isn't.

CORSAIR QUINOA WHISKEY
46% ABV

Quinoa is a South American supergrain grown for its seeds, which have become a staple of the healthy person's salad bowl. Corsair founder Darek Bell has remarked, tongue in cheek, that if you're trying to sell anything in California these days, you need to have quinoa in it: hence this whiskey. Quinoa comes in several colors, and this whiskey is made with red and white grains. This is one of Corsair's least assertive and relatively flat whiskeys. It has a nutty, earthy, grassy core, and a soft, clean finish.

CORSAIR RYEMAGEDDON
46% ABV

One of the most attractive things about much of the craft drinks sector is that its core figures are happy and enjoying themselves. There is little pretentiousness, and part of the fun is that if there are rules, they're there to be broken. The team behind Corsair is doing as it pleases, and if that means using puns in names, so be it. Ryemageddon is a chocolate rye and malted rye, an aged version of the distillery's white whiskey, Wry Moon. The spice mix is split between savory kitchen spices and sweet Christmas ones.

CORSAIR TRIPLE SMOKE
69.35% ABV

Corsair has been going up through the gears in recent years, focusing on its best expressions, and taking them to ever-higher levels. This is a single malt whisky, with three equal parts of malt smoked individually, one part over peat, one part over cherrywood, and one part over beechwood. The resulting spirit is then matured in new charred oak barrels, from which it picks up candy and vanilla notes. The final product is a sweet and sour blackcurrant cheesecake of a whiskey, with wafts of campfire smoke.

FEISTY SPIRITS BETTER DAYS BOURBON
ABV VARIES

Many Feisty Spirits products come in single barrels or very small batches, and some of its bottlings never leave the tasting room. The distillers also experiment with new ways to present their whiskeys. Better Days Bourbon is one of their single-barrel whiskeys, so it is variable, but whatever version you get will have little of the vanilla candy sandalwood associated with conventional bourbon: this whiskey is distinguished by notes of maple syrup through its center, and by the almost rum-like quality of its finish.

FEISTY SPIRITS RHAPSODY BLUE CORN BOURBON
ABV VARIES

Blue corn is increasingly popular in America, where many now swear by its health benefits. It has become a staple in the production of some speciality foods. Several micro-distillers now use it to make whiskey, especially in Colorado, New Mexico, and Texas. Feisty Spirits Rhapsody is a single-barrel offering. Its nutty taste may be due to the blue corn, but it's also quite velvety and soft. There are additionally soft buttery and toffee notes in the mix. Spices, presumably from some rye, are also present.

FEISTY SPIRITS ROCKIT RYE
ABV VARIES

Feisty Spirits is experimenting with different grains and woods. It's still a very young distillery, so it's no doubt learning as it goes. Rye is probably not the best idea, because it is one of the toughest grains to work with. This is a nearly-but-not-quite whiskey that needs additional work or time, or both. There are fruity notes, mainly apricot and peach, a distinctive and sharp rye spice, and some caramel notes. But there is also some harshness, and the components within the whiskey do not yet join up fully.

FEW BOURBON WHISKEY
46.5% ABV

Illinois is one of a handful of states that are producing some of the most exciting craft distilleries. Few Spirits is right at home here, subtly bringing a twist to America's flagship whiskey style. This bourbon has a larger than average rye content, bringing what Few calls a Northern flavor to a traditionally Southern whiskey style. A sugar and spice one–two combo sets this whiskey apart, adding a herbal, rootsy quality to more traditional bourbon flavors. The effect is to give depth and complexity to a young whiskey.

FEW RYE WHISKEY
46.5%

The term 'sugar and spice' might have been coined for this little gem. Few Rye Whiskey is made up of a heavy portion of rye and a much smaller amount of corn. The high rye content ensures a top-drawer, hard, spicy hit, but you've got to wait to experience it, because up front there are some weird, oily, vegetal things going on. It takes a while for the palate to accustom itself to these peculiarities, but basically this product is a jagged rye whiskey coated in sweetcorn. It's unusual and distinctly un-European.

FIRESTONE & ROBERTSON TX BOURBON
45% ABV

Firestone & Robertson is pure Texas, and so is their whiskey. TX Bourbon is made with Texan ingredients: #2 yellow dent Texas corn; Texas soft red winter wheat; six-row distillers malt; Texas water; and (amazingly) its own proprietary strain of yeast captured from a Texas pecan. It has been barreled for about four and a half years. This is a delicious, soft, rounded bourbon, with candy and dark fruits. The oaky spices could be turned up a notch, but this is still impressive stuff.

FIRESTONE & ROBERTSON TX WHISKEY
45% ABV

'American whiskey' may be a bland and broad descriptor, but an increasing number of craft distillers are taking the whiskey category into new and exciting areas that can't be defined under existing headings. This is described as a blend, but the distillery is not giving too much away about what that means. No matter: it's excellent. Texan it may be, but this is a featherbed of a whiskey, all soft butterscotch, gentle honey, and orange fruits. The finish is short, soft, and rounded. A new star is born in the Lone Star State.

HIGH WEST AMERICAN PRAIRIE RESERVE
46% ABV

High West shows how lucrative independent thinking and a fresh approach to making whiskey can be. In 2016, the distillery was bought by Constellation Brands for $160 million. Not bad for a ranch-like operation that began in the mountains of Park City, Utah. American Prairie is a blend of three sourced whiskeys of different ages and mash bills. It's well made, with tropical fruit, banana, and toasted oak on the nose, fruit and vanilla on the palate, and a spicy rye finish.

HIGH WEST CAMPFIRE
46% ABV

High West has attracted criticism for using stock bought in from elsewhere. This is a bit harsh, because that's what highly acclaimed alchemists Compass Box do. Campfire is a blend of bourbon, rye, and peated Scotch—whiskey's version of supergroup The Highwaymen, with each of the components bringing something special to the party. At times feisty, at times gnarly, at times smooth and dapper, this is smoky honey with a touch of cinnamon and pepper, a delightful meeting of whiskey styles. Utterly irresistible.

HIGH WEST RENDEZVOUS RYE
46% ABV

Rendezvous Rye is High West's flagship brand and arguably its most famous product. It is a blend of straight rye whiskeys, and although the company keeps its mash bill secret, it makes a point of emphasizing that the whiskey has a higher than normal rye content to maximize the traditional spicy rye flavors. It's a full-bodied, slightly oily, and highly assertive whiskey, with chili and menthol in the mix. There's a subtlety to the rye, too, with toffee and sweet spices lightening proceedings. The finish is spicy and chewy.

HILLROCK SOLERA AGED BOURBON WHISKEY
46.3% ABV

There is a danger that craft distillers will try to force their spirits to age fast for commercial reasons. Whiskeys matured in small casks to accelerate maturation can be one-dimensional and lack depth or flavor. Whiskey consultant Dave Pickerell has taken a different approach, using the solera system to mix sourced aged whiskeys with new spirit from Hillrock. The youthfulness shows, but the core components—fruit, toffee, vanilla, spice, and oak—are all present.

HUDSON BABY BOURBON WHISKEY
46% ABV

Tutlhilltown Spirits says that Baby Bourbon is its most sought-after whiskey, and it certainly captured the imagination of the trendy bar crowd in downtown New York, providing a genuinely different option to traditional bourbon, and fitting in comfortably with the burgeoning cocktail scene. It is made with New York corn, and matured in tiny 9-liter (2-gallon) barrels while being agitated by heavy bass music. It is feisty and sweet, with caramel and fruit, but little depth or spiciness. Different though.

HUDSON FOUR GRAIN BOURBON WHISKEY
46% ABV

Hudson whiskeys are made by Tuthilltown Spirits, a New York distillery that made waves early in the micro-distilling boom and was promptly snapped up by Scottish family distillers William Grant & Sons, a company adept at spotting a trend and taking full advantage of it. Four Grain is a bourbon made of corn, barley, rye, and wheat. It's matured in small casks: you can tell because there's a sappiness from the oak. But there are plenty of pluses, and the light oak, soft caramel, and cinnamon are nicely balanced.

HUDSON MANHATTAN RYE WHISKEY
46% ABV

Hudson Manhattan Rye Whiskey re-
establishes the link between New York and
rye whiskey. Before Prohibition, rye was the
drink of choice, and the key ingredient in the
Manhattan cocktail. Now the spirit is back
in vogue, and it seems fitting that Hudson
Manhattan Rye Whiskey has found its place
on the current cocktail scene. It has none of
the depth and body of a classic big rye, and
is lighter than you might expect. The spices
are peppery and the fruitiness thin. It is
perfectly pleasant, although unexciting.

IRONROOT REPUBLIC HARBINGER
58.3% ABV

Ironroot Republic is the creation of the
Likarish brothers from Texas, and these
guys are taking no prisoners. They use the
heaviest glass bottles that money can buy,
they are brash in their branding, and they
deliver oily, feisty whiskey at cask strength.
All their whiskeys need a big dollop of water
and time to settle. Even then, they might
not win you over, but the bourbon flavors do
start to make sense, with masses of vanilla,
butterscotch and popcorn. There is also an
oiliness that appeals to many drinkers.

IRONROOT REPUBLIC HUBRIS
58.9% ABV

There is some debate about whether whiskeys are developed to suit local palates and hence seem alien to people in more traditional whisky-producing regions. Ironroot Republic seemed to exemplify an American/European split until Hubris won top awards in England and San Francisco. It is an acquired taste though. Add a lot of water and leave for 15 minutes. Then you'll discover sweet buttered popcorn, vanilla, and fudge fighting their way through the oily spiciness that makes initial sips so testing.

IRONROOT REPUBLIC ICARUS
53.75% ABV

Drinking this distillery's whiskeys is like listening to Iron Maiden or Metallica: to some it's just a nasty load of noise. But once you get it, it's like being in a scuzzy and loyal club. Icarus won a silver medal in the 2018 Wizards of Whisky World Whisky Awards, so someone's getting it. It's a straight corn whiskey, meaning at least 80 per cent corn and two years in casks—in this case, casks that previously contained peated whiskey or port. With water it's campfire and candy, an earthy and youthful grain with dark fruits.

IRONROOT REPUBLIC TEXAS LEGATION BATCH NO. 2
45% ABV

In diplomacy, a legation is like an embassy but at a less formal level. When Texas was seeking independence from Mexico in the 1840s, it set up a legation in London, in a building owned by wine and spirits merchant Berry Bros & Rudd (BBR). To mark the link, BBR's whisky-maker Doug McIvor worked with the Likarish Brothers at Ironroot Republic to create their best whiskey yet, in which banana and orange flavors accompany chili oil and woody spices.

I.W. HARPER
45% ABV

Isaac Wolfe Bernheim immigrated from Germany to America in 1867 with $4. After a few years he had enough money to bring his brother over, and they opened the Bernheim Distillery in Louisville. They chose the name Harper because it sounded more American. This whiskey is a modern version of one that was discontinued but is now made at Stitzel-Weller Distillery. It is thinner and fruitier than many bourbons, but excellent. Banoffee pie on the nose gives way to butterscotch, zingy fruit, spices and nuts.

JEFFERSON'S GROTH RESERVE CASK FINISH
45.1% ABV

Jefferson's is a historical whiskey name which disappeared in the 1990s and is now back on the map as part of the Kentucky Artisan Distillery at Crestwood. The company makes traditional American whiskeys, but also experiments. This product spent about six years in virgin oak casks, then nine months in cabernet sauvignon casks from Groth vineyards in Napa Valley. It is a plummy, fruity delight, with nuttiness, sweetness, and a pleasant wave of spices. Fresh and summery.

JOHN EMERALD SINGLE MALT WHISKEY
43.8% ABV

Alabama's first legally produced whiskey in 100 years, this is a good example of the American style of single malt, with the new-make spirit matured in new oak casks that may have been toasted or charred. It contains 100 per cent malted barley that has been smoked with peach and pecan wood. It's made in very small batches so there are differences between bottles. I tasted Batch 5, a three-pronged whiskey, with smoky, savory notes, an earthy, malty heart, and sweetness, vanilla, and toffee from the oak maturation.

JOHNNY DRUM BOURBON
50.5% ABV

Johnny Drum is one of a number of whiskeys made by the Willett Distillery, which operates on the edge of Kentucky's bourbon capital, Bardstown. It's the flagship bourbon and used to be bottled as a 15-year-old. There is no age statement now, but this is well aged. The team here knows what it is doing, and all its whiskeys are of a good standard. This is classic bourbon, its mix of candy, vanilla, spice, leather saddle, and sandalwood all present and correct. It's bottled at a weighty ABV and has a lovely long and spicy finish.

KENTUCKY PEERLESS RYE
53.7% ABV

Brave guys. Kentucky Peerless was one of the earliest distilleries in the state, and it has a low registration number to prove it. Now reopened in Louisville's Whiskey Row, it's turning heads with its bourbon and this rye. Controversially, both are made using a sweet rather than a sour mash, and the spirit is put into the cask at a lower strength than normal. This may not please traditionalists, but is the distillery making great whiskey? You betcha! This one came 15th in *Whisky Advocate*'s top whiskeys of 2017.

KINGS COUNTY DISTILLERY STRAIGHT BOURBON WHISKEY
45% ABV

Founded in 2010, two years later Kings County Distillery moved into the 118-year-old Paymaster Building in Brooklyn Navy Yard, where it produces handmade moonshine and other whiskeys. Its straight bourbon is made with New York corn, but has strong links with Britain, too. The distillery's traditional copper pot stills were made in Scotland, and its barley is imported from all over the United Kingdom. It is matured for at least two years.

KOVAL SINGLE BARREL BOURBON WHISKEY
47% ABV

Koval was set up in Chicago by Robert and Sonat Birnecker. The former's Austrian heritage is thought to have influenced his unconventional approach to distilling. This is bourbon because it meets the legal requirement of having a mash containing 51 per cent corn. But its other main constituent is millet. The resulting whiskey is different, with tropical fruits and a sweet, starchy body. It's extraordinary, with a unique soft and rounded finish.

KOVAL SINGLE BARREL RYE WHISKEY
40 % ABV

This turns conventional wisdom about rye whiskey on its head. It's not sharp, over-spicy or aggressive. But it is very nice. It's a 100 per cent rye whiskey (in itself a challenge), made with locally sourced grain and matured in casks of oak from Minnesota. The result is surprisingly gentle, fresh, sweet, and approachable, with just enough rye spice late on to stop it from becoming sloppy or cloying. The sample I tested was, like all Koval bottlings, from a single barrel, so it may have been a rogue batch. I hope not.

LEOPOLD BROS STRAIGHT BOURBON
45% ABV

Few distilleries pay as much attention to detail as Leopold Bros does. It goes to great lengths to recreate pre-Prohibition-style whiskeys and to introduce subtlety to some of America's greatest whiskey styles. It is working with Colorado farmers to grow heritage grains. Its bourbon, launched late in 2017, is made with 64 per cent corn, and its 15 per cent rye content is partly chocolate rye. The wash is double-distilled, and the new spirit matured for 33 months. The result is well balanced with an intense, sweet finish.

LEOPOLD BROS MARYLAND-STYLE RYE WHISKEY
43% ABV

Maryland-style rye is less well known than the big spicy ryes that formed the basis of the cocktail boom. They taste so different that it's hard to believe that both are from the same family. Maryland-style rye doesn't necessarily come from Maryland: Leopold Bros is in Denver, Colorado. This whiskey contains a modest 65 per cent rye and 20 per cent malted barley, and is an elegant drink with notes of citrus and pine forest, a strong vanilla and chocolate theme, and restrained rye notes.

MICHTER'S KENTUCKY STRAIGHT RYE WHISKEY
55% ABV

Michter's has been on a (barrel) roll in recent years. One of America's oldest distilleries is well and truly back in business, and its 2018 arrival in Louisville's Whiskey Row felt like a victory parade. It's making great whiskey, too. This barrel-strength bottling has been matured conventionally in new charred oak barrels but finished in casks made from naturally seasoned virgin oak, this time toasted rather than charred. The result is spicy enough to need water.

MICHTER'S UNBLENDED AMERICAN WHISKEY
41.7% ABV

Part of the fun of micro-distilling is working out what has gone into different whiskeys, and in some cases trying to determine whether they really are whiskeys at all. But it is not easy to resist the conclusion that distillers who want to call their product 'American whiskey' should be allowed to do so, just so long as it tastes great. This whiskey is a real mystery. Michter's tells you little about it, but if you've got a sweet tooth, this is for you—all candy and butterscotch.

NEW HOLLAND BEER BARREL BOURBON
40% ABV

Every New Holland whiskey comes with a twist: a single malt matured in new oak casks; an aged single malt finished off in a sherry cask. In some ways, this is its most conventional product, a bourbon matured in casks that previously contained Dragon's Milk stout. The result is soft and biscuity with traces of oak and some savory notes. Gimmick or genuine attempt at innovation? It works—just—and won a gold in the 2018 Wizards of Whisky World Whisky Awards.

NEW HOLLAND BEER BARREL RYE
44% ABV

Beer has frequently been matured in ex-whiskey barrels, so why not do the same thing the other way round? New Holland is a pioneer in this field, and with bourbon it made sense. Rye matured in its Dragon's Milk stout though? That was a riskier and altogether more provocative idea. Undoubtedly the barrel softens the rye, and there is little sweetness. Overall, this is really fun. Bizarrely, I'm reminded of a spicy tomato beef stew. There's certainly a lot going on here.

NOAH'S MILL BOURBON
57.15% ABV

Noah's Mill Bourbon is another whiskey from the Willett Distillery. Small production and big demand after countless outstanding reviews make it very hard to get hold of. If you get the chance to taste it, this is how great bourbon should be. The first thing to note is the age: at 15 years it's very old for any bourbon, let alone a craft one. It's a faultless whiskey, with a beguiling nose and a full-throttle taste. Bottled at cask strength, it's a tour de force of toffee, corn, oak, chilli spice, hickory, leather saddle, and dark cherry.

NOR' EASTER BOURBON
44.4% ABV

Nor' Easter Bourbon is made at the Triple Eight Distillery, which is part of Cisco Brewers in Nantucket. The name refers to the storms that batter the region each year, bringing heavy rain, strong winds, and snow. This bourbon is matured 48km (30 miles) out to sea, typically for from four to eight years in 240-litre (53-gallon) charred American oak barrels sourced from the Buffalo Trace Distillery in Kentucky. Nor' Easter is easy drinking with an unusual tangy note that the distillery says is from the ocean maturation.

NOTCH
44.4% ABV

The name seems to invite you to preface it with the word 'top,' and that is what this is—a superlative single malt that holds its own with any malt produced anywhere, including Scotland. It is made at the Triple Eight Distillery and the word is a portmanteau of 'not' and 'Scotch.' The attention to detail here is staggering. Notch is made from a special beer made with Maris Otter barley, then matured for a decade. It has lots of the characteristics of a great Speyside whisky: it is subtle and brilliant.

OLD BARDSTOWN BOTTLED IN BOND
50.0% ABV

Bardstown—a pretty little place an hour south of Louisville—is considered the capital of bourbon. Kentucky Bourbon Distillers (or Willett) is based just outside the town, and its Old Bardstown is one of the state's most iconic bourbons, having been launched just a few years after the end of Prohibition. It has a relatively high malt content of 15 per cent, and it stands apart from modern bourbons insofar as it is not oversweet. Yet its youth lets it down: at four years old, it shows promise but remains sappy, thin, and grainy.

OLD POTRERO 18TH CENTURY STYLE WHISKEY
63.64% ABV

San Francisco's Anchor Distilling says that in the 18th century hot oak chips were used to heat barrel staves so that they would bend. The chips toasted the barrel but did not char it. That's what's been done here, and a 100 per cent rye mash has been used, giving the whiskey an oily texture. It's bottled at barrel strength, but water unlocks a subtle mix of evolving flavors. This has a big nose of oil, peat, liquorice, and sea salt, and the palate is medicinal, with cloves, hickory, anisette, and spices. Hard to find but very special.

OLD POTRERO HOTALING'S WHISKEY
50.0% ABV

Old Potrero is a range of whiskeys made by Anchor Distilling in San Francisco. Each of them is based on a traditional 18th-century recipe, and they are all quite unlike any other whiskey on the planet. Their taste is unforgettable, and they are massively sought after. If you get a chance to try any of them, take it. They are savory delights, mouth-coating, with a complex mix of spices including chili, cinnamon, ginger, and cumin. A rhubarb sweetness underlines everything. Weird and wonderful.

DIAMOND STATE STRAIGHT BOURBON WHISKEY
44.0% ABV

One of the challenges for craft distillers is to anticipate demand. When Painted Stave launched its first bourbon, it sold out in 45 minutes, and it was several months before a second batch matured. Diamond State Bourbon is aged for two years, but it has the gentlest and most inoffensive nose and taste you're ever likely to find in bourbon. It is almost floral, with some oak, pepper, and honey. Some notes of cloves and cinnamon make an appearance late on.

DIAMOND STATE STRAIGHT RYE WHISKEY
44.0% ABV

Painted Stave uses the latest technology to combine regional ingredients with traditional recipes. This limited edition rye has a mash bill of 65 per cent rye, 25 per cent corn, 5 per cent six-row barley, and 5 per cent rye malt. It is a straight rye, having spent two years in new American oak barrels. The nose has smoke and citrus among the more prevalent vanilla and spice, but the spice never really develops on the palate, and there is honey and fruit upfront, with pepper coming later. Pleasant but no showstopper.

PAPPY VAN WINKLE'S FAMILY RESERVE 20 YEARS OLD
46% ABV

The Van Winkle dynasty has legendary status in Kentucky, having produced great wheated bourbons at the Stitzel-Weller Distillery in Louisville. The distillery is owned by Diageo now, and is distilling again, but Van Winkle's whiskeys are made at Buffalo Trace. The whiskeys are beautiful. Twenty years is very old for a bourbon, and it shows. There is a lot going on here: green and orange fruit, a Rumtopf-like rum heart, burned raisins, sharp oak, tannins, and a soft, delicate finish.

PIKESVILLE STRAIGHT RYE WHISKEY
55.0% ABV

Pikesville is a brand with a history stretching back to 1895, when it was made in Maryland. Today's version is made by Heaven Hill in Louisville, Kentucky, and warrants inclusion here because it is one of the truly outstanding American whiskeys. Six years in the cask have given it a rich, full body, but haven't tamed the zestiness of the flavors. The rye content isn't high, but add some water and the spicy notes surf over a wave of honey and fruit. Balanced, flavorful, and chewy: whiskey at its finest.

RANSOM RYE, BARLEY, WHEAT WHISKEY
46.7% ABV

Ransom does things differently when it comes to making whiskey. The distillery has a whiskey called The Emerald, which is made to an Irish recipe of 1865, impressively given to them by drinks expert David Wondrich. Its Rye, Barley, Wheat offering contains six grains—three different barleys, two different ryes, and wheat—and the spirit is matured in ex-French wine casks. It tastes like an oddball mix of damp forest and black and red berries, but the grains come through with biscuity, earthy, and nutty notes.

REBEL YELL SMALL BATCH
45.3% ABV

Rebel Yell has been given a complete overhaul under its latest owners. Gone is the outdated Southern imagery, and in its place is a pleasant, well-packaged, biker-friendly bourbon. Of the whole Rebel Yell range this small batch version is the best. The nose is soft and sweet, with classic vanilla, honey, and caramel notes. The bourbon itself is easy-drinking, medium-bodied, and well-balanced, with vanilla, toffee, and honey on the palate. Perhaps a little more bite and tang wouldn't go amiss, but it is good value.

RITTENHOUSE RYE
50% ABV

Rittenhouse Rye is made to a recipe which is close to the old Pennsylvania style of rye, and it is named after a square in Philadelphia. It's made by Heaven Hill, and it's one of the few ryes that kept the flag flying while the whiskey style was out of fashion. Now, of course, the opposite is true, and this provides a benchmark: a rye that mixes savory, sweet, and exotic spices with a big, fruity punch. What makes it a heavyweight whiskey is the delightful charred oak and dark cherry mix at its core.

ROCK TOWN ARKANSAS BOURBON WHISKEY
46.0% ABV

This bourbon is the flagship whiskey from the Arkansas Rock Town Distillery, but if you get the chance to explore any of its single-barrel offerings, take it. Its bourbons are assured and innovative, with malted and unmalted grains used together in the mash bill, adding a certain Irishness to traditional bourbon flavors. The standard bourbon is surprisingly plummy, with some pleasant licorice and berry fruit notes. Oak gives the mix a tangy note, and the whole shebang culminates in a long, warming finish. Classy.

ROUGHSTOCK MONTANA BOURBON WHISKEY
45.0% ABV

Montana still has some unusual alcohol laws. Only one liquor-retailing lease is allowed for every 1,500 citizens in a township, so some outlets are paying astronomical fees or relying on raffles to obtain one. Distilling is just as tough, and Roughstock lost its lease in 2017 and is now closed. That is a shame, because this is a full-on, smooth whiskey that evolves on the palate, with honey and vanilla giving way to gentle oak, leather, cigar box, and sandalwood. Why stop production of such a gem?

ROWAN'S CREEK
50.5% ABV

First a warning: this whiskey is made in batches, and customer reviews suggest that these vary considerably. But I've never tasted a bad sample, and on a good day Rowan's Creek is another wonderful whiskey from Kentucky Bourbon Distillers (Willett), which has honed its skills by distilling and bottling for other companies and perfected its own range of premium whiskeys. This is a smooth combination of exotic fruits, toffee sauce, and diced hazelnuts on vanilla ice cream and sweet spices. The finish is an oaky delight.

SONOMA COUNTY RYE
48.0% ABV

The jury is out on Sonoma County's whiskeys. Some bloggers have expressed disappointment that little progress has been made by the distillery since it first launched, but this is harsh: the amateur spirity notes have gone, and the use of direct fire stills and of cherrywood to dry the barley (and on occasion, wheat) is both different and ground-breaking. Treat this as an introductory rye: not too big and spicy, pleasantly sweet, smooth, and complex with a long finish. The smoky notes are a bonus.

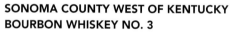

SONOMA COUNTY WEST OF KENTUCKY BOURBON WHISKEY NO. 3

47.8% ABV

For many, details of age and expression are secondary to the name of the distillery, and for this reason care should be taken with craft distillers, especially if each batch of whiskey is different from the previous one. Sonoma County whiskey is evolving batch by batch, and the distillers are tinkering with the mash bill. Batch No. 3 is better than Batch No. 1, and spicier than Batch. No 2, which had a higher wheat content. There's a gentle smokiness from the barley, too.

SONS OF LIBERTY BOURBON WHISKEY

45.0% ABV

Sons of Liberty's smart image is based on its New England heritage. Its sometimes weird and wonderful whiskey expressions are smartly packaged, and the distillers shout that this is a Rhode Island whiskey made with Rhode Island ingredients. Its bourbon is matured in oak barrels of three sizes—45, 68, and 112 liters (10, 15, and 25 gallons). This is the most traditional of the distillery's whiskeys, but it still tastes little like the typical Kentucky bottling. Toasted oak, treacle, and burned caramel are in the mix.

SONS OF LIBERTY UPRISING
46.0% ABV

I wasn't sure at first, but this whiskey has grown on me. Uprising is described as a single malt, but it isn't under European rules, because it is made from a stout beer, and beer contains hops. That's nitpicking, though, because in Europe it isn't even whiskey, having been matured for only two years in casks 'enhanced' with toasted French oak staves. The result is a whiskey like no other: with chili chocolate, deeply roasted coffee, and milky malt. Best of all is the bitter cherry note that comes when water is added.

STAGG JR.
67.2% ABV

George T. Stagg is one of the world's best whiskeys. Released in batches each Fall, it is an aged bourbon with huge and complex depth, served up at a high ABV. Junior refers to the fact that this version is younger, but don't let that put you off. It's still aged for nearly a decade, and that's old for bourbon. It's unfiltered, and bottled at barrel strength. The result is an absolute monster, as robust a bourbon as you will find, with lashings of oak, cherry, orange, and pepper spices. Unfortunately, it's as rare as its dad.

STRANAHAN'S COLORADO WHISKEY

47.0% ABV

Many whiskey enthusiasts hold Stranahan's up as an example of just how much craft distillers are capable of. The distillery was ahead of the craft distilling revolution, and one of the first to produce single malt whiskey. Dedication, enthusiasm, and attention to producing quality spirits made Colorado Whiskey America's biggest-selling American single malt. And with good reason: it's a cracker, with a delightful balance of sugar and spice. Utterly irresistible.

STRANAHAN'S DIAMOND PEAK

47% ABV

Diamond Peak is made in small batches as an ongoing limited edition series, so no two batches will be the same. You can expect high quality, though, because Stranahan's doesn't do poor. This whiskey is made from some of the distillery's older barrels, with a No. 3 char specially selected by the master distiller. Among the most likely flavors are malt, toffee, and candy. There should be a good balance between the bourbon notes from the barrel and the single malt qualities of the whiskey. Not easy to find, but worth seeking out.

● SMOKE ● FRUIT ● WOOD ● SPICE ● CONFECTIONERY

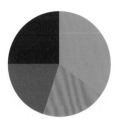

SYNTAX STRAIGHT BOURBON WHISKEY
47.5% ABV

The head distiller at Syntax is former
engineer Heather Bean, who not only runs
the stills, but also built them, having been
inspired by craft distilleries in Portland,
Oregon. Syntax has grown up in public, and
its move from chaotic cartoon packaging to
premium presentation is an apt metaphor for
this bourbon, early bottlings of which were
ordinary at best, poor and sulfury at worst.
But since 2016 they have improved into a
grainy, sweet drink with gentle yellow fruit
notes and a touch of oak and spice.

TATOOSH RYE
43.0% ABV

Not only is this not typical of a rye whiskey,
but it is something of a curiosity. It tastes
more like an aperitif, and is light and flighty.
The mash bill is 70 per cent rye and 30
per cent corn, and while there is no age
statement, it's not described as a straight
rye, so we can conclude that it is under two
years old. It is matured in conventional new
American oak 240-liter (53-gallon) barrels.
The nose is slight, the palate feels thin,
and the flavors include honey, cereal, wood
shavings, fresh herbs, and tropical fruits.

TEMPLETON RYE
40.0% ABV

You have to admire the chutzpah of the producers. Until they were stopped from doing so by a court ruling, they claimed that this liquor was made to a pre-Prohibition recipe in Templeton, Iowa. In truth, it's whiskey bought in from Indiana and flavored with modern chemicals. They are no longer allowed to claim that it's small batch, either, because it isn't. But questionable marketing should not be permitted to obscure the fact that Templeton Rye is an utterly irresistible balance of sugar and spice.

TROY & SONS BLONDE
47.0% ABV

Troy & Sons is a woman named Troy with bright blonde hair and her sons making corn whiskey in North Carolina. In the past, their whiskeys tended to be pretty unsubtle, with an oiliness and a harsh alcoholic bite. Blonde isn't like that at all, though. It's a mellow and sweet whiskey, probably due to a mash bill that combines white corn with rare Turkey Red Wheat. It is a simple, straightforward whiskey, with milk chocolate notes, some delicate oak, and a sweet grain heart. The finish is medium-long and warming.

TROY & SONS OAK RESERVE
40.0% ABV

It's not easy making a 100 per cent whiskey, and to kick-start the fermentation an enzyme is used. The resulting spirit is aged in ex-bourbon barrels, so it can be defined as a corn whiskey. It is a sweet, grain-powered whiskey with bourbon, butterscotch, and vanilla notes. One online review described it as rum-like, which it is, with sweet molasses dominant. Oak and pepper spice are in the mix, but another year in the barrel would have given the whiskey more shape and depth. But perfectly acceptable.

VAN WINKLE SPECIAL RESERVE 12 YEARS OLD
45.2% ABV

Van Winkle specializes in aged bourbon, mixing the oldest stocks of whiskey from Buffalo Trace into distinctive and much sought-after products. Twelve years is a good age for bourbon, and this one is marked by strong tannins and oak notes. Much of the fruitiness has been dried out. The sweet confectionery nose gives way to a more savory taste, with chicory, burned beef, and gentle spices. The unusual finish is mainly candy but with a citrusy undertone.

**VIRGINIA DISTILLERY PORT CASK
FINISHED VIRGINIA-HIGHLAND WHISKY**
46.0% ABV

This port cask-finished whiskey is Virginia
Distillery's flagship release and it is described
as a Highland whisky. It's a mixture of whiskey
from the distillery and some Scottish whisky.
The core whiskey is 100 per cent malt, and
the taste suggests that it's been matured
in new American oak barrels. The finishing
process is more evident in this whisky than in
many others, with dried fruits, rich wine and
raisin notes, some oaky tannins, and milk
chocolate-covered toffees.

WHISKEY DISCOURSE A
47.0% ABV

Oola is a small distillery that is growing
in confidence and challenging whiskey
conventions with experimental bottlings in
its Discourse series. This bourbon is a four-
grain delight, with a high rye content adding
spiciness that is deliciously offset by organic
white winter wheat. Matured in both 45-liter
(10-gallon) and 240-liter (53-gallon) barrels,
the resulting bourbon is balanced, with light
tannins and oak under a mix of toffee, maple
syrup, vanilla, and cherries. For extra wallop,
there's also a barrel-strength version.

WASMUND'S SINGLE MALT WHISKY
48.0% ABV

Before launching Copper Fox Distillery and his own single malt whiskey, Rick Wasmund toured Scotland and served an internship at Bowmore. He then struck out on his own, drying his barley with apple and cherrywood, and putting toasted hardwood chips into the barrel for maturation. The resulting malt whisky is a delight, with a strange mix of palma violets, cocoa, and banana. The finish is malty and smoky, with orange, milk chocolate, and pepper. The finish is long, with pepper, milk chocolate, and some smoke.

WESTLAND AMERICAN OAK WHISKEY
46.0% ABV

This is one of the finer examples of the new American single malt whiskey style, whereby single malt whiskey is made in much the same way as Scottish single malt, but the spirit is matured in new American oak barrels. This requires resetting your taste radar, because you're hit on one side by savory malt, spice, and possibly peat, and on the other by vanilla, toffee, and candy. When this method works—as it does here, probably due to a decent length of time in the barrel—it makes a delightful experience.

WESTLAND PEATED WHISKEY
46.0% ABV

Westland does single malt very well indeed, but the distillery team seems to have a special affection for peat. It holds a peat week, and there have been several different special releases where peat has been a big part of the story. This is a fine whisky, but it is a bit of a curio. Despite having the word 'peat' in its name, there is more fruit on the nose, and on the palate the effect is more sweet smoke than reeking peat. It does rise up, though, mixing with milk chocolate and vanilla, and offering a stylishly different malt.

WESTLAND SHERRY WOOD WHISKEY
46.0% ABV

It's all well and good saying you're bringing New World thinking to an Old World idea, but a sherry cask's a sherry cask, right? Well no, actually. I'm not sure what they've done here, but this doesn't taste like an Old World whisky at all, although the sherry influence is most certainly there. This has raisins and Danish pastry in its flavor profile; there are large dollops of sweet yellow fruit, and hints of blood orange. More of a confectionery delight than some other sherry whiskies, with only a hint of spice and oaky tannins.

WHISTLEPIG STRAIGHT RYE WHISKEY 111
55.5% ABV

WhistlePig is another distillery that at best raises the eyebrows and at worst gets people genuinely angry. That's because WhistlePig buys its rye from Alberta, Canada, from casks selected by David Pickerell, and brings it to Vermont, where it is finished in ex-bourbon barrels. And it calls the product American rye. But while you might have an issue with that, you can't have an issue with the drink. Called 111 because of its proof strength, it's aged for 11 years, and it is classic spicy fruity rye, with a perfect balance of oak and spices.

WHISTLEPIG STRAIGHT RYE WHISKEY 15 YEAR OLD
46% ABV

There are two ways to create an older whiskey. A distillery can either take one of its existing whiskeys and simply age it for longer, or it can do what WhistlePig has done here. Introduced in 2016, this expression is made up of different stocks from its 11-year-old—toasted Vermont oak barrels rather than bourbon casks. The result is less spice, and more caramel and vanilla notes, tobacco pouch, and a trace of orange. *Wine Enthusiast* gave it a score of 97, and it's a worthy addition to the WhistlePig range.

WHISTLEPIG FARMSTOCK
43.0% ABV

WhistlePig has started distilling rye on the farm where it is based, but in view of the company's exacting standards, it may be several years before we see any bottles of Vermont rye. In the meantime we have this—new spirit from the farm mixed with the best of its five- and six-year-old ryes and some of its award-winning 12-year-old. It's certainly different, with a nose of wood shavings and green fruit, a thinner palate than other WhistlePig whiskeys, and then a sugar-and-spice two-step, with pastry notes late on.

WHISTLEPIG THE BOSS HOG IV RYE
59.6% ABV

WhistlePig's 15-year-old was a hard act to follow, but with this product the company excelled itself again, picking up Best in Show at the San Francisco World Spirits Competition in 2017, beating the cream of the world's best spirits. Boss Hog IV is finished in Armagnac casks and doesn't come cheap, but it is a huge and flavorful rye that pits cinnamon and clove spiciness with figs, plums, citrus, and nuts. There are sweet notes, earthy notes, herbal notes, and savory notes. Incredibly complex and wonderful.

WILLETTS POT STILL RESERVE
47.0% ABV

Willett is the family name behind Kentucky Bourbon Distillers and was the name of the distillery before 1984. The company is in the process of reviving the Willett name, and the family business is now reasserting its position among Kentucky's distillers. As with so many of its releases, Pot Still Reserve is an outstanding small-batch bourbon. It's been aged for eight to ten years. Dried fruits and some refreshing notes are wrapped up in a pleasant candy and oak casing. There is a nice mouth feel, and a long fruity finish.

WOOD'S HIGH MOUNTAIN TENDERFOOT AMERICAN MALT WHISKEY
45.0% ABV

The word 'single' in the term 'single malt' means that the product comes from one distillery. It does not mean that it is from a single cask. And, as this whiskey demonstrates, it does not necessarily mean that it contains one grain, although all the grains must be malted. This liquor is made with a mash bill of malted barley, malted rye, and malted wheat. Freshly cut wood is on the nose and the palate, and the tannins are joined by spiciness and smokiness.

CHAPTER 5

THE WORLD'S BEST AMERICAN WHISKEY BARS

What makes a great bar? Has the American Bar in London's swanky Savoy Hotel a right to be included any more than a pinky, rocky whiskey Aladdin's cave such as Delilah's in Chicago?
A few years ago, whiskey sat unloved and unwanted on the back bar. Now, no self-respecting bar can be without a proper selection of not just Scotch, Irish and American whiskeys, but whiskies from all over the world. So this list is highly subjective, but it is mixed enough so that there is a bar for everyone to feel at home in.

CC LOUNGE AND WHISKY BAR

TORONTO, CANADA

The Canadians spell 'whisky' the Scottish way, but make no mistake, the CC Lounge and Whisky Bar promotes North American whisk(e)y of all types, and the list of American whiskeys on offer here is extraordinary.

Located in the Beardmore building in St Lawrence Market, the bar is designed to reflect the opulence of the 1920s. It is Prohibition-themed, with original brick walls, a cascade of sparkling crystal chandeliers, and lush velvet drapery throughout.

What sets CC apart is its whisky tunnel. This feature was inspired by an underground secret passage built in 1891 and used by Hiram Walker, founder of Canadian Club Whisky, to transport and smuggle whisky and other prohibited spirits from Toronto to bootleggers in the United States.

The tunnel in the bar contains more than 450 whiskeys from all over the world, but there is a heavy bias toward Canada and the United States. Whisky tunnel tours are hosted nightly by the bar's historian.

If you're lucky enough to visit, ask about Burnside Bourbon, Black Saddle 12 Year Old, and Tincup American Whiskey.

WELL FANCY THAT

Hiram Walker & Sons produced and supplied Canadian Club to many thirsty Americans during Prohibition. Walker was personal friends with Henry Ford and Thomas Edison, and held meetings with Al Capone and the Purple Gang that ran the illegal whiskey trade in Detroit.

CC LOUNGE AND WHISKY BAR
45 FRONT ST E
TORONTO, ON M5E 1B3
CANADA, +1 416-362-4777
WWW.CCONFRONT.COM/

EMMET RAY

TORONTO, CANADA

There's an air of mystery about Emmet Ray. Some people don't believe that he ever existed; others claim that he was a talented but little-known gypsy jazz guitarist of the 1930s and 1940s. He has been described as an anti-hero, a hard drinker, and a bit of an ass—but above all, he was a stellar guitarist.

The bar named after him was opened by brothers Andrew and Derek Kaiser in 2009. Five years earlier, Andrew, who had developed a love of whisky, decided to further his career in pubs and bars by heading to Europe. After only a few years on the continent, he was running 22 venues in six countries. But he was determined to have his own business, so he headed back to Toronto and opened the Emmet Ray.

Today the bar hosts live music acts, and offers an eclectic menu that includes burgers, salads, and Thai food.

But the whisky is the center of attention, and the range of American makes is highly impressive. Blanton's and Weller Stagg are among the big-shot names; some of Buffalo Trace's Experimental Series also make the list, and there are several newcomers, such as New Holland and Black Saddle.

WELL FANCY THAT

Woody Allen's 1999 romantic comedy Sweet and Lowdown attempted to shed some light on the life and times of Emmet Ray. Sean Penn was nominated for an Oscar for his performance as Ray; also nominated was Samantha Morton, who played Ray's mute love interest. Uma Thurman co-starred.

THE EMMET RAY
924 COLLEGE STREET
TORONTO, ON M6H 1A4
CANADA, +1 416-792-4497
WWW.THEEMMETRAY.COM

In Canada, all alcohol is state-controlled and must be purchased at state-owned liquor stores. Whiskey from America or Scotland must be approved by the liquor board, and as a consequence many wonderful whiskeys are not available to Canadians.

Shortly before the 2018 Victoria Whisky Festival, police and liquor board officials raided Fets Whisky Kitchen and three other Vancouver bars and confiscated hundreds of bottles of whisky. According to the bars, the whisky was purchased legitimately, and all due tax was paid. It seems, though, that the authorities took a dim view of the bars buying whisky from the Scotch Malt Whisky Society. The raid followed a press report that Fets Kitchen had grown into Canada's biggest whisky bar, with more than 1,300 bottles and a hugely impressive whisky wall.

Until the raid, Fets had a fine range of single-cask, cask-strength Scotch whiskies. Its collection of American whiskeys is still pretty special, and the bar doesn't only serve it straight or in cocktails—it also cooks with it. Try its Southern fried chicken with whiskey gravy.

WELL FANCY THAT

During the notorious swoop by the government authorities, only Scotch Malt Whisky Society products were seized—but that alone meant that Fets Whisky Kitchen forfeited a staggering 242 bottles.

FETS WHISKY KITCHEN
1230 COMMERCIAL DR,
VANCOUVER, BC V5L 3X4,
CANADA, +1 604-255-7771
WWW.WHISKYKITCHEN.CA

CANON WHISKEY AND BITTERS EMPORIUM

SEATTLE, WASHINGTON, USA

Canon has only seven tables, but it's big in every other dimension: it offers a full restaurant menu, a complex cocktails list, and a great choice of wines. It also has 4,000 spirits, and more American whiskeys than anywhere else on Earth.

Owner James Boudreau spends much of his time seeking out the latest releases. He welcomes the craft revolution up to a point, but believes that there needs to be a shakeout of distillers producing under-aged and inferior spirits. He says: 'Locally, Westland Distillery is the star standout in our community. I'd mention more but I'm discovering that there are still great deviations that are occurring from batch to batch, and I'm concerned that a brand that I mention now might be putting out garbage in a year, or may not even exist at all, as the weaker distilleries are beginning to drop out.'

What are Canon's best offerings? Boudreau says that, while it's not a fair question, in view of his vast range, he would pick out any Willett Family Reserve with a wax top, any Old Fitzgerald's from the era when Pappy Van Winkle was running the distillery, and, 'for those wanting a bottle that is fairly easily accessible,' Old Medley 12 year.

WELL FANCY THAT

Canon has a vast vintage spirit collection—'more than 400 labels of whiskies from the 1870s forward,' according to James Boudreau. 'To put that in perspective, whiskey bottles didn't come along until the 1860s. We have things like bourbon and American rye from Canada and Mexico, which is obviously not a possibility in today's world.'

CANON WHISKEY AND BITTERS EMPORIUM
928 12TH AVE, SEATTLE,
WA 98122, USA
WWW.CANONSEATTLE.COM

and rare and sought-after whiskeys.

Ever since it was opened by Alan Davis and Greg Goodman it has been in demand, with long lines to get in and applications for membership stretching forward months and even years.

It's easy to understand why. The bar boasts 1,800 different spirits products, the majority of which are, unsurprisingly, whiskey. They are displayed behind the bar on shelves from floor to ceiling, and are accessed by rolling ladders.

The wide range of spirits is due to the tenacity of the owners and the bar manager. Oregon exercises state control, so it is hard to source rarer bottles. And the current high demand for the best whiskeys means that there is a fight across the United States for special releases and whiskeys released on allocation.

The bar itself is a work of genius and dedication. Bottles are displayed by genre and then through subdivisions such as region, and finally in alphabetical order. The drinks menu reflects the backbar exactly. All well and logical until you think of the nightmare of moving everything to accommodate a new set of Buffalo Trace annual special releases.

The bar serves food made using locally sourced products and ranging from snacks including salt and pepper fries and Pacific Northwest oysters, through to supper dishes including 40-day dry-aged ribeye and bison flank steak. The bar also does an exciting range of cocktails.

isn't snobbish about mixing good whiskeys into long drinks—offering a high-end cocktail menu called Scholar's List with vintage cocktails including one made from a 1960s'-era bottling of Rittenhouse Rye Whiskey.

MULTNOMAH WHISKEY LIBRARY
1124 SW ALDER ST, PORTLAND, OR 97205, USA
+1 503-954-1381
WWW.MWLPDX.COM/

BLIND DONKEY

PASADENA AND LONG BEACH, CALIFORNIA, USA

Blind Donkey is the brainchild of local entrepreneurs Brandon Bradford and Alen Aivazian, and beer and spirits expert Ryan Sweeney.

Whiskey is at the heart of everything Blind Donkey does, and while it has impressive selections of Scottish, Irish, Japanese, and world whiskies, it is with American whiskey that it really excels.

The name is a reference to the days when donkeys, blindfolded so that they didn't get scared, were used to pull the millstones that crushed grains to make whiskey. The two current venues are gastropubs designed to serve the best of everything. There is a strong range of craft beers on tap, and the bar food includes a choice of quality burgers and imaginative takes on the standard bowl of fries.

The pub theme is maintained by a standing bar area, and there are pub games, tasteful background music, and some televised sport.

Blind Donkey attracts beer lovers, but it's the whiskey list that sets it apart. Its whiskey flights—selections of three or four different whiskeys—include offerings from Angel's Envy and other new craft distilleries.

WELL FANCY THAT

Blind Donkey describes itself as a 'whiskey bar and game room also serving craft cocktails, beer & elevated bar food,' and it is indeed a multi-functional bar and diner. Or rather, they are, since Blind Donkey now operates at Long Beach and Pasadena.

BLIND DONKEY
149 LINDEN AVE,
LONG BEACH, CA 90802, USA
+1 562-247-1511
WWW.THEBLINDDONKEY.COM

Messhall Kitchen is primarily a restaurant and, judging from the reviews, an extremely good one. Based on an American summer camp theme, it attracts a young, smart, casual, hipster crowd. Set up to bring customers a fresh take on regional American dining, it opens for breakfast, lunch, and dinner, and its menu includes fresh oysters and innovative interpretations of American favorites using local, sustainable, organic, and seasonal ingredients. Among its offerings are twists on simple, traditional dishes such as mac and cheese, local trout, and a burger made with organic turkey, as well as a range of healthier options, including a wide choice of salads.

Behind the foodie front is an impressive drinks list that emphasizes craft beers, small batch and craft American spirits, and well thought-out cocktails. Prominent too are more than 500 whiskeys, including 13 expressions of Willetts. You can also try whiskey flights, offering a selection of different whiskeys from across the world. The many accolades this bar has received include being picked as one of America's best bourbon bars by liquor.com, and a top ten best bar nomination from USA Today.

MESSHALL KITCHEN
4500 LOS FELIZ BLVD, LOS ANGELES, CA 90027, USA
+1 323-660-6377
WWW.MESSHALLKITCHEN.COM

SEVEN GRAND

LOS ANGELES AND SAN DIEGO, CALIFORNIA, AND AUSTIN, TEXAS, USA

In the owners' account, Seven Grand's three venues were opened 'to create an experience that appealed to those just looking for a drink with friends [and] to those seeking something a bit more special.'

The places feel like bars, and offer hand-crafted cocktails along with good beer, live music, and pool tables. They have an old-fashioned, clubby feel: the only thing stuffy about them is the taxidermy that decorates the rooms.

Then there's the whiskey. Seven Grand has one of the biggest selections on America's West Coast, with scores of bottles displayed on shelves that reach to the ceiling and are accessed by ladders.

And if that's not enough, the bar is home to the Whiskey Society, a unique organization that offers members a program of tastings and seminars. Seven Grand regularly hosts events attended by master distillers, visiting brand ambassadors, and industry experts.

The whiskey choice is a mixture of well-known brands; rare bottlings, such as single barrel and small batch bourbons; and newer craft releases. If you like an Old Fashioned cocktail, the bar offers ten different versions.

SEVEN GRAND
515 W 7TH ST #200, LOS ANGELES, CA 90014, USA
+1 213-614-0736
WWW.SEVENGRANDBARS.COM

ANVIL BAR & REFUGE

HOUSTON, TEXAS, USA

'Anvil Bar & Refuge is casual,' says the team behind it. 'We don't take reservations or hold a line at the door. The building is modern and industrial, but the vibe is warm, inviting, and friendly.'

It also happens to be a great place to come for a drink. It was originally opened as a cocktail bar in 2009, and still serves a choice of around 100 different combinations. To make sure that each of these is the best that it can be, the bar seeks out superior spirits and craft beers.

The whiskey list is fabulous. It covers the whole world of whiskey—its Irish section is particularly appealing—and even the most accomplished American whiskey expert would struggle to find gaps in its list of expressions from the country's larger producers.

It's not as thorough when it comes to craft distillers, because the bar staff won't take on any whiskey that doesn't meet their exacting standards, but Westland, Koval, Rieger's, and St George do make the list.

There are also some ultra-rare blended whiskeys, and a large number of single-barrel bottlings.

WELL FANCY THAT

The Anvil uses its own house-made sodas, infusions, liqueurs, and even flames. All the bartenders are highly trained and skilled, and many former employees have gone on to open their own bars.

ANVIL BAR & REFUGE
1424 WESTHEIMER RD,
HOUSTON, TX 77006, USA
+1 713-523-1622
WWW.ANVILHOUSTON.COM

DELILAH'S

CHICAGO, ILLINOIS, USA

Delilah's has carved out an international reputation through the efforts of its owner, Mike Miller. You'll struggle to find any bar or pub host as knowledgable as he, but there's nothing affected about him. On the contrary, he's the sort of regular guy you'd find in any dive bar in America.

Delilah's is a bit scuzzy, but it qualifies as an iconic whiskey bar because it was doing bourbon before bourbon was a thing, specializing in American whiskey when it was considered a low-class drink. Miller was bourbon's friend when it didn't have many.

Now, in addition to offering some of the best whiskey anywhere, Delilah's has its own bottled bourbon, rye, and Scotch. And Miller and his team have worked with John Glaser of Compass Box to release Compass Box Delilah's, which was sold internationally.

The thing about the venue is that, although it isn't much to look at on the outside, it attracts rock fans as well as the fashionable Chicago set, maintaining a happy biker ambience. The bar holds film and art evenings as well as live music events, and for 20 years has helped to define Chicago's bar scene.

WELL FANCY THAT

In 2017 Delilah's was voted Chicago's best mainstay bar in *Time Out*, and was picked as one of America's top ten bourbon bars by smart fashion mag *Men's Journal*. Not bad for a place whose clientele are mainly T-shirt-and-jeans guys.

DELILAH'S
2771 N LINCOLN AVE,
CHICAGO, IL 60614, USA
+1 773-472-2771
WWW.DELILAHSCHICAGO.COM

OLD SEELBACH

LOUISVILLE, KENTUCKY, USA

Across Kentucky there are throwbacks to its past, the past alluded to in the song 'My Old Kentucky Home' and represented by places like the Seelbach, a grand hotel that was opened at the start of the 20th century. Today it is a luxurious Hilton, with modern facilities and the finest cuisine, but it retains its old-world charm.

It has a history as a playground of the great and good. It hosted wild parties in the 1920s, and it was here that they invented the heart attack on a plate that is The Hot Brown, served in the early hours after a hard night's dancing. Al Capone was a regular here, drinking and gambling during the Prohibition years. King bootlegger George Remus was a frequent guest who became Scott Fitzgerald's inspiration for *The Great Gatsby*.

There's a more unsavory past to it, too, though. For many years it barred black guests, so when Muhammad Ali first won the world heavyweight boxing championship in 1964 he hired an entire floor of the hotel, probably to make a point in the year of the Civil Rights Act.

A visit to the Seelbach Bar is a must for anyone seeking out the roots of bourbon, especially if they're doing so at someone else's expense. Some of the rarest and finest bourbons are on offer, and you can while away an hour or so soaking in all the history of the place as you sip a Mint Julep.

WELL FANCY THAT

Today one can dine in a small alcove in The Oakroom where Al Capone used to play cards. Still here is the large mirror that the gangster had brought from Chicago and positioned so that he could watch his back while sitting at the table. Behind two panels in the room are hidden doors leading to secret passageways through which he could make his escape if necessary.

OLD SEELBACH
500 S 4TH ST, LOUISVILLE, KY 40202, USA
+1 502-585-3200
WWW.SEELBACHHILTON.COM/DINING

JOCKEY SILKS

LOUISVILLE, KENTUCKY, USA

One of the great traits of whiskey is that you can be tasting it in a downtown biker bar in Chicago one moment, and enjoying it in a stylish bourbon bar in one of Louisville's swishiest hotels the next.

Actually, it says all you need to know about the way bourbon has gone from zero to hero since 2010. Back then, not only would the idea of a dedicated bourbon bar in a top hotel have been greeted with laughter, but you'd have struggled to find bourbon anywhere else in Kentucky's biggest city—even though the state is home to most of the leading whiskey producers.

Jockey Silks is now a member of the Louisville Urban Bourbon Trail. In 2012 that trail consisted of just five members; it currently has more than 30.

The name is a nod toward the world-famous Kentucky Derby horse race, which is held in Louisville. The bar is on the second floor of the Galt House Hotel. It doesn't have the most comprehensive whiskey menu, but it offers whiskey flights, has an impressive white whiskey listing—raising the status of this drink from moonshine to something more establishment—and includes products of the best new distilleries.

WELL FANCY THAT

The birthplace of Muhammad Ali, Louisville was built as a trading post on the banks of the Ohio River. Some of the world's largest canal locks were installed here to enable freight barges to avoid the nearby series of waterfalls. In the bar that is now Jockey Silks, actor John Wayne used to knock back shots of tequila.

JOCKEY SILKS
140 N FOURTH ST, LOUISVILLE, KY 40202, USA
+1 502-589-5200
WWW.GALTHOUSE.COM/
DINING/JOCKEY-SILKS-
BOURBON-BAR

THE SILVER DOLLAR

LOUISVILLE, KENTUCKY, USA

During the Great Depression of the 1930s, thousands of impoverished, out-of-work residents of the Midwest headed to California, where they believed there were plenty of jobs. There weren't. Unwelcome to many Californians, the newcomers developed something of a ghetto mentality and created a subculture of their own.

Prejudice against the people known as Okies helped to spawn one of the great musical styles of the 20th century—the Bakersfield sound, which by the 1950s had supplanted Nashville as the grittiest form of country music. Stewed in the cauldrons of local roadhouses, the Bakersfield sound was characterized by explosive electric guitar and tough, rockabilly attitudes.

The Silver Dollar is situated inside a former firehouse, and models itself on the old dives that spawned the Bakersville sound. The bar proudly plays honky-tonk music, and serves only Kentucky whiskey. It's as good a place as any to drink bourbon. You can pair your drink with hearty dishes, such as Cajun shrimp and oyster stew, hickory-smoked beef brisket, chicken and waffles, and brunch specialties, such as cornbread pancakes and fried oyster sandwiches.

WELL FANCY THAT

The Bakersfield style still influences acts ranging from rock bands to Los Angeles-based contemporary country artists such as Dwight Yoakam. A version of it became known as 'the California sound,' and influenced The Flying Burrito Brothers, Poco, Eagles, Emmylou Harris, Gram Parsons, and Creedence Clearwater Revival.

THE SILVER DOLLAR
1761 FRANKFORT AVE,
LOUISVILLE, KY 40206, USA
+1 502-259-9540
WWW.WHISKEYBYTHEDRINK.COM

PROOF ON MAIN

LOUISVILLE, KENTUCKY, USA

Proof on Main is part of the stylish boutique hotel Museum, which is just a bit off the wall. It holds art exhibitions in its foyer, and shows weird films such as a tortoise-eye view of the world. The art is combined with quirky extras, such as colored penguin statuettes placed at various points in the hotel (guests are encouraged to move them as they see fit); a urinal beside the hotel's main corridor with a wall which is a one-way mirror so that you can look at people walking past while using it; and some strange noose art around the lifts.

Proof itself is staid and ordinary by comparison. It is half fine dining restaurant serving award-winning and not cheap quality food, and half casual bar area, serving fine craft beer and cider and some fine American whiskey.

The bourbon list is not the most extensive, certainly not now that the whole city's gone bourbon crazy, but the selections—to use Proof's words—'reflect a dedication to quality, diversity, and originality.' Nevertheless, a choice of 120 different bourbons isn't to be sniffed at.

'Our spirit collection emphasizes small batch, artisanal craftsmanship from around the world,' says the bar. 'Given our proximity to bourbon country, it is naturally highlighted by an impressive selection of fine bourbons, some bottled exclusively for Proof on Main, including special barrels of Woodford Reserve and Van Winkle.'

WELL FANCY THAT

Proof's signature cocktail list includes original recipes inspired by the season and, on occasion, by the art exhibitions in the hotel. Fresh juices, inventive infusions, and home-made tonic are among the highlights of the bar's offerings.

PROOF ON MAIN
702 W MAIN ST, LOUISVILLE,
KY 40202, USA
+1 502-217-6360
WWW.PROOFONMAIN.COM

OLD TALBOTT TAVERN

BARDSTOWN, KENTUCKY, USA

Bardstown is widely regarded as the capital of bourbon. It is home to the annual Kentucky Bourbon Festival, and it has a quaint bourbon museum. Heaven Hill's visitor center is nearby. The town is pretty but, truth be told, away from festival time, pretty dead too.

The place to head to if you find yourself there is the Old Talbott Tavern. It was built in 1779 and has a rich history. Abraham Lincoln stayed there when five years old while his parents settled a land dispute. Alexander Walters, cofounder of the National Association for the Advancement of Colored People, was born in the kitchen area, where his mother was a slave. Among other famous guests was Kentucky State founder Daniel Boone. A dozen bullet holes in the wall of one room are said to have been put there by Jesse James.

The link with bourbon is also strong. Regulars included: William Heavenhill; Mr Ed' Shapiro, who founded Heaven Hill; and William Samuels and Leslie Samuels, who founded Maker's Mark. T D Beam, brother of Jim Beam, purchased the Old Talbott Tavern from the Talbotts in 1916. Another distiller, Tom Moore, also owned it for a time.

WELL FANCY THAT

Talbott Tavern is said to have played host to King Louis Philippe and his two brothers on their tour of the New World. They arrived at the Tavern on October 17, 1797, and during their stay some members of the royal entourage are believed to have painted the murals which were uncovered in 1927.

OLD TALBOTT TAVERN
101 W STEPHEN FOSTER AVE,
BARDSTOWN, KY 40004, USA
+1 502-348-3494
WWW.TALBOTTS.COM

BARREL PROOF

NEW ORLEANS, LOUISIANA, USA

You don't normally associate New Orleans with whiskey. Its climate and Cajun, French, and Creole culture traditionally sit uneasily with the spirit, although the city's penchant for hedonism might lead you to conclude that anything goes, and the Sazerac, which includes rye whiskey, was invented here.

In fact, the link is strong, not least because New Orleans has always received goods from Kentucky transported down the Mississippi River. According to one account, whiskey, shipped by distillers as a clear liquid but taking color from the barrel on its journey south, found its way into bars on Bourbon Street, and became known as the Bourbon Sreet Spirit, and eventually as Bourbon.

For all that, opening a whiskey bar in the city in 2014 was a brave move, and one reviewer visiting shortly after its launch questioned its viability. But its success is further proof—pun intended—of how far whiskey has come.

Barrel Proof is a cavernous room with a long bar and corrugated metal walls. Its comprehensive list of American whiskeys totals nearly 300 different expressions. The atmosphere is informal, the bar staff knowledgable and eager to help, and there are quality craft beers to go with your whiskey choice.

WELL FANCY THAT

Barrel Proof has a simple but tasty menu designed to match the whiskeys on offer. Staff are always happy to make recommendations.

BARREL PROOF
1201 MAGAZINE ST, NEW
ORLEANS, LA 70130, USA
+1 504-299-1888
WWW.BARRELPROOFNOLA.
COM

The main achievement of craft distilling in America has been to introduce whiskey to a new generation. Every generation wants to drink something that their mothers and fathers didn't, and for most early-21st-century 20-somethings, whiskey in general would fall into that category—it may have been drunk by their grandparents, but not by 40–55-year-olds. And obviously craft whiskey opens a whole new world to smart city slickers. That's best witnessed in New York, which tuned in to the whiskey trend early on, and has embraced it ever since, with a number of new distilleries springing up in and around the Big Apple.

American Whiskey—let's get straight to the point, shall we guys?—is tapping in to this trend right in the center of New York (one block away from Madison Square Garden). It is embracing new producers, and pairing its whiskeys with high-quality food, thus appealing to a mixed crowd of whiskey aficionados and curious novices. It's a large, spacious bar that stocks more than 350 whiskeys. The venue offers whiskey flights that mix new producers with some classics, and it has an appealing and exciting range of cocktails.

WELL FANCY THAT

Examples of this bar's imaginative whiskey flights include: two Scottish single malts pitted against Stranahan's and Westward whiskeys; whiskeys from Medley Brothers (102 proof), James E. Pepper (100 proof), and Sonoma County (92 proof) versus Russell's Reserve Single Barrel offering from Wild Turkey.

AMERICAN WHISKEY
247 W 30TH ST, NEW YORK, NY 10001, USA
+1 212-967-1070
WWW.AMERICANWHISKEYNYC.COM

MAYSVILLE

NEW YORK, NEW YORK, USA

Whiskey isn't the cheapest drink to experiment with, so all credit to Maysville for its Early Bourbon initiative: every Saturday and Sunday between 3pm and 6pm, the bar offers a range of expensive whiskeys at discounted prices.

'It is a great opportunity to reach for those bottles on the top shelf or just relax with a reliable favorite,' says the bar. 'And in case you or any of your compatriots are non-bourbon drinkers, there will also be discounted beer, cocktails, and wine by the glass.'

Sounds great, doesn't it? And to cap it all, Maysville's half-dozen oysters are offered at half price, along with selected hot snacks.

Maysville offers more than 150 American whiskeys: classic bourbons and an impressive selection of newer products. But it also recognizes that, while exploring whiskey is a lot of fun, some people prefer to stay with just one choice. So it offers 24-cl (8-ounce) and 48-cl (16-ounce) decanters of some of the bar's favorite whiskeys. The pricing is modest, the choice of American whiskeys excellent, and the menu includes a healthy number of American single malts and American whiskeys that fall outside conventional categories.

WELL FANCY THAT

Maysville is named for the Kentucky birthplace of bourbon, and the grits and poached eggs on the menu are an homage to that state. Much of the food is smoked over hay, reminiscent of charring bourbon barrels.
Maysville is also the birthplace of country legend Rosemary Clooney, aunt of the now even more famous George Clooney.

MAYSVILLE
17 W 26TH ST, NEW YORK, NY 10010, USA
+1 646-490-8240
WWW.MAYSVILLENYC.COM

Noorman's Kil made its name by excelling in two different areas: whiskey and fashionable cheese sandwiches. Like the word 'whiskey,' the term 'cheese sandwiches' doesn't tell much of a story on its own. So how about trying The Jane, which features New York sharp cheddar and locally produced mustard on sourdough; or The Maefred, consisting of Brie, local mushrooms, and rosemary on ciabatta? In neither case will you be disappointed.

The bar—named after a creek that once flowed through northern Brooklyn—is the creation of four respected names in the New York bar scene.

The bar itself is a 19th-century-saloon-style bar salvaged by the owners. It is now decorated with a mix of modern and traditional millwork and metal fixtures. There is also a large garden backyard.

It takes a lot to stand out in New York, but Noorman's Kil does so with its impressive and diverse range of whiskeys. It has more than 400 of them, and the American list is an impressive combination of bourbon classics and other styles, many of them from craft distilleries. With a fantastic selection of craft beer on offer, too, the whole outfit is outstanding.

WELL FANCY THAT

Since 2010 New York has been as good a place as any to taste American whiskey. A number of downtown areas now have bars offering a wide range of whiskeys. The best of them, including Noorman's Kil, are helping to fuel the current micro-distilling boom.

NOORMAN'S KIL
609 GRAND ST, BROOKLYN,
NY 11211, USA
+1 347-384-2526
WWW.NOORMANSKIL.COM

THE FLATIRON ROOM

NEW YORK, NEW YORK, USA

Even by the high standards of the New York bar scene, The Flatiron Room is special. This is one of the world's greatest whiskey bars, with walls lined with bottles, and decor a stylish mix of classical, theatrical wood and Italian-style wallpaper. There are more than 1,000 drinks available at this venue, and the staff are outstanding and knowledgable. If a new whiskey is being launched in the city, the chances are that the event will take place here. In an upstairs room, the venue stages regular events, including tastings and seminars. There is also a whiskey school with a number of courses aimed at everyone from beginners to connoisseurs.

The establishment offers an extensive list of tasting flights, but it's much more than just a whiskey bar. It also has an award-winning food offering, which includes flatbreads, steaks, cheeseboards, and ribs. And the management is keen to emphasize that The Flatiron Room offers the whole gamut of traditional liquors, including many kinds of vodka, tequila, and rum, as well as wine and champagne.

WELL FANCY THAT

The Flatiron Room has ambient live jazz on some occasions, and the decor has been put together to give a sense of timelessness. The chandelier once hung in the Smithsonian Institution. Numbers are limited to maintain a relaxed feel.

THE FLATIRON ROOM
37 W 26TH ST, NEW YORK, NY 10010, USA
+1 212-725-3860
WWW.THEFLATIRONROOM. COM

LLOYD WHISKEY BAR
PHILADELPHIA, PENNSYLVANIA, USA

It would be easy to get carried away by the micro-distilling revolution and forget the great but more traditional whiskeys that have evolved in America over the last 200 years. Thankfully, though, that's where bars such as this come in. Good bar owners understand the importance of heritage and provenance, and appreciate good quality. Indeed, if anything, they can be cautious about embracing craft whiskeys.

The link with the past is strong at the Lloyd Whiskey Bar. It is named after Lloyd Coudriet, who opened it in 2012 with his son and daughter-in-law Scott and Taylor. The bar is reminiscent of the family sitting room, where Lloyd would enjoy a Miller High Life and the occasional shot of Old Grandad Bourbon: 'Hence our Citywide Special, which combines a bottle of the beer with a shot of the whiskey for $6,' says Scott.

Lloyd's celebrated its fifth birthday in 2017 by doubling the length of its happy hours, and offering discounts on craft beers and bar snacks. Many of its food offerings have a Southern twist: examples include bourbon-chili-glazed chicken wings, and blackened catfish sandwiches.

WELL FANCY THAT

The Lloyd Whiskey Bar puts an emphasis on local drinks, and stocks a wide range of craft beers. On its whiskey menu is a section dedicated to Philly whiskeys, including expressions from Kinsey, New Liberty, Bluebird, Dad's Hat, and Brothership.

LLOYD WHISKEY BAR
529 E GIRARD AVE,
PHILADELPHIA, PA 19125, USA
+1 215-425-4600
WWW.LLOYDWHISKEYBAR.COM

VILLAGE WHISKEY
PHILADELPHIA, PENNSYLVANIA, USA

Village Whiskey is one of around a dozen restaurants and bars across the United States currently owned by renowned Ecuadorian American chef Jose Garces. His aim here was to create the sort of place in which he and his staff would want to drink, eat, and relax after a hard night at work in the kitchen. Since his favorite spirit is whiskey, he stocked the Village Whiskey bar with some 200 different expressions.

It's a simply furnished venue and it's not big, offering only around 30 covers, but it has a relaxed, Prohibition speakeasy feel about it. Certainly, that era has influenced the cocktail menu.

The fundamental aim is simple: the best whiskeys and the best burgers, together in a single place. But not just burgers. When Garces talks about snacks, he doesn't mean simple nuts and chips. Unsurprisingly for an award-winning chef who has written two renowned books on Latin food, his creations are rather more ambitious than that. The dishes on offer at Village Whiskey include truffled cauliflower pickles, fried shrimp, and deviled eggs. How about Kentucky fried quail anyone?

WELL FANCY THAT

Chef Garces has ensured that his bar staff are as outstanding at drinks as he is at food. Check out the imaginative cocktail list. Offerings include The Philadelphia Fish House Punch—a winning mixture of peach brandy, dark rum, cognac, tea, and lemon juice.

VILLAGE WHISKEY
118 S 20TH ST, PHILADELPHIA,
PA 19103, USA
+1 215-665-1088
WWW.PHILADELPHIA.
VILLAGEWHISKEY.COM

BOURBON DC

WASHINGTON, DC, USA

America might have gone whiskey crazy in recent years, and enthusiasts have certainly embraced their country's new distillers with a passion, but the city of Washington, DC, has always considered itself a whiskey town, and unsurprisingly there are plenty of venues to choose from in the national capital now that whiskey is big news. Even the city's most modest bar is likely to have some form of whiskey offering.

The complex that houses Bourbon DC contains at least three other whiskey options. But Bourbon DC stands out from the competition, partly because of its multilevel layout with patio, but mainly because of its extensive range of whiskeys and new craft distillers' expressions. There are all sorts of unusual and exciting gems on offer here. Among the most enticing examples are: cask-strength versions of both Maker's Mark and Maker's Mark 46; Wild Turkey Tribute (15-year-old Wild Turkey, to mark Jimmy Russell's 50th anniversary) bottled at the classic 101 proof; and Wild Turkey Master's Keep (a very rare 17-year-old bottling). The craft distillery bottlings stocked at Bourbon DC also make impressive reading.

WELL FANCY THAT

There are whiskey lists and there are whiskey lists. Bourbon DC's is one of the most impressive, mixing quantity with quality, and major producers with minor ones. There are 20 different whiskeys from Kentucky Bourbon Distillers alone, and more than 30 expressions from Heaven Hill

BOURBON DC
2321 18TH ST NW,
WASHINGTON, DC 20009, USA
+1 202-332-0800
WWW.BOURBONDC.COM

JACK ROSE DINING SALOON

WASHINGTON, DC, USA

On the home page of the Jack Rose website is a counter showing the number of different whiskey bottles currently on the saloon's shelves. At the time of writing, the total stood at just over 2,700.

I don't know if that counter ever goes down, but reading old reviews of the venue you would expect not. And 2,700 is a lot: indeed, it is claimed to be the biggest whiskey offering in the Western Hemisphere.

But size can be intimidating. There's a famous Scottish whisky bar that displayed all its bottles without description or price; its staff would come to your table and expect you to know what you wanted. It was plain scary, even for someone in the industry.

By contrast, the staff of Jack Rose are trained to be approachable, amenable, knowledgable, and agile—agile because they need to run up and down ladders to fetch some of the highest bottles.

The Saloon serves everything from light bites and supper to full dining-room cuisine; there's an intimate cellar room, a rentable private party room, and when weather permits, a tiki bar and outside terrace.

WELL FANCY THAT

Jack Rose owner Bill Thomas scours the shelves of liquor stores for unrecognized gems. He once paid $114 for six bottles of Pappy Van Winkle's Family Reserve 15-year-old bourbon that he found in a clearance bin in Kentucky. You'd currently pay around $800 for each bottle.

JACK ROSE DINING SALOON
2007 18TH ST NW,
WASHINGTON, DC 20009, USA
+1 202-588-7388
WWW.
JACKROSEDININGSALOON.
COM

Confidence flows through this bar's menu—and with good reason. The team here has evidently thought long and hard about its drinks offerings, and you get the sense that they know they have got it absolutely right.

Bourbon is a restaurant specializing in Cajun and Creole food, especially Southern classics such as gumbo, jambalaya, and étouffée, as well as dishes based on locally sourced ingredients. But there is also a passion here for whiskey, and the bar stocks some 350 American whiskeys, together with a growing collection of whiskeys from other parts of the world.

But Bourbon also appreciates that if you want to do well in today's climate, the cocktails have to step up to the plate and deliver every time. The team explains how it achieved this aim:

'We traveled all over the United States to sample cocktails at some of the top bars in the country, and came back with a deep appreciation for the "craft of the cocktail" and those who practice it at their establishments, from tiny dive bars to opulent places with unlimited budgets. The common themes from the best were always the same…well-balanced, thoughtful cocktails served in a timely manner and with a heightened level of care and hospitality.

'So, our cocktails are simple, yet elegant. We LOVE a good cocktail. So we go out of our way to make sure our cocktails are good. However, we also LOVE our whiskey, so most of the time, you'll see us with a couple ounces of it, with a bit of ice or water…but mostly not.'

WELL FANCY THAT

Bourbon has some of the most unusual bourbons you'll find anywhere in America. Unusual offerings include whiskeys from Belle Meade, Bib and Tucker, Medley Bros, New Southern Revival, and Smooth Ambler.

BOURBON
1214 MAIN ST, COLUMBIA,
SC 29201, USA
+1 803-403-1404
WWW.BOURBONCOLUMBIA.
COM

From the outside it looks just like any other Glaswegian pub. Certainly it doesn't look like it's a great place for American whiskey. But The Pot Still is an institution, one of the world's greatest pubs, and an essential stopover for all whisky tourists.

The Pot Still's not exactly huge on the inside, either, but what could be called a cosy space becomes even cosier once a mix of regulars and guests turn up, pack its floor, and perch on the edge of the seats by the tables, where invariably conversations with strangers will be struck up.

Unsurprisingly, the main trade is in Scottish single malts, and there are a lot of them. But The Pot Still's owners see the world of whiskey as one big family, and they're curious about what is being launched elsewhere in the world. The staff are all extremely knowledgable, down-to-earth, and approachable. And athletic, too. Whiskey bottles stretch high to the ceilings on the wall behind the bar, and regular trips up a ladder are all part of the service. Regular music sessions and whiskey tastings are held in the pub, and there are some tasty craft beers if you fancy a refresher.

WELL FANCY THAT
The Pot Still is on Hope Street in the center of Glasgow, and attracts a wide range of customers. It has long been associated with the drinks trade, and the famous McCall family ran a public house there from 1870 to 1981.

THE POT STILL
154 HOPE ST, GLASGOW,
G2 2TH, SCOTLAND
+44 141 333 0980
WWW.THEPOTSTILL.CO.UK

DICK MACK'S PUB & BREWERY

DINGLE, COUNTY KERRY, IRELAND

No one does hospitality quite like the Irish do. They call it the Craic, and it's a heady mix of music, beer, whiskey, laughter, and talk with people who start out as strangers and end up as friends. If you go to Dublin, find a local and get him or her to point you away from the tourist areas and to the real bars of the city. Elsewhere in the country, though, traditional Irish bars are still easy to find. To stand out as a bar or pub in this sort of environment takes some doing, but Dick Mack's manages to do it. It has been serving up liquid refreshments since 1899 and, as is so often the case with the Emerald Isle, it's an odd sort of place, with one half of it offering beer and a fine selection of whiskeys, and the other half of it selling leather. It's a family business currently run by Dick Mack's grandson, Finn Mac Donnell. It attracts tourists and celebrity drinkers from all over the world.

Mac Donnell and Peter White set about turning the pub into a destination whiskey bar a few years back, and they have been building up the choice of whiskeys ever since. The bar now has an extensive collection of whiskeys, and in 2018 hosted the first meeting outside Dublin of the Irish Whiskey Society.

WELL FANCY THAT
Dingle punches well above its weight when it comes to whiskey: it has one of Ireland's best new distilleries; it has Dick Mack's, and there is a Dingle Whiskey Bar in the whiskey golden triangle in Dublin. It also has its own chapter of the Irish Whiskey Society.

DICK MACK'S PUB & BREWERY
46 GREEN ST, DINGLE, CO.
KERRY, V92 FF25, IRELAND
+353 66 915 1787
WWW.DICKMACKSPUB.COM

Jake's Bar is a highly atmospheric and snug watering hole named after heavyweight mixologist Jake Burger, one of a team of three partners who own five venues, most of which are in Leeds, although the Portobello Star in London's Notting Hill district is also a part of the group.

Jake's Bar is a great all-rounder, but it made its name on the quality of its cocktails. Such concoctions require spirits of the highest quality, and the American whiskeys used here are the veritable cream of the cream. As if not content with the best available, Jake's Bar has gone one further: in 2012 the management installed Tabitha, a 30-liter (6.6-gallon) copper pot still on which are made a unique range of spirits and liqueurs called The Distilled Spirit of Leeds. The range is updated regularly to reflect the different flavors of the changing seasons.

Jake's is located on one of the busiest streets in Leeds, and attracts a trendy weekend crowd, so you may have to line up to gain entry. But American-inspired food and an eclectic selection of music ensure a lively, club-like atmosphere and make it worth the wait.

WELL FANCY THAT

London's Portobello Star is more than just a bar. It is home to the Ginstitute, a museum that offers training courses and hosts tastings, and also to the distillery that makes the highly acclaimed Portobello Gin. The bar here serves some of Jake's very best cocktails.

JAKE'S BAR
27 CALL LANE, LEEDS,
LS1 7BT, ENGLAND
+44 113 243 1110
WWW.JAKESBAR.CO.UK

BUNNY JACKSON'S JUKE JOINT

MANCHESTER, ENGLAND

'Your local dive bar and home of the 10p wing, live music, free hot dogs and good times,' announces the home page of Bunny Jackson's website. You can add American whiskey to that list, says the venue's manager.

'BJ's is as close as we dare get to an authentic American dive bar,' he continues. 'Live music, cold beer, a mix of classic and party cocktails, relaxed and friendly service, massive sandwiches, fried chicken, and loads of bourbon. Whiskey is our key product, and our range is our unique selling point.'

Bunny Jackson's is a colorful bar with a caged stage on which blues, country, and Americana acts perform at weekends. The sandwich menu includes burger and Po'boys as well as 'loads of crazy, mixed-up creations.' There is an impressive selection of American craft beers, and, of course, whiskey.

'Whiskey as a category has taken off hugely in the last few years, and is becoming much less for stuffy old men sipping in the boozer than it was a decade ago,' says the manager. 'Nowadays it seems to appeal to a much broader demographic, and is used a lot more readily as a mixing ingredient on cocktail menus.'

WELL FANCY THAT

Want to try something new and different? Bunny Jackson's suggests one of their Brand New York Sours. It's made up of Buffalo Trace, lemon, and maple syrup shaken together with a late bottled vintage (LBV) port float.

BUNNY JACKSON'S JUKE JOINT
1 JACK ROSENTHAL STREET,
MANCHESTER, M15 4RA,
ENGLAND
WWW.BUNNYJACKSONS.CO.UK

NQ stands for Northern Quarter, a small and compact area of Manchester packed with the city's coolest bars. It is one of those neighborhoods that seems to start waking up only at lunchtime, hitting its stride in the evening, and peaking late at night, especially at weekends.

Trof, though, is a little bit different. It is an all-day cafe bar that offers breakfast, brunch, beer, bourbon, coffee, and cocktails, though, it says, 'not necessarily in that order.' The menu is extensive, evolving during the day from full English breakfast (with vegetarian and vegan options) through an upmarket burger and sandwich lunch to stylish restaurant-quality dinner. Unsurprisingly, cocktails are at the core of the bar operation, but the American whiskey list is impressive, with Kentucky Bourbon Distillers well represented, Wasmunds flying the flag for American single malt, and the rye selection including a rare 2011 bottling of Sazerac 18 year old.

The bar operates over three levels, and is laid back and informal, with stripped wood, industrial fixtures, and sofas. From time to time the venue hosts special events, such as The Big Bourbon Blowout.

WELL FANCY THAT

Manchester has a fantastic bar scene, but if you love Scotch whisky you should head to The Briton's Protection. It looks like a normal North English pub, and in many ways it is. But it also has a fantastic whisky collection. It's reasonably priced, and the staff really know their whiskies and are happy to advise.

TROF NQ
8 THOMAS ST, MANCHESTER, M4 1EU, ENGLAND
+44 161 833 3197
WWW.TROFNQ.CO.UK

BLUES KITCHEN

LONDON, ENGLAND

This is another concept that has been rolled out to more than one venue, in this case three outlets in the British capital. And another place that gets its offering spot on. So much so that when Wild Turkey's Eddie Russell came over to England to do media interviews, the Blues Kitchen in Camden was the venue chosen to host him. The Blues Kitchen describes itself as 'London's very own home of the barbecue, blues, and rock and roll' and, like All Star Lanes, its image is of a bygone era of American cool.

The Blues Kitchens are in Shoreditch, Camden, and Brixton. Each has an extensive program of live music, with evenings of soul, blues, country, and bluegrass. The venues are big enough to attract quality acts, such as Seasick Steve and Kent DuChaine.

All three venues are set in special spaces; each has its own distinctive personality, and operates in a slightly different way. But the core menu in each—based on classic barbecue American food—is the same, and this extends to the drinks list. The bourbons are unexceptional, but there is an impressive selection of corn and wheat whiskey, and the list of ryes is excellent.

WELL FANCY THAT

As recently as 2010, whiskey was rarely used in cocktails. Now it is at the center of any good bar operation. At the Blues Kitchen, why not try a Marmalade Cup: Four Roses Yellow Label, grapefruit liqueur, lemon juice, marmalade, egg white, sage, and peach bitters?

THE BLUES KITCHEN
111—113 CAMDEN HIGH ST, LONDON, NW1 7JN, ENGLAND
+44 20 7387 5277
WWW.THEBLUESKITCHEN.COM

ALL STAR LANES

LONDON, ENGLAND

All Star Lanes is a group of outlets that are mainly London-based, although there is also a branch in Manchester. We're talking about American retro chic here: 1950s-style bowling alleys that are part leisure center and part cool and trendy bar. In fact, these venues have a sort of Jekyll and Hyde feel. In the day, they're all families, shakes, and burgers; in the evenings, they're after-work groups, beers, and bourbons.

All Star Lanes is not a chain-like bowling alley such as the ones you find in most major British cities. The lanes themselves are flown in from America, so they're the real deal, and the food is cooked fresh to order, making good use of local butchers' and fishmongers' produce. The bar is a serious enterprise, too, with highly experienced mixologists employed to create outstanding cocktails. And when the mood takes them, they pride themselves on having some much sought-after American whiskey, including an extensive range of old and rare bourbons.

In addition to the main bowling alleys, all the venues have smaller rooms that can be hired for private birthday, hen, or stag parties. The London branches are in Holborn, Spitalfields, and Westfield Stratford.

WELL FANCY THAT

All Star Lanes was launched in 2006 by Mark von Westenholz and Adam Breeden. Their theory was that people like bowling but had been put off by scruffy, sticky, sweaty, bowling alley centers with reheated hotdogs and overpriced cola as their catering options. They changed the game by bringing in proper bars with quality drinks menus.

ALL STAR LANES
95 BRICK LANE, LONDON,
E1 6QL, ENGLAND
+44 20 7426 9200
WWW.ALLSTARLANES.CO.UK

DEMON, WISE & PARTNERS

LONDON, ENGLAND

Ah, the wonderful world of whiskey! On the one hand, you can get loud and sweaty, with burger in one hand and bourbon in the other. Alternatively, you can visit Demon, Wise & Partners, which sounds like a firm of solicitors but is actually a plush, very British, and incredibly stylish venue with leather chairs and cosy booths tastefully decorated in subdued copper and red.

It describes itself as 'a classic cocktail bar,' and you'll find it beneath The Arbitrager in the heart of the City of London. Reservations are recommended because the bar is seated only.

As you might expect in such a stylish establishment, the drinks list is of the highest quality. The only Jack Daniels on offer is Single Barrel, for instance, and the list of ryes and bourbons is small but perfectly formed. There is a great selection of absinthes, too, and if you're in the mood for a cocktail, why not try a Drunken Pumpkin, which is comprised of Wild Turkey 81 bourbon, pumpkin and pecan nut purée, almond milk, and coffee liqueur? Or how about a Goodnight Sweetheart, made with Wild Turkey 81 bourbon, dry curacao, winter cordial, and Angostura and orange bitters?

WELL FANCY THAT

At the time of writing, the house specials were the Demon and the Wise. The owners describe the former as 'reflecting our inner wickedness and daring'; the latter as showing 'maturity of years, wisdom and complexity.' Each of these drinks will be made only 100 times before being replaced by other recipes.

DEMON, WISE & PARTNERS
27A THROGMORTON ST,
LONDON, EC2N 2AN,
ENGLAND
+44 20 3774 7654
WWW.DEMONANDWISE.CO.UK

HARRILD AND SONS

LONDON, ENGLAND

Harrild and Sons is a bar and restaurant operating in the Farringdon district of the British capital. It has a main bar and dining area on the ground floor, and a cosy cocktail room in the basement. It's stylishly furnished, and pitched perfectly between informal bar and informal restaurant, with wooden tables and floorboards and exposed brickwork. The subdued decor is broken up by bright neon cocktail signs.

The mixed bar-restaurant theme is reinforced by the food menu. Snacks go from chips and fish finger sandwiches to smoked aubergine purée, seeded flatbread, cauliflower pakora and mango chutney. If you want a main course, there's a choice of stylish offerings such as red mullet fillets, chargrilled vegetables, red pepper sauce, and olive tapenade or Portland crab, squid ink tagliatelle, samphire, mascarpone & dill. There's also good old fish and chips.

The drinks list is impressive, too, particularly the craft beer. The American whiskey list is off the wall, with selected Heaven Hill bourbons alongside the likes of Westland Sherry, Michter's, Sonoma County, and a modestly priced Smooth Ambler 8 Year Old Single Barrel whiskey.

WELL FANCY THAT

Harrild and Sons has been created in the former premises of a printing-press manufacturer, and is named in memory of Robert Harrild, who manufactured hot metal type or rotary printing drums for many of the daily newspapers that used to be based in nearby Fleet Street.

HARRILD AND SONS
26 FARRINGDON ST, LONDON, EC4A 4AB, ENGLAND
+44 20 3714 2497
WWW.HARRILDANDSONS.COM

The Lexington is a great example of how, with a little imagination, a venue can be relaunched as something new and exciting. Situated near Pentonville Prison, it was once a classic example of a London drinking pub. Today, it describes itself as 'a classic London boozer-turned-lounge bar, with a hint of Kentucky charm and lashings of rock & roll excess.'

It boasts the best bourbon selection in London, has an impressive list of American craft beers, and upstairs there is a regular program of live music and DJs playing a wide range of music. You can learn to swing dance here, watch class American acts such as The Hold Steady, or enjoy indie music nights.

The menu consists of upmarket burgers and fries, and an array of different sauces, including chili and peanut butter and a very hot Scotch bonnet sauce.

But we're here for the American whiskey, and the list is impressive, with distinguished classic bourbons such as Old Grandad and Very Old Barton (you don't see the latter very often anywhere) listed alongside Garrison Brothers, Ezra Brooks, and Old Overholt. Elsewhere on the list you'll find WhistlePig and High West.

WELL FANCY THAT

With its American nostalgia theme and its reputation for staging some of the hottest new acts, The Lexington has become a sought-after venue by more established bands warming up for impending tours.Check the web page for 'secret' gigs.

THE LEXINGTON
96—98 PENTONVILLE ROAD, LONDON, N1 9JB, ENGLAND
+44 20 7837 5371
WWW.THELEXINGTON.CO.UK

HARRY'S NEW YORK BAR

PARIS, FRANCE

Harry's New York Bar has iconic status, an institution with more than 100 years at its site on Rue Daunou near the Opéra. It is there because a former American jockey persuaded a friend who owned a bar in New York to dismantle it and move it to Paris. Harry MacElhone was approached to run it, and it opened its doors on Thanksgiving Day in 1911.

'It is a mythical place,' say its owners. 'Authors such as Hemingway and Sartre came to taste a few of the most famous cocktails in the world, including those which were created here, such as the Bloody Mary or the White Lady. A century later, it is still an inescapable place in Paris.'

Unsurprisingly, a bar with so much in its past has become something of a tourist trap, and it's in an expensive part of Paris. You need to be prepared for a hefty bill, but even that can't detract from the charm and ambience of the place. And it doesn't get much better than having a barman make you a personalized cocktail at the underground piano bar, where, legend has it, George Gershwin composed *An American in Paris*, and where jazz concerts are currently held every Thursday and Friday night.

WELL FANCY THAT

In the run-up to every US Presidential election since 1924, Harry's Bar has conducted a straw poll of the voting intentions of its American expatriate clientele. It's picked the winner on all but three occasions: Jimmy Carter in 1976; George W. Bush when he ran for a second term in 2004, and Donald Trump in 2016.

HARRY'S NEW YORK BAR
5 RUE DAUNOU, 75002 PARIS, FRANCE
+33 1 42 61 71 14
WWW.HARRYSBAR.FR

THE BEAST RÉPUBLIQUE

PARIS, FRANCE

Is opening an American smokehouse in the center of Paris a stroke of genius, or an act of extreme folly? There's an assumption that France makes world-class food and the United States doesn't—so who's going to go to an American smokehouse in the capital of haute cuisine?

But there is another way of looking at it. If you're going to chance your arm by owning a restaurant in Paris, you wouldn't go for a traditional French theme, would you? And maybe there are Parisians who like the idea of American food and drink.

People such as Thomas Abramowicz. He's a Frenchman, but while working in New York he fell in love with the taste of barbecue food. So he made the decision to give up a highly paid job, rented a car, and headed to Texas, where he visited scores of barbecue joints. He also worked in one, and learned all about cooking beef the American way.

He is also a huge bourbon fan, so, never one to do anything by half, he set off for Kentucky to visit distilleries and to start buying up the liquor he would add to his bar offering. Beast currently has more than 50 American whiskeys available—not the biggest collection, but here it's all about quality, not quantity. The food menu's not extensive, either, but ask anyone who has eaten there about the pulled brisket and you'll get a sense of why this bar is such a success.

Among the whiskey delights are a 22-year-old Elijah Craig and a 23-year-old Pappy Van Winkle. And at the other end of the age scale you'll find True Blue, an un-aged whiskey from Texan craft distillery Balcones.

WELL FANCY THAT

Thomas Abramowicz must be doing something right, and certainly his thoroughness and hard work to ensure an authentic Texan barbecue offering have paid off. There are now three Beast outlets in Paris—at République, Belleville, and one called Son of a Beast, at the same site as the Belleville one.

THE BEAST RÉPUBLIQUE
27 RUE MESLAY, 75003 PARIS, FRANCE
+33 7 81 02 99 77
WWW.THEBEAST.FR

J.D. WILLIAM'S WHISKY BAR

AMSTERDAM, NETHERLANDS

J.D. William's is a smart, compact whisky bar and very much a labor of love. It's in Amsterdam's beautiful Jordaan neighborhood, and it's a concept bar that seeks to bring together whisky, whisky cocktails, and gourmet Asian fusion-style bar food in an industrial chic setting.

'Our aim is quite simple,' says Daniel, co-owner with his wife. 'We want to spread our passion for whisky! Whether you are an expert looking for one of Scotland's rarest single malts or a novice looking to try whisky for the first time, J.D. William's is the place.'

Naturally, Scotch whisky is at the heart of the whisky offering, but a good range of American whiskey is also on offer.

'American whiskey is very important to us,' Daniel continues. 'I am from the States, and a big lover of ryes and bourbons. We try to find as many different American whiskeys that are rare or hard to find in the Netherlands. We normally keep our USA stock of whiskey at around 40 to 50 different whiskeys. And of course we pour many ryes and bourbons in our cocktail menu.'

Not only do the couple think that American whiskey will continue to thrive, but they also want to start distilling for themselves in the near future. Daniel is sure: 'For us, the demand for American whiskey is up there with the Japanese whisky trend. And it will continue to grow. The whiskey market in general is growing, and I think the American whiskeys will continue that trend.'

Daniel says that customers have been wary about embracing the new craft American producers, accepting that there are some bad whiskeys on the market. But he points out that if you search for them, there are many good new producers too. He's a fan of Michter's, Stag, Corsair, and Catoctin Creek.

WELL FANCY THAT

Who was or is J.D. William? Sounds like some historical American whiskey character, doesn't it? It's not. 'J.D. William's Whisky Bar is our bar,' says the owner. 'J is for our oldest son, Jackson; D is for our youngest son, Donovan, and William is my father's name.'

J.D. WILLIAM'S WHISKEY BAR
PRINSENSTRAAT 5, 1015 DA
AMSTERDAM, NETHERLANDS
+31 20 362 0663
WWW.JDWILLIAMSWHISKYBAR.
COM

Some cities are whiskey cities and others are not. Berlin definitely is. When it wants to, whiskey can hitch up its skirts and get all down and dirty, and the hedonistic, indulgent bar scene of Berlin is just the place for it to do so. There are lots of options here, and lots of different whiskey styles rubbing shoulders with each other across the German capital.

Madonna isn't the coolest or the flashest place to drink in Berlin. It's a simple neighborhood bar with clusters of wooden tables, whitewashed walls, and a large main bar area. However, it came to wider public attention when it appeared as a location in the 2003 movie *Herr Lehmann* (English-language title: *Berlin Blues*).

It has a lively pub-like feel, and attracts a casual and friendly local clientele, as well as music lovers of all ages on band nights.

But many come here for the whiskey, too. Madonna has a selection of more than 250 expressions, including a substantial number of American whiskeys. Knowledgable bar staff will offer help if it's needed, and there are tasting sessions on Sunday nights.

WELL FANCY THAT

The movie that made Madonna famous was directed by Leander Haussmann and based on a novel by Sven Regener, who also wrote the screenplay. It's about a bar in East Berlin just before the fall of the Wall that divided the city until 1989.

MADONNA
WIENER STRASSE 22, 10999
BERLIN, GERMANY
+49 30 6116943
WWW.MADONNA-BAR.DE

BASCULE WHISKY BAR

CAPE TOWN, SOUTH AFRICA

If drinking whiskey in opulent surroundings is your thing, then you could do worse than visit the Bascule at the Cape Grace Hotel on a private quay between Cape Town's bustling V&A Waterfront and the tranquil yacht marina. The Bascule offers breathtaking views, and a choice of more than 400 whiskeys.

The Bascule morphs over the course of the day. It attracts businessmen for meetings over coffee in the morning and early afternoon, a smart crowd at lunchtime, and visitors and tourists for afternoon tea. But it really comes into its own from the early evening and at night, when it is transformed into a lively bar that attracts after-work business folk, whiskey enthusiasts, and fashionistas who gather to enjoy sundowners and lively music.

Whiskey is the bar's main attraction, but there's also a good selection of signature cocktails, including the delightful Spiced Apple Julep—Maker's Mark blended with spiced apple purée, fresh lime, and mint.

The tapas-style menu includes biltong, marinated olives, freshly shucked oysters, salt and pepper squid with sweet chili, and smoked ostrich, served with balsamic-poached pear, goats' cheese, and pine nuts.

WELL FANCY THAT

South African company Distell— owner of the country's James Sedgwick Distillery, which makes Three Ships single malt whisky—is now one of the world's biggest drinks companies, having bought Scottish distillery group Burn Stewart in 2013.

BASCULE WHISKY BAR
CAPE GRACE HOTEL, W QUAY
RD, V & A WATERFRONT, CAPE
TOWN, 8002, SOUTH AFRICA
+27 21 410 7082
WWW.CAPEGRACE.COM/

THE WHISKYBROTHER

JOHANNESBURG, SOUTH AFRICA

Whiskey is booming in South Africa, where an emerging black middle class has adopted the finest single malt and bourbon as their spirits of choice. The country's whiskey festivals are among some of the best in the world, and a good whiskey list is essential for any hotel or restaurant bar worth its salt. Whiskybrother was the Twitter handle of Marc Pendlebury, who moved to London and took to social media to talk about his passion for whiskey. When he returned to his native South Africa he took the plunge and opened a whiskey shop in 2012, building a strong and loyal customer base. Since then whiskey has taken off in the city and several whiskey shows have been launched but in 2017 Whiskybrother launched another one, offering excellent value for money and some rare and special whiskeys. Just a few months later Pendlebury teamed up with business partners to open a dedicated whiskey bar in 2018. Scotch whisky is the main focus—the bar has more than 600 of them—but a growing number of people are discovering American whiskey, too. The new bar has room for 28 covers and there is a tasting room which can accommodate eight people.

WELL FANCY THAT

Johannesburg has hoisted one of the most successful whiskey festivals for some years now. Whisky Live is also geld in Cape Town and is regarded as one of the highlights of the whiskey year. And now Whisky Brother, which owns a dedicated shop and bar in the city, has added a new whiskey festival too.

THE WHISKYBROTHER
MORINGSIDE SHOPPING
CENTRE, RIVONIA RD,
MORNINGSIDE, SANDTON,
2196, SOUTH AFRICA
+27 11 883 3762
WWW.WHISKYBROTHER.COM

ROGIN'S TAVERN

MORIGUCHI, OSAKA, JAPAN

You'd expect Japan to be in the mix when it comes to the world's best bars, but you might not expect to find one of the most American whiskey bars in Moriguchi, a satellite city of Osaka. It was brought to our attention by Owen Lang, who visited it and described it as 'the ultimate in bourbon destinations.'

Ever since owner Seiichiro Tatsumi opened the tavern in 1977, he has been growing his collection by visiting Kentucky and driving around the state scouring liquor stores for rare and forgotten bottles. One suspects there's more to it than that, though, because there are bourbons here dating back more than a century—and you don't find those sitting on the shelves at Binny's.

Rogin's Tavern occupies premises from which Tatsumi-San's family has run a business for 16 generations. It has hundreds of bottles of whiskey, and is also overflowing with whiskey memorabilia. On the first floor is a traditional bar that would not look out of place anywhere in the United States. A jukebox plays in the corner, and a wide selection of whiskey covers the bar. There is also a simple bar menu. The collection of pre-Prohibition bottles provides a unique opportunity to sample history.

WELL FANCY THAT

Rogin's Tavern occupies three floors. The top floor includes all sorts of rarities. It looks like an old Western saloon, and the rare whiskeys here include ancient Pappy Van Winkle, the original Jack Daniel's Gold Medal Old. 7, and an 1849 bottle of Fitzgerald's. Visiting master distillers have signed their names on the walls.

ROGIN'S TAVERN
1, CHOME-2-15, HONMACHI,
MORIGUCHI, 570-0028 OSAKA,
JAPAN
+81 6-6997-3200

SHOT BAR ZOETROPE

TOKYO, JAPAN

That everyone who has ever been to Shot Bar Zoetrope ranks it as one of their favorite bars anywhere in the world tells you pretty much everything you need to know about it. You'll find it on the third floor of a commercial building in the Shinjuku district of Tokyo, and you get to it by using a rickety old elevator. It is small and cramped—only a handful of seats at the bar—and notable for two things, reflecting owner Atsushi Horigami's twin passions: lots and lots of whisky, and old American movies. In the evenings, black-and-white silent or animated movies provide a backdrop.

We'd be lying if we claimed that this was a temple to American whiskey—its main offerings are rare Japanese whisky and Scottish single malts—but you can drink outstanding American whiskeys here, and the chances are that, if you do, the experience will be indelibly engraved in your memory. The place gets very busy, and it is on every whisky lover's 'to do' list, so two pieces of advice—if you're planning to go, go soon, because a lot of those rarer whiskeys are disappearing forever. And visit early in the evening, to ensure that you get in without undue difficulty.

WELL FANCY THAT

Japan probably has more whisky bars than any other country on the planet. If you're going to Tokyo, do your research in advance because, like Shot Bar Zoetrope, many of the best bars are hidden away and you're unlikely to chance upon them. Expect to pay a cover charge in many such places.

SHOT BAR ZOETROPE
7–10–14, NISHISHINJUKU,
TOKYO 160-0023, JAPAN
+81 3-3363-0162
WWW.RYDEN.WAY-NIFTY.COM/
ZOETROPE

THE BEAST SOUTHERN KITCHEN AND BOURBON BAR

SINGAPORE

The Beast, say its owners, is 'a slice of the dirty South in Singapore.' That's the South of the United States. They continue: 'You can almost imagine yourself sitting on your porch swing, glass of sweet tea in hand, with cosy interior elements such as our rusted oil drums, farmhouse lighting, and salvaged wood countertops making you feel right at home.' And certainly, if cornbread, bacon, country fried steak, pimento cheese, and buttermilk fried chicken served on top of crispy waffles drizzled with bourbon maple butter sauce are collectively your thing, you are indeed going to feel right at home here.

And you'll be even happier if it's whiskey that floats your boat. The choice here is said to be among the finest in Singapore, and the bar also has an extensive selection of American craft beers, together with bourbon and rye specialty cocktails. Among the many additional attractions, The Beast makes its own version of Southern Comfort, and has a barrel-aging program that showcases a rotating selection of classic cocktails. In the heart of Southeast Asia, The Beast is a cure for any American's homesickness and an unexpected treat for lovers of Americana, wherever they may come from.

WELL FANCY THAT

The Beast occupies three floors and is based on an American barn. The first level of a barn is where animals graze and play, so the ground floor is a casual bar. Animal feed is stored on the second level, so this is the dining area. The top level is where farmers gather, so this is a loft event space.

THE BEAST SOUTHERN KITCHEN AND BOURBON BAR
17 JLN KLAPA, SINGAPORE
199329
+65 6295 0017
WWW.THEBEAST.SG

THE FLAGSHIP

SINGAPORE

According to the team at The Flagship, this cool and stylish bar offers 'solid cocktails with an invigorating sexy vibe, run by a badass crew at their best behavior. Armed with an all-embracing whisky list, Flagship is the home of the Old Fashioned, the misfits, and the rebels.'

Pedants may question some of the use of English in this description, but there's no doubt that the folk behind The Flagship know a thing or two about running a successful watering hole. They have three other establishments that regularly appear in the Top 50 of Asian bars, and at The Flagship, in the basement of a 'three-in-one' bar building, they have created an informal and intimate, stripped-back, dive bar. On the bar's website you'll find an extensive list of rap and rock selections, and these musical genres are at the heart of the whole enterprise.

The bar staff are on a mission to resurrect the cocktail as a drink of choice, but there's a very impressive whiskey list here, too. There is a particularly good selection of ryes, with all the big names joined by the likes of Few, Dad's Hat, High West, a single-barrel Michter's, and a cask-strength Catoctin Creek Roundstone. The menu is unambitious but satisfying, majoring in chicken wings, fried chicken, fried calamari, and fish and chips.

WELL FANCY THAT

The Flagship offers four versions of the Old Fashioned cocktail, including three made with American whiskey. The best of them is Cowboy Blues, which comprises Michter's Small Batch Bourbon, Providore black tea, sugar, mint, and peach bitters.

THE FLAGSHIP
20 BUKIT PASOH RD,
SINGAPORE 089834
+65 9011 8304
WWW.THEFLAGSHIP.SG

The Roadhouse Bar & Grill is located in the Atura Hotel in the Blacktown district of Sydney, and according to its owners, The American Whiskey Collection, it offers 'a unique experience where New York-style loft meets Tennessee Whiskey House.'

The bar claims to have western Sydney's largest collection of American whiskey, including many varieties that are normally found only in the United States. The bar has an extensive whiskey menu, and is proud of the choice of bourbons and ryes on offer. It also specializes in whiskey-based cocktails, including its own Old Fashioned, the liquor in which is decanted directly into your glass from the barrel in which it has aged.

The Roadhouse tells customers: 'Take your time to wander through the list of imported whiskeys, and if you have a question or two, ask at the bar. Our helpful staff have a passion for whiskey.'

The mix of whiskeys covers a large range of prices, and you can select four standard or premium products on a tasting plate served up with a juicy Angus beefburger from the Roadhouse Bar & Grill kitchen.

WELL FANCY THAT

Now with hotels across Australia, the Atura group promotes itself as a purveyor of premium quality at budget prices. The owners describe the interior decor throughout the chain as 'urban, industrial, art-inspired.' The Sydney Whiskey Bar adds stylishness to an already chic operation.

THE ROADHOUSE BAR AND GRILL
32 CRICKETERS ARMS ROAD, PROSPECT NSW 2148, AUSTRALIA, +61 2 9421 0000
WWW.ATURAHOTELS.COM/ BLACKTOWN/EAT-DRINK

SHADY PINES SALOON

SYDNEY, AUSTRALIA

The web page tells you nothing. A weird color picture of a ranchero on the back of a rabbit looking out over cattle. A link to hours, contacts, and bookings. And that's it.

Click on bookings, though, and there's an angry-looking bull with enormous horns and next to it the words: 'Absolutely no bookings, functions or door list. Everyone is welcome.'

So now we know that Shady Pines is informal, accommodating, and friendly. And comfortable in its own skin. It knows that it will get talked about, and that drinkers will seek it out. It's in the Darlinghurst area of Sydney, and you get into it through two unmarked doors on a gloomy street.

They make fine cocktails, but they don't mind if you want a beer tinny and a shot. In other words, it is succeeding at being all things to all people, and is welcoming, no matter what you choose to drink.The decor is kitsch, with stuffed animals around the room, and a stag's head on the wall. But the staff are on the ball, and while everything appears relaxed and informal, the cocktails are delivered perfectly. Some great bourbon choices, too.

WELL FANCY THAT

Shady Pines has a smaller sibling called The Baxter Inn in Sydney's central bar district.You have to go down a small lane and round the back to where a staircase leads you down to the action. It is less kooky and quieter than Shady Pines, and has more than 300 bottles of whisky.

SHADY PINES SALOON
4/256 CROWN ST, DARLINGHURST NSW 2010, AUSTRALIA, +61 405 624 944
WWW.SHADYPINESSALOON. COM

If you've been reading through these bar pages carefully, you'll have noticed that American whiskey is most commonly found either in the most upmarket locations or in dive bars. So The Smoking Panda offers a pleasant third way.

It offers Asian-influenced decor and environment, with dark wood, exposed brickwork, timber-beaded curtains, Chinese lanterns, and an illuminated seawater tank full of jellyfish. Behind the bar, a flashing neon sign advertises Marlboro cigarettes.

'We renovated, created, and cooked, and The Smoking Panda was born,' says the team proudly.' Fusing LA hip with all the charm of a retro Chinese eatery, The Smoking Panda is cool, quirky, and one helluva a good time. Drop by The Hotel Coronation on Park Street for world-class cocktails, a cracking wine list, and irresistible pan-Asian bites…See you at the bar!'

The bar staff have joined the battle to become Sydney's number one destination for an Old Fashioned, and they offer this classic cocktail with a range of base spirits. The Smoking Panda claims to have Australia's biggest range of bitters—232 of them—and more than 260 spirits.

WELL FANCY THAT
In addition to more than 80 whiskeys and numerous whiskey cocktails, The Smoking Panda offers bourbon infusions such as the Cherry Chocolate Knob (Creek), the Berry Basil Buffalo (Trace), Makin Bourbon (Maker's Mark), and the Two Smoking Barrels with chili and lime.

THE SMOKING PANDA
5—7 PARK ST, SYDNEY NSW 2000, AUSTRALIA
+61 2 9264 4618
WWW.THESMOKINGPANDA.COM.AU

KODIAK CLUB

MELBOURNE, AUSTRALIA

The Kodiak says that it is Melbourne's only bourbon bar, and while its bourbon selection is impressive, it doesn't do badly with ryes and other whiskeys, either.

This inclusive bar in the Fitzroy district of the city offers hearty, solid food rather than flash bites, so you get chicken wings doused in hot buffalo sauce, cheese-stuffed jalapeños, grilled corn, and weighty burgers with fries. The American beer selection is pretty impressive, and the bar staff are dab hands at cocktails. The Kodiak Club keeps the prices down, so customers are more inclined to experiment a bit. And then there are the bourbons and the ryes—they're not mucking about here, with six rare Pappy Van Winkles, for instance, exciting whiskeys from Michter's and Buffalo Trace's Experimental range, and oddballs such as Belle Meade, which is trailed as a bourbon but its region is described as 'international.'

Exciting ryes include Rittenhouse 25 year old, Sazerac 18 year old, Thomas H. Handy Sazerac Rye, and a single-barrel rye from Michter's. It's also good to see the likes of California's Sonoma County, Pennsylvania's Dad's Hat, and Yellow Rose from Texas finding their way Down Under.

WELL FANCY THAT
Not content with being Melbourne's only bourbon bar, the Kodiak Club encourages its patrons to explore tequila. The venue has what it calls 'a secret tequila bar' called Little Blood, which offers a range of authentic tequila on Friday and Saturday nights.

THE KODIAK CLUB
272 BRUNSWICK ST, FITZROY VIC 3065, AUSTRALIA
+61 3 9417 3733
WWW.THEKODIAK.CLUB

CHAPTER 6

WHISKEY COCKTAILS

Cocktails and craft spirits work in tandem with each other: where once there was a limited demand for classic cocktails and for garishly coloured sweet concoctions with a sparkler and/or umbrella stuck in the middle, almost exclusively consumed after too many lagers on a cheap package holiday, the modern cocktail is something of an art form. To make a cocktail unique, you need unique ingredients, so what better than spirits made by you and you alone? Conversely, a good cocktail, perhaps made with home-produced bitters and locally soured fruits, may help mask the taste of some of the more ordinary whiskeys in the warehouse.

WHISKEY COCKTAILS

It is no coincidence that the surge in new micro-distilleries has happened at the same time as cocktails have come back into fashion. While the two trends do not mirror each other exactly, they are interrelated. Many craft distilleries publish cocktail recipes on their websites, serve them in their tasting rooms, and encourage visitors to concoct their own through masterclasses and workshops. Some have gone even farther, forming partnerships with local bars, or working closely with mixologists to offer unique cocktail offerings. A few bars have even turned to micro-distilling themselves.

The new wave of cocktail-makers have been in the vanguard of a grass roots revolution. When the big producers saw what was happening, they encouraged innovation, hosting competitions, and in many cases cherry-picking the best competitors, taking them on as brand ambassadors and educators.

It all adds up to a remarkable transformation in the drinks industry since the start of the millennium. Before 2000, it was almost unheard of for a barman or woman to make mixed drinks using whiskey or whisky. There was no real demand for it, and cocktail-makers preferred to stay with vodka, gin or rum, rather than battle with the strong flavors of bourbon or Scotch. When *Whisky Magazine* set out to break new ground by staging a whisky cocktail competition, three-quarters of the entrants attempted to mask the flavor of the whisky, effectively creating an expensive version of a vodka cocktail.

The picture's very different today, and there has been a huge increase in demand for cocktails. And it's not just flashy new cocktails that are doing well—traditional cocktails such as the Manhattan, the Sidecar, and the Mint Julep have been reappraised and reinvented.

The following cocktails have been chosen to give a flavor of what's happening in the world of micro-distilling. They reflect the exciting, innovative, and optimistic approach of the new craft distillers. Many recipes include specific spirits or mixers, but they should be used merely as a guide, and experimenting with your own preferred expressions could lead you to a new favorite drink. For further ideas, check out the websites of the distilleries featured in this book.

BLUE BONNET

Ingredients
45ml (1½ fl oz) UHDCO. Reserve
    Straight Bourbon Whiskey
30ml (1 fl oz) grapefruit juice
15ml (½ fl oz) honey-cinnamon syrup
2 dashes Angostura bitters
Dry sparkling white wine

Method
• Combine all ingredients, apart from the sparkling wine, into a mixing glass
• Fill with ice, and cap with a shaker tin
• Shake well, and strain into a champagne flute
• Top with sparkling white wine

Honey-cinnamon syrup prep:
Place four cinnamon sticks in a small saucepan containing 600ml (1 pint) of cold water. Bring to the boil; simmer for 5 minutes. Add 2 cups of honey, then reduce heat. Let cool, keep in jar, refrigerate.

BLUE BONNET

BOULEVARDIER

Ingredients
1 part OYO Bourbon Whiskey
1 part Campari
1 part Carpano Antica Sweet Vermouth
2 dashes bitters

Method
• Build in a Collins glass over ice; garnish with orange peel.

(Middle West Spirits, Columbus, Ohio)

CAMPFIRE

Ingredients
60ml (2 fl oz) Colkegan Whiskey
15ml (½ fl oz) lime juice
15ml (½ fl oz) maple syrup
Ginger beer to taste

Method
• In a cocktail shaker filled with ice, combine the Colkegan, lime juice, and maple syrup
• Shake a strain into a rocks glass filled with ice
• Top with a good ginger beer
• Garnish with a lime wedge

(Santa Fe Spirits, Santa Fe, New Mexico)

BURNING MAN

Ingredients
60ml (2 fl oz) Syntax Bourbon
Splash of maple syrup to taste
6 dashes of chocolate bitters
Scorched orange rind

Method
• Mix the bourbon, maple syrup, and chocolate bitters; garnish with orange rind

(Syntax Spirits, Greeley, Colorado)

BURNING MAN

CHOCOLATE MILK SHAKE

Ingredients
3 scoops chocolate ice cream
170ml (⅓ pint) milk
2 shots Chocolate Moon Pie Moonshine to taste
Chocolate syrup (to taste)
Marshmallow fluff
Biscuit crumbs
Whipped cream
Cherry for garnish

Method
• Combine first four ingredients in a blender, and blend until smooth
• Dip the rim of a Mason jar in marshmallow fluff, and roll in the biscuit crumbs
• Pour milkshake into the Mason jar
• Garnish with whipped cream, chocolate syrup, and a cherry

(Limestone Branch Distillery, Lebanon, Kentucky)

CAMPFIRE

LEFT_**CODY ROAD FLOAT**

BELOW_**DORADO SLING**

CRUSTA

Ingredients
45ml (1½ fl oz) Leopold Bros American
   Small Batch Whiskey
30ml (1 fl oz) Leopold Bros American
   Orange Liqueur
15ml (½ fl oz) Leopold Bros
   Maraschino Liqueur
15ml (½ fl oz) lemon juice
3 dashes bitters

Method
• Combine all ingredients in a cocktail
shaker with ice
• Shake until cold; strain into a sugar-
rimmed lowball glass
• Garnish with a lemon twist

(Leopold Bros, Denver, Colorado)

CODY ROAD FLOAT

Ingredients
30ml (1 fl oz) Cody Road Rye
30ml (1 fl oz) Iowa Coffee Company
   Liqueur
30ml (1 fl oz) Iowish Cream Liqueur
Root beer to taste

Method
• Shake until frothy (use plenty of ice;
the high alcohol content of the spirits
may cause the cream to curdle)
• Top with root beer

(Mississippi River Distilling, Le Claire,
Iowa)

DORADO SLING

Ingredients:
45ml (1½ fl oz) Whiskey Del Bac Dorado
10ml (⅓ fl oz) fresh lemon juice
2 dashes Cajun bitters
Ginger ale to taste

Method
• Shake first three ingredients in a
cocktail shaker with ice; pour over ice
into a Collins glass
• Top with ginger ale
• Garnish with a lemon half wheel and
a cherry

(Hamilton Distillers, Tucson, Arizona)

GETTING FIGGY WIT IT

Ingredients
45ml (1½ fl oz) Foolproof Hop Whiskey
25ml (⅘ fl oz) fig demerara
15ml (½ fl oz) fresh lemon juice
Dash of aromatic bitters

Method
• Shake and double-strain into rocks
glass over a big cube of ice
• Garnish with a lemon twist

(Sons of Liberty Spirits Co., South
Kingstown, Rhode Island)

THE INVERSION LIFTER

Ingredients
3 parts 8 Feathers Whiskey
1 part peach schnapps
3 parts orange juice
2 parts cranberry juice
1 splash club soda

Method
• Mix the ingredients into a long glass
• Stir
• Serve over ice

(8 Feathers Distillery, Boise, Idaho)

OSAKI'S SMASH

Ingredients
2 parts Minnesota 14 Whiskey
1 part simple syrup
1 part lemon juice
Fresh mint
Ice

Method
• Add the whiskey, simple syrup, lemon juice, and 4 mint leaves into shaker and SHAKE!
• Strain and pour into a rocks glass filled with ice
• Garnish with mint leaves

(Panther Distillery, Osakis, Minnesota)

MANRESA'S "THE DAVID"

Ingredients
60ml (2 fl oz) Charbay Whiskey R5 (Lot No. 4)
30ml (1 fl oz) Carpano Antica
30ml (1 fl oz) Aperol
1 dash orange bitters
Juice of half a Cara Cara orange

Method
• Combine ingredients in a beaker, stir with a large ice cube, and strain into a rocks glass
• Garnish with the peel of the orange

(Charbay Winery & Distillery, St Helena, California)

ABOVE_**THE INVERSION LIFTER**

RIGHT_**OSAKI'S SMASH**

BELOW_**MIDNIGHT MANHATTAN**

RIGHT_**RYE CHAI**

MIDNIGHT MANHATTAN

Ingredients
60ml (2 fl oz) Rye or Bourbon Whiskey
30ml (1 fl oz) sweet vermouth
1 half dropper of coffee & cacao bitters
Spiced orange bitters

Method
• Put the ingredients in a mixing glass
• Stir with ice, strain in a chilled
cocktail glass
• Garnish with a brandied cherry at the
bottom of the glass, and, if desired,
add expressed orange peel to the rim
• To make an expressed orange
peel: take a strip of orange peel, and
squeeze the peel in half above the
drink to release the oil from the peel,
then drop the peel into the glass!

(Sugar House Distillery, Salt Lake City,
Utah)

RODGER THAT ROY

Ingredients
60ml (2 fl oz) Cherry Wood
    Smoked Whisky
180–240ml (6–8 fl oz) cherry cola
1 tsp Luxardo syrup
1 Luxardo cherry

Method
• Mix ingredients with ice in a tall glass
• Garnish with a cherry

(Do Good Distillery, Modesto,
California)

REBECCA'S BET

Ingredients
60ml (2 fl oz) Rebecca Creek Whiskey
15ml (½ fl oz) Grenadine
15ml (½ fl oz) lemon juice
15ml (½ fl oz) grapefruit juice
3 dashes of orange bitters

Method
• Mix all ingredients; serve over ice

RYE CHAI

Ingredients
45ml (1½ fl oz) Diamond State
Rye Whiskey
40ml (1⅓ fl oz) chai tea syrup
30ml (1 fl oz) light cream
Fresh cinnamon

Method
• Put the whiskey, tea syrup, and cream
into a shaker
• Shake well (6–8 seconds), then strain
• Garnish with cinnamon

Chai tea syrup
• Add high-quality chai teabags to
boiling water (one bag per cup)
• Let steep for about 30 minutes, then
take out the teabags
• Add sugar (equal to the water by
volume) and bring back to the boil
• Allow the syrup to cool before using

SLEEPY HOLLOW

Ingredients
6 parts Prichard's Double Barreled
Bourbon Whiskey
1 part fresh lime juice
4 parts pumpkin purée
4 slices fresh ginger

Method
• Muddle ginger and lime juice in
shaker
• Add all other ingredients; shake well
• Strain into chilled cocktail glass
• Garnish with toasted pumpkin seeds

(Prichard's Distillery, Kelso, Tennessee)

SMOKED BUCK

Ingredients
60ml (2 fl oz) Seven Brothers
    Hickory Smoked Whisky
45ml (1½ fl oz) ginger beer
25ml (⅘ fl oz) lime juice
25ml (⅘ fl oz) simple syrup

Method
• Shake over ice; strain into copper
mug
• Garnish with a lime wedge

(Seven Brothers Distilling Co,
Cleveland, Ohio)

SNUFFLEUPAGUS

Ingredients
60ml (2 fl oz) Mammoth Whiskey
150g (⅛ oz) lemon ginger shrub
150ml (¼ pint) simple syrup
3 dashes bitters
3 mint leaves

Method
• Put the mint leaves into rocks glass
• Add syrup and bitters; muddle
• Add lemon ginger shrub, ice, and
  whiskey

(Mammoth Distilling, Torch Lake,
Michigan)

SMOKED BUCK

TEX MEX

Ingredients
30ml (1 fl oz) brown sugar syrup
6 small lemon wedges
6 mint leaves
30ml (1 fl oz) limoncello
60ml (2 fl oz) Yellow Rose Outlaw
    Bourbon Whiskey
90–120ml (3–4 fl oz) club soda

Method
• In a pint glass, place sugar syrup
• Squeeze and drop in the lemon
wedges, mint leaves and limoncello
• Muddle slightly
• Add the bourbon, and fill with ice
• Shake and add more ice if needed
• Top with club soda and stir. Garnish
with a sprig of fresh mint and a lemon
wedge on the rim
• Serve with a long straw

(Yellow Rose Distilling, Houston, Texas)

VERPLANK AVE

Ingredients
30ml (1 fl oz) Beacon Bourbon
30ml (1 fl oz) apple brandy
30ml (1 fl oz) passion fruit juice
Dash of pomegranate juice
Dash of orange bitters

Method
Shake over ice
Strain into cocktail glass

(Denning's Point Distillery, Beacon,
New York)

WHISKEY DIRECTORY

ALASKA

Amalga Distillery, Juneau
www.amalgadistillery.com
Alaska Single Malt Whiskey

Arctic Harvest, North Pole
www.arctichaevestak@gmail.com
Whiskey

High Mark Distillery, Sterling
www.highmarkdistillery.com
Blind Cat Moonshine

Port Chilkoot Distillery, Haines
www.portchilkootdistillery.com
Wrackline Rye, Boatwright Bourbon, 6
Volts Moonshine

WASHINGTON

2 Loons Distillery, Loon Lake
www.2loonsdistillery.com
Corn whiskey

2bar Spirits, Seattle
www.2barspirits.com
Moonshine

3 Howls Distillery, Seattle
www.3howls.com
Single malt whiskey, hopped and rye
whiskey

Admiralty Distillers, Port Townsend
www.admiraltydistillers.com
Whiskey

Bad Dog Distillery, Arlington
www.baddogdistillery.com
American whiskey, bourbon, rye, wheat

Bainbridge Organic Distillers,
Bainbridge Island
www.bainbridgedistillers.com
Whiskey, rye, bourbon

Batch 206 Distillery
Seattle; www.batch206.com
Barrel Raider Whiskey

Black Heron Spirits, West Richland
www.blackheronspirits.com
Whiskey, moonshine, bourbon

Black Sam Bellamy Distillery,
Montessano
www.blacksamdistillery.com

Blackbird Distillery, Brookville
www.blackbirddistillery.com
Flavored moonshine

Blackfish Spirits Distillery, Auburn
www.blackfishdistillery.com
Whiskey

Blind Pig Spirits, Olympia
www.blindspirits.com
Moonshine, whiskey, smoked whiskey

Blue Spirits Distilling, Everett
www.bluespiritsdistilling.com
Whiskey

Cadee Distillery, Clinton
www.cadeedistillery.com
Bourbon, whiskey, single malt whiskey

Carbon Glacier Distillery, Wilkeson
www.carbonglacier.com
Moonshine, Pump Trolley Whiskey

Caudill Bros Distillery, Port Angeles
www.caudillbrosdistillery.com
Whiskey

Chambers Bay Distillery, University Place
www.chambersbaydistillery.com
Chambers Bay Straight Bourbon,
Greenhorn Bourbon, Ghost Dog Whiskey

Chuckanut Bay Distillery, Bellingham
www.chuckanutbaydistillery.com
Whiskey

Copperworks Distillery, Seattle
www.copperworksdistilling.com
American Single Malt Whiskey

Cowlitz River distillery, Toledo
www.cowlitzriverdistillery.com
Smoky Valley Moonshine

Cultus Bay Distillery, Clinton
www.cultusbaydistillery.net
Poitin, Mulligan XXX Whiskey

Double V Distillery, Battle Ground
www.doublevdistillery.com
Colonel Cobb Moonshine,
Colonel Cobb Dirty Dog Aged Corn
Whiskey, Wedeye Malt Whiskey, JS
Tallman Bourbon

Dry Fly Distilling, Spokane
www.dryflydistilling.com
Wheat whiskey, wheat bourbon, triticale
whiskey

Evil Roy's Elixirs, Carnation
www.evilroyselixirs.com
Corn whiskey

Fremont Mischief Distillery, Seattle
www.fremontmischief.com
Whiskey, bourbon

Heritage Distilling Co, Gig Harbor
www.HeritageDistilling.com
Whiskey

It's 5 Artisan Distillery, Cashmere
www.its5distillery.com
Moonshine Corn Whiskey, bourbon

JP Trodden Distillery, Woodinville
www.jptrodden.com
Bourbon

Lodgepole Distilling, Seattle
Whiskey

Mutiny Bay Distillery, Freeland
www.mutinybaydistillery.com
Whiskey

Old Soldier Distillery, Tacoma
www.oldsoldierdistillery.com
Old Soldier Traditional Corn Whiskey

Oola Distillery, Seattle
www.ooladistillery.com
Bourbon, whiskey

Sandstone Distillery, Tenino
www.sandstonedistillery.com
Whiskey

Scratch Distillery, Edmonds
www.scratchdistillery.com; Whiskey

Seabeck Spirits, Seabeck
www.seabeckspirits.com
Whiskey, moonshine

Skip Rock Distillers, Snohomish
www.skiprockdistillers.comRye

Skunk Brothers Spirits, Stevenson
www.skunkbrothersspirits.com
Moonshine

Swede Hill distilling, Yakima
www.swedehilldistilling.com
Apple Pie Moonshine

Tatoosh Distillery & Spirits
www.tatooshdistillery.com
Whiskey, bourbon

The Ellensburg Distillery, Ellensburg
www.ellensburgdistillery.com
Wildcat White Whiskey

The Hardware Distillery, Hoodsport
www.thehardwaredistillery.com
Whiskey

Tinbender Craft Distillery, Spokane
www.tinbendercraftdistillery.com
Whiskey

Valley Shine Distillery, Mount Vernon
www.valleyshinedistillery.com; Bourbon

Walla Walla Distilling Co, Seattle
www.wallawalladistillingcompany.com
Whiskey

Westland distillery, Langley
www.westlanddistillery.com
American Single Malt Whiskey, Peated
American Single Malt Whiskey

Whiskey Gap Distillery, Ritzville
www.whiskeygapdistillery.com
Whiskey

Wishkah River Distillery, Aberdeen
www.wishkahriver.com; Malt whiskey

XO Alambic, Dayton
www.xoalambic.com; Five grain whiskey

OREGON

Abiqua Spirit Distillery
www.abiquaspiritdistillery.com; Whiskey

Bendistillery, Bend
www.craterlakespirits.com
Crater Lake Rye, Black Butte Whiskey

Big Bottom Distilling, Hillsboro
www.bigbottomdistilling.com
Blended whiskey

Bull Run Distilling Co., Portland
www.bullrundistillery.com
Blended whiskey, bourbon

Eastside Distilling, Portland
www.eastsidedistilling.com
Burnside Bourbon and Whiskey, Barrel
Hitch American Whiskey, Cherry Bomb
Whiskey

Hard Times Distillery, Monroe
www.hardtimesdistillery.com
Moonshine, whiskey

Hood River Distillers, Hood River
www.hrdspirits.com
Trail's End Bourbon

House Spirits Distillery, Portland
www.housespirits.com
Whiskey

III Spirits, Talent
www.iiispirits.com
Whiskey

Immortal Spirits, Medford
www.immortalspirits.com
Whiskey

Indio Spirits, Portland
www.indiospirits.com
Whiskey, James Oliver Rye

McMenamins, Troutdale
www.mcmenamins.com
Whiskey

McMenamins Cornelius Pass Distillery,
Hillsboro; www.mcmenamins.com
Whiskey

Oregon Grain Growers Brand Distillery,
Pendleton; www.oregongrain.com
American Single Malt, moonshine,
whiskey

Pilot House Distilling, Astoria
www.pilothousedistilling.com
Whiskey, bourbon, moonshine

Ransom Spirits, Sheridan
www.ransomspirits.com
Whiskey

Rogue Ales & Spirits, Portland
www.rogue.com
Whiskey

Sinister Distilling, Albany
www.sinisterdeluxe.com
Whiskey

Stein Distillery, Joseph
www.steindistillery.com
Rye

Sundance Distilling, Grants Pass
www.sundancedistilling.com
Whiskey

Swallowtail Spirits Distillery, Springfield
www.swallowtailspirits.com
Whiskey

Trail Distilling, Oregon city
www.traildistilling.com
Whiskey

CALIFORNIA
1848 Distillery, Placerville
www.1848distillery.com

35 Maple Street Spirits, Sonoma
www.35maplestreet.com
Masterton's Whiskey, Bib & Tucker
Bourbon

Alchemy Distillery, Arcata;
www.alchemydistillery.com
Clear whiskey

Alley 6 Craft Distillery, Healdsburg
www.alley6.com
Rye, single malt

Blinking Owl Distillery, Santa Ana
www.blinkingowl.com
Whiskey

Bowen's Spirits, Bakersfield
www.bowenspirits.com
Whiskey

Channel Island Distillery, Ventura
www.cistill.com
Whiskey, moonshine

Cobble Ridge Distillery, Oroville
www.cobbleridgedistillery.com
Moonshine

Cutler's Artisan Spirits, Santa Barbara
www.cutlersartisan.com
33 Straight Bourbon Whiskey

Cutwater Spirits, San Diego
www.cutwaterspirits.com
Whiskey

Denny Bar Co, Etna
www.dennybarcompany.com
Whiskey

Devils Creek Distillery, Mammoth Lakes
www.devilscreekdistillery.com
Whiskey, bourbon

Do Good Distillery, Modesto
www.dogooddistillery.com
Bourbon, single malt

Domaine Charbay Distillery, St Helena
www.charbay.com
Whiskey

Drift Distillery, San Clemente
www.driftdistillery.com
Wheat whiskey

Dry Diggings Distillery, El Dorado
www.drydiggings.com
Bourbon, rye, single malt

Goleta Red Distilling Company, Goleta
www.goletared.com
Whiskey

Graton Distilling Co., Graton
www.gratondistilling.com
Rye whiskey

Greenbar Craft Distillery, Los Angeles
www.greenbardistillery.com
Whiskey

Greenway Distillers/American Craft Whiskey Distillery, Redwood Valley
www.greenwaydistillers.com
Low Gap Whiskey

Griffo Distillery, Petaluma
www.griffodistillery.com
Whiskey

HelloCello & Prohibition Spirits, Sonoma
www.prohibition-spirits.com
Hooker's House Bourbon, rye, corn

Home Base Spirits, Oakland
www.homebasespirits.com
Bourbon, American Single Malt

Hotaling & Co, San Francisco
www.hotalingandco.com
Old Potrero 18th Century Whiskey,
Straight Rye, Hotaling's Whiskey

Humboldt Craft Spirits, Eureka
ww.humboldtcraftdistillers.com
Redwood Rye

J Riley Distillery, Redlands;
www.jrileydistillery.com; Whiskey

Kalifornia Distilleries, Temecula
www.kaliforniadistilleries.com
Whiskey, moonshine

Kill Devil Spirit Co, San Diego
www.killdevilsspiritco.com; Moonshine

Krobar Craft Distillery, Paso Robles
www.krobardistillery.com
Bourbon, rye

Liberty Call Distilling, Spring Valley
www.libertycalldistilling.com
Moonshine

Lost Spirits Distillery, Los Angeles
www.lostspirits.net
Peated single malt

Mosswood Distillers, Berkeley
www.drinkmosswood.com
Aged whiskeys

Moylan's Spirits, Petaluma
www.stillwaterspirits.squarespace.com
Moylan's American Single Malt,
bourbon, rye

Oakhurst Spirits, Oakhurst
www.oakhurstspirits.com
Wheat, corn whiskey

Old trestle, Truckee
www.oldtrestle.com
American malt, bourbon, rye

Old World Spirits, Belmont
www.oldworldspirits.com
Rye

Patio29 Spirits Company, Winters
www.patio29.com; Rye

R6 Distillery, El Segundo
www.r6distillery.com
Whiskey

ROK Distillery, Jackson
www.ROKstars.com; Rye, bourbon

Savage & Cooke, Vallejo;
www.savageandcooke.com
Bourbon, whiskey, rye

Seven Caves Spirits, San Diego
www.the7caves.com; Whiskeys

Sonoma Brothers Distilling, Windsor
www.sonomabrothersdistilling.com
Bourbon

Sonoma County Distilling County, Rohnett Park
www.sonomacountydistilling.com
Aged rye, wheat and bourbon

South Bay Spirits, San Jose
www.southbayspirits.squarespace.com
Whiskey

Spirit Works Distillery, Sebastopol
www.spiritworksdistillery.com
Whiskey

St George Spirits, Alameda
www.stgeorgespirits.com
Single malt whiskey

St James Spirits, Irvingdale
www.saintjamesspirits.com
Peregrine Rock Single Malt Whiskey

Stark Spirits Distillery, Pasadena
www.starkspirits.com
American whiskey

Sutherland Distilling Company,
Livermore; www.sutherlanddistilling.com
Bourbon

TreeCraft Distillery, San Francisco
www.treecraftdistillery.com/
Aged whiskey, bourbon

Venus Spirits, Santa Cruz
www.venusspirits.com
Whiskey

Wright & Brown distilling, Oakland
www.wbdistilling.com
Whiskey

Young & Yonder Spirits, Healdsburg
www.youngandyonder.com
Bourbon

IDAHO
8 Feathers Distillery, Boise;
www.8feathers.com; Corn whiskey,
moonshine, vanilla bean whiskey, bourbon

Grand Teton Distillery, Driggs
www.tetondistillery.com
Bourbon, American whiskey, moonshine

Koenig Distillery & Winery, Caldwell
www.koenigdistilleryandwinery.com
Whiskey

Old Flatbed Distillery, Meridian
www.oldflatbeddistillery.com
Whiskey, bourbon

NEVADA
Depot Distilling, Reno
www.thedepotreno.com
Whiskey, bourbon

Frey Ranch Estate Distillery, Fallon
www.freyranch.com; Bourbon

Las Vegas Distillery, Henderson
www.lasvegasdistillery.com
Whiskey, bourbon

N.Scott Distillery, Las Vegas
www.lasvegasdistillery.com
Whiskey, bourbon

Vapour Point, Goldfield
www.vapourpoint.com
Whiskey

Verdi Local Distillery, Verdi
www.verdilocaldistillery.com; Apple
cinnamon whiskey, garlic whiskey

UTAH
Alpine Distilling, Park City
www.alpinedistilling.com; Lafayette
Spiced Bourbon, Spur Blended Whiskey

Dented Brick Distillery, South Salt Lake
www.dentedbrick.com
Hugh Moon White Whiskey

ARIZONA
Arizona Distilling, Tempe
www.azdistilling.com
Bourbon, wheat, malt, rye

Arizona High Spirits Distillery, Flagstaff
Whiskey

Elgin Distillery, Elgin
www.azcraftbev.com; Whiskey

Forward Brands, Carefree
ray.klemp@gmail.com
Bourbon

Hamilton Distillers, Tucson
www.hamiltondistillers.com
Smoked single malt whiskey

Lucidi Distilling, Peoria
www.lucididistilling.com; Whiskey

Three Wells Distilling, Tucson
www.threewellsdistilling.com
Bourbon, whiskey

Thumb Butte Distillery, Prescott
www.thumbbuttedistillery.com
Whiskey, bourbon

MONTANA
Bozeman Spirits Company, Bozeman
www.bozemanspirits.com
Whiskey

Dry Hills Distillery, Bozeman
www.dryhillsdistillery.com
Whiskey

Glacier Distilling, Coram
www.glacierdistilling.com
Whiskey, Bad Rock Rye

Headframe Spirits, Butte
www.headframespirits.com
Orphan Girl Bourbon, whiskey

Steel Toe Distillery, Bonner
www.steeltoedistillery.com
Uncle Carl's Prohibition Whiskey

Trailhead Spirits, Billings
www.trailheadspirits.com
Highwood Rye Malt Whiskey, flavoured
whiskey, wheat whiskey

Whistling Andy, Bigfork
www.whistlingandy.com;
Bourbon, whiskey

Wildrye Distilling, Bozeman
www.wildryedistilling.com; Bourbon

Willie's Distillery, Ennis
www.williesdistillery.com
Bourbon, moonshine

WYOMING
Geyser Distilling, Cody
www.geyserdistilling.com
Whiskey

Koltiska Distillery, Sheridan
www.koltiska.com; Whiskey

Pine Bluffs Distilling, Pine Bluffs
www.pinebluffsdistilling.com; Bourbon

Single Track Spirits, Cody
www.singletrackspirits.com
Wheat whiskey

Wyoming Whiskey, Jackson
www.wyomingwhiskey.com
Whiskey, bourbon

COLORADO
10th Mountain Whiskey & Spirit, Vail
www.10thwhiskey.com
Whiskey, bourbon, moonshine

3 Hundred Days of Shine, Monument
www.3hundreddays.com
Moonshine and flavoured moonshine

Altitude Spirits, Boulder
www.altitudespirits.com
Highland Harvest Single Malt and
Blended Malt

Bear Creek Distillery, Denver
www.bearcreekdistillery.com
Whiskey, bourbon

Big Fat Pastor Spirits, Loveland
www.bigfatpastorsspirits.com
Whiskey

Black Bear Distillery,
Green Mountain Falls;
www.blackbeardistillery.com
Moonshine, corn whiskey

Black Canyon Distillery, Longmont
www.blackcanyondistillery.com
Black Canyon Corn Whiskey

Boathouse Distillery
www.boathousedistillery.com
Whiskey, bourbon

Bouck Brothers Distilling, Idaho springs
www.bouckbros.com
Corn whiskey, bourbon

Breckenridge Distillery, Breckenridge
www.breckenridgedistillery.com
Bourbon, whiskey

Cockpit Craft Distillery, Colorado
Springs; www.cockpitdistillery.com
Whiskey, moonshine

Colorado Gold Distillery, Colorado
Springs
www.coloradohighvodka.com
Colorado Gold Straight Bourbon, Rocky
Mountain Rye Whiskey

Dancing Pines Distillery
www.dancingpinesdistillery.com
Straight bourbon, straight rye

Deerhammer Distilling, Buena Vista
www.deerhammer.com
Barrel aged single malt, white whiskey

Distillery 291, Colorado springs
www.distillery291.com
291 Colorado Whiskey, Fresh Colorado
whiskey

Downslope Distilling, Centennial
www.downslopedistilling.com
Double Diamond Whiskey

Durango Craft Spirits, Durango
www.durangospirits.com
Cinder Dick Straight Bourbon, Mayday
Moonshine

Elwood Distilling Co, Boulder
www.elwooddistillingco.com
Single malt whiskey

Feisty Spirits Distillery, Fort Collins
www.feistyspirits.com
Seasonal bourbon, grain whiskey, hybrid
whiskey

Highlands Craft Distillery, Grand
Junction
www.coloradohighlandsdistillery.com
Bourbon, whiskey

Iron Horse Distiling, Durango
www.ironhorsedistilling.com
Whiskey, bourbon

KJ Wood Distillery, Ouray
www.kjwooddistillers.com
Dead Drift Whiskey

Laws Whiskey House, Denver
www.lawswhiskeyhouse.com
AD Laws Straight Whiskey, Four Grain
Bourbon, Hordeam Malt, Triticum Wheat

Leopold Bros., Denver
www.leopoldbros.com; Whiskey

Longtucky Spirits, Longmont
www.longtuckyspirits.com; Bourbon, rye

Mad Rabbit Distillery, Westminister
www.madrabbitdistillery.net
Mad Rabbit Light Rye Malt Whiskey

Mile High spirits, Denver
www.drinkmhs.com
Fireside Whiskey

Mystic Mountain Distillery, Larkspur
www.mysticmtnspirits.com
Whiskey, bourbon, moonshine

Peach Street Distillers, Palisade
www.peachstreetdistillers.com
Bourbon

Rising Sun Distillery, Denver
www.risingsundistillery.com
Rye, bourbon, whiskey

Rocker Spirits, Littleton
www.rockerspirits.com
Whiskey

Rocky Mountain Distilling, Colorado
Springs; www.rockymountaindistilling.com
Whiskey

Sand Creek Distillery, Hugo
www.sandcreekdistillery.com; Malt whiskey

Spirit Hound distillers, Lyons
www.spirithounds.com; Whiskey

Spring44 Distillery, Loveland
www.spring44.com
Whiskey

Steamboat Whiskey Company,
Steamboat Springs
www.steamboatwhiskeyco.com
Warrior Whiskey

Still Cellars, Longmont
www.stillcellars.com; Organic whiskey

Stoneyard Distillery, Dotsero
www.stoneyarddistillery.com
Laws Whiskey

Syntax Spirits, Greeley
www.syntaxspirits.com; Bourbon, whiskey

The Family Jones Spirit House, Denver
www.thefamilyjones.co; Bourbon

Wood's High Mountain Distillery, Salida
www.woodsdistillery.com
Rye, American Malt Whiskey

NEW MEXICO
Algodones Distillery, Algodones
www.algodonesdistillery.com
Whiskey

Don Quixote Distillery, Jaconita
www.dqdistillery.com
Blue corn bourbon

Glencoe Distillery, Glencoe
www.glencoedistillery.com
Single malt whiskey

KGB Spirits, Alcalde
www.kgbspirits.com
Rye, bourbon

Left Turn Distilling, Albuquerque
www.leftturndistilling.com
Blue Corn Whiskey

Santa Fe Spirits, Santa Fe
www.santafespirits.com; Whiskey

Three Rivers Brewing Co, Farmington
www.threeriversbrewery.com; Whiskey

NEBRASKA
Brickway Brewery & Distillery, Omaha
www.drinkbrickway.com; Whiskey

Cooper's Chase Distillery, West Point
www.cooperschase.com; Whiskey

Cut Spike Distillery, La Vista
www.cutspikedistillery.com; Whiskey

Patriarch Distillers, La Vista
www.patriachdistillers.com
Patriarch Whiskey

KANSAS
Boot Hill Distillery, Dodge City
www.boothilldistillery.com
Bourbon, white whiskey

High Plains Distillery, Atchison
www.highplainsinc.com; Whiskey

Union Horse Distilling Company,
Lenexa; www.unionhorse.com
Rye, bourbon, white whiskey

Wheat State Distilling, Wichita
www.wheatstatedistilling.com
Whiskey, bourbon

TEXAS
Acre Distilling, Fort Worth
www.acredistilling.com
Bourbon

Alamo Premium Distillery, San Antonio
www.alamopremiumdistillery.com
Whiskey, moonshine

Andalusia Whiskey Co, Blanco
www.andalusiawhiskey.com
Single malt whiskey

Austin Whiskey Company, Austin
www.9bandedwhiskey.com; Whiskey

Balcones Distillery, Waco
www.balconesdistilling.com
American single malt, bourbon, rye,
Blue Corn whiskey

Banner Distilling Company, Manor
www.bannerdistilling.com; Whiskey

Ben Milam Whiskey, Blanco
www.benmilamwhiskey.com
Whiskey

Bone Spirits, Smithville
www.bonespirits.com
Fitch's Goat Corn Whiskey

Buffalo Bayou Distilleries, Houston
www.buffalobayoudistilleries.com
Whiskey, bourbon

Coastal Bend Distilling, Beeville
www.coastalbenddistillingco.com
Bourbon, blended whiskey

Crystal Creek Moonshine, Spicewood
www.crystalcreekmoonshine.com
Moonshine

Dallas distilleries, Garland
www.dallasdistilleries.com; Whiskey

Fire Oak Distillery, Liberty Hill
www.fireoakdistillery.com
Small batch whiskey, bourbon

Firestone & Robertson Distilling, Fort
Worth; www.frdistillling.com
Blended whiskey, straight bourbon

Five Points distilling, Forney
www.fivepointsdistilling.com; Whiskey

Flanagan's Texas Distillery & Winery,
Bertram
www.flaniganspirits.com
Whiskey

Front Porch distillery, Nacogdoches
www.frontporchdistillery.com
Blended whiskey, moonshine

Garrison Brothers Distillery, Hye
www.garrisonbros.com
Straight bourbon

Ironroot Republic Distillery, Denison
www.ironrootrepublic.com
Corn whiskey, moonshine

JEM Beverage Co., Pilot Point
www.jembevco.com
Whiskey, moonshine

Kiepersol, Tyler
www.kiepersol.com; Bourbon

Kooper Family Whiskey, Dripping
Springs; www.kooperfamily.com; Rye

M. Wells Distilling, Cedar Creek
www.mwellsdistilling.com
Bourbon, moonshine, Four Grain White
Whiskey

North Texas Distillery, Fort Worth
www.northtexasdistillers.com
1835 Bourbon

Old Humble Distilling Company,
Humble; www.oldhumbledistilling.com
Whiskey, bourbon, corn whiskey

Powderfinger Spirits, Buda
www.powderfingerspirits.com; Whiskey

Ranger Creek Brewing & Distilling,
San Antonio; www.drinkrangercreek.com
Whiskey, bourbon

Real Spirits Distilling Co., Blanco
davin@realalebrewing.com; Hopped beer

Rebecca Creek Distillery, San Antonio
www.rebeccacreekdistillery.com
Whiskey

Red River Republic Distillery, Denison
www.redriverrepublic.com; Whiskey

Rio Brazos Distillery, College Station
www.boxcarwhiskey.com
Whistlestop and Boxcar Whiskeys

Rocking M Ranch Distillery, Henrietta
www.rockingmranchdistillery.com
Bourbon, Moonshine

Swift Distillery, Dripping Springs
www.swiftdistillery.com
Single malt whiskey

Tate & Co. Distillery, Waco
www.tatedistillery.com
Single malt whiskey, corn whiskey

The Texas Legend Distillery, Orange
www.texaslegenddistillery.com
Blended whiskey

Treaty Oak Distilling Co, Austin
www.treatyoakdistilling.com
Bourbon, whiskey

Trinity River Distillery, Forth Worth
www.trinityriverdistillery.com; Whiskey

Whiskey Hollow Distillery, Valley View
www.whiskeyhollowdistillery.com
Whiskey, bourbon, moonshine

Whitmeyer's Distilling, Houston
www.whitmeyers.com
Straight bourbon, flavoured whiskey,
moonshine

Witherspoon Distillery, Lewisville
www.witherspoondistillery.com
Bourbon, single malt whiskey

Yellow Rose Distillery, Houston
www.yellowrosedistilling.com
Whiskey, bourbon

MINNESOTA
11 Wells Spirits, St Paul
www.11wells.com
Wheat whiskey, rye, bourbon

Bent Brewstillery, Roseville
www.bentbrewstillery.com
Whiskey

Chankaska Creek Ranch & Winery,
Kasota; www.chankaskawines.com
Light whiskey

Copperwing Distillery, St Louis Park
www.copperwingdistillery.com
Light whiskey

Du Nord Craft Spirits, Minneapolis
www.dunordcraftspirits.com
Appleseed whiskey

Far North Spirits, Hallock
www.farnorthspirits.com; Whiskey

IOWA
3 OaksDistillery, Holy Cross
www.3oaksdistillery.com; Whiskey

Artisan Grain Distillery, Davenport
www.artisangraindistillery.com
Bourbon, whiskey

Broadbent Distillery, Norwalk
www.twojaysiowa.com; Corn whiskey

Cedar Ridge Distillery, Swisher
www.crwine.com/whiskey
Single malt, bourbon, rye, wheat

Dehner Distillery, Clive
www.dehnerdistillery.com; Whiskey

Iowa Distilling Co., Cumming
www.iowadistilling.com; Whiskey

Iowa Legendary Rye, Carroll
www.iowalegendaryrye.com
Rye

Lonely Oak distillery, Earling
www.lonelyoakdistillery.com
Backstreet Bourbon

Templeton Rye, Templeton
www.templetonrye.com
Rye

MISSOURI
Copper Run Distillery, Walnut Shade;
www.copperrundistillery.com; Moonshine

Holladay distillery, Weston
www.holladaydistillery.com
Bourbon, whiskey

Mid-Best Distillery, Gravois Mills
www.midbestdistillery.wordpress.com
Whiskey, moonshine

Missouri Ridge Distillery, Branson
www.missouriridgedistillery.com
American single malt, bourbon, corn,
moonshine

Missouri Spirits, Springfield
www.missourispirits.com
Whiskey

Ozark Distillery, Osage Beach
www.ozarkdistillery.com
Bourbon, moonshine

Pinckney Bend Distillery, New Haven
www.pinckneybend.com
Malt whiskey

Restless Spirits Distilling Company,
Kansas City
www.restlessspiritsdistilling.com
Irish-style whiskey, poteen

Rockin' A Distillery, Creighton
www.rockinadistillery.com
Corn whiskey

S.D. Strong Distilling, Parkville;
www.sdstrongdistilling.com
Straight Rye, Big Boom Bourbon

Square One Brewery & Distillery,
St Louis
www.spiritsofstlouisdistillery.com
JJ Neukomm Whiskey, Urban Bourbon,
hybrid

StilL 630 distillery, St Louis
www.still630.com
Whiskey

Tom's Town Distilling, Kansas City
www.toms-town.com
Whiskey, bourbon

Wood Hat Spirits, New Florence
www.woodhatspirits.com
Bourbon, whiskey

ARKANSAS
Arkansas Moonshine, Newport
www.arkansasmoonshine.com; Moonshine

Rock Town Distillery, Little Rock
www.rocktowndistillery.com; Bourbon, rye,
single malt, hickory smoked whiskey

White River Distillery, Gassville
www.whiteriverdistillery.com
Corn whiskey, moonshine

WISCONSIN
45th Parallel Spirits, New Richmond
www.45thparalleldistillery.com
Whiskey

Central Standard Cruft Distillery,
Milwaukee; www.thecentralstandard.com
Bourbon, oat whiskey

Dancing Goat Distillery, Cambridge
www.dancinggoat.com
Whiskey

Death's Door Spirits, Middletown
www.deathsdoorspirits.com
Whiskey

Door County Distillery, Carlsville
www.doorcountydistillery.com
Whiskey, moonshine

Driftless Glen Distillery, Baraboo
www.driftlessglen.com
Moonshine

Great Lakes Distillery, Milwaukee
www.greatlakesdistillery.com
Bourbon, small batch whiskey

Great Northern Distilling, Plover
www.greatnortherndistilling.com
Whiskey

Henry Farms Prairie Spirits, Dane
www.henryfarmsllc.com
Bourbon

Infinity Beverages, Eau Claire
www.infinitybeverages.com
Whiskey distilled from beer

Minhas Craft Brewery, Monroe
www.minhasbrewery.com
Whiskey, moonshine

Northern Waters Distillery, Minocqua
www.northernwatersdistillery.com
Bourbon, moonshine

St. Croix Spirits, New Richmond
www.stcroixspirits.com
Whiskey, moonshine

State Line Distillery, Madison
www.statelinedistillery.com
Whiskey

Twisted Path Distillery, Milwaukee
www.twistedpathdistillery.com; Rye

Two Tall Distilling, Sun Prairie
www.twotalldistilling.com; Whiskey

White Wolf Distillery, Shell Lake
www.whitewolfdistillery.com

ILLINOIS
Blaum Bros distilling Co, Galena
www.blaumbros.com
Bourbon, rye, malt whiskey

CH Distillery, Chicago
www.chdistilllery.com; Whiskey, bourbon,
whiskey distiled from beer

Chicago Distilling Company, Chicago
www.chicagodistilling.com; White whiskey

Copper Fiddle Distillery, Lake Zurich
www.copperfiddledistillery.com
Bourbon

Fox River Distilling Co, Geneva
www.foxriverdistilling.com
Malt whiskey

Frankfort Spirits, Frankfort
www.frankfortspirits.com
Bourbon

Grand River Spirits, Carbondale
www.grandriverspirits.com
Grand River Whiskey, moonshine

JK Williams Distilling, East Peoria
www.jkwilliamsdistilling.com
Corn whiskey, Young Buck Bourbon

Koval Distillery, Chicago
www.koval-distillery.com;
Whiskeys

Oppidan Spirits
www.oppidanspirits.com
Whiskey
bourbon

Quincy Street Distillery, Riverside
www.quincystreetdistillery.com
Bourbon

Rumshine Distilling, Tilton
www.rumdistilling.com
Flavoured moonshine

Rush Creek Distilling, Harvard
www.rushcreekdistilling.com
Whiskey

Soltis Family, Columbia
www.soltisfamilyspirits.com; Old Monroe
Bourbon, flavoured whiskey, white whiskey

Whiskey Acres Distilling, DeKalb
www.whiskeyacres.com
Whiskey

Wondertucky Distillery & bottling,
Woodstock
www.wondertuckydistillery.com; Corn,
whiskey

MICHIGAN
American Fifth Spirits, Lansing
www.americanfifthspirits.com
White whiskey

Bier Distillery, Comstock Park
www.bierdistillery.com; Rye, moonshine

Civilized Spirits, Traverse City
www.civilizedspirits.com, Whiskey

Copper Kettle Distilling, Prudenville
www.copperkettledistilling.com
Whiskey

Coppercraft Distillery, Holland
www.coppercraftdistillery.com; Bourbon

Detroit City Distillery, Detroit
www.detroitcitydistillery.com
Bourbon, rye

Entente Spirits, Baroda
www.roundbarndistillery.com; Bourbon

Ethanology, Elk rapids
www.ethanologydistillation.com; Whiskey

Flat Lander's Barstillery, Grand Rapids
www.flatlandersbar.com
Whiskey, bourbon

Grand River Distillery, Jackson
www.grandriverbrewery.com
Whiskey

Grand Traverse Distillery, Traverse City
www.grandtraversedistillery.com
Rye, bourbon

Green Door Distilling, Kalamazoo
www.greendoordistilling.com
First Ascent Whiskey

Iron Fish Distillery, Thompsonville
www.ironfishdistillery.com
Whiskey, bourbon

Journeyman Distillery, Three Oaks
www.journeymandistillery.com
Organic rye, wheated whiskey, white
whiskey, bourbon

Long Road Distillers, Grand Rapids
www.longroaddistillers.com
Whiskey

Luca Mariano Distillery, Plymouth
www.lucamariano.com
Bourbon, rye

Mammoth Distilling, Central Lake
www.mammothdistilling.com
Whiskey

Motor City Gas Distillery, Royal Oak
www.motorcitygas.com
Motor City Gas Whiskey

New Holland Artisan Spirits, Holland
www.newhollandbrew.com
Bourbon, hopped whiskey

Northern United Brewing & Distilling,
Traverse City; www.nubco.net; Whiskey

Red Cedar Spirits, East Lansing
www.redcedarspiritsdistillery.com
Bourbon

Sanctuary Spirits, Grand Ledger
www.sanctuaryspirits.com
Malt whiskey, rye, white whiskey

Traverse City Whiskey, Traverse City
www.tcwhiskey.com
Straight bourbon, straight rye

Two James Spirits, Detroit
www.twojames.com
Grass Widow Bourbon, whiskey,
single malt

Valentine Distilling Co, Ferndale
www.valentinedistilling.com
Mayor Pingree Bourbon and Rye

INDIANA
1205 Distillery, Indianapolis
www.1205distillery.com
Four Finger Rye Whiskey, White On The
Line Wheat Whiskey, Corn Star Corn
Whiskey

176 Spirits/Little Pot Spirits, Columbus
www.littlepotspirits.com
Bourbon

Bear Wallow Distillery, Nashville
www.bearwallowdistillery.com; Rye, corn
whiskey, white whiskey

Dusty Barn Distillery, Mount Vernon
www.dustybarndistillery.com
Single Barrel Rye, Casked Corn Whiskey,
blended whiskey

Edwin Coe Spirits, Churubusco
www.edwincoespirits.com; Bourbon, rye

French Lick Wine & Spirits, West Baden
Springs; www.spiritsoffrenchlick.com
White bourbon

Lucky 7 Distillery, Batesville
lucky7distillery@gmail.com
Bourbon

Oakley Brothers Distillery, Anderson;
www.oakleybrothersdistillery.com
Moonshine

Old 55 Distillery, Newtown
www.old55distillery.com
Whiskey, bourbon

Outlaw Lickers, Floyds Knobs
www.outlawlickers.com
Whiskey, bourbon, moonshine

The Indiana Whiskey Co., South Bend;
www.inwhiskey.com; Silver Sweet Corn
Whiskey, wheated bourbon whiskey

Tipton Spirits, Brazil
www.tiptonspirits.com
Harrison Brothers Bourbon

West Fork Whiskey Company,
Indianapolis
www.westforkwhiskey.com
Whiskey

OHIO
25 Street Spirits, Cleveland
www.25stspirits.com; Whiskey

451 Spirits, Columbus
www.451spirits.com; Whiskey

Candella Micro-distillery, Boardman
www.candellamicro-distillery.com
Bourbon, whiskey

Cleveland Whiskey, Cleveland
www.clevelandwhiskey.com
Bourbon, whiskey, hybrid whiskey

Ernest Scarano Distillery, Fremont
www.esdistillery.com
Old Homicide Oak Aged Rye Whiskey

Fifth Element Spirits, Shade
www.fifthelementspirits.com
Whiskey

Flat Rock Spirits, Fairborn
www.flatrockspirits.com
Bourbon, whiskey, moonshine

Indian Creek Distillery, New Carlisle
www.staleymillfarmanddistillery.com
Legendary Ohio Frontier Whiskey, white
rye, bourbon, white corn

Iron Vault Distillery, Galion
www.ironvaultdistillery.com
Whiskey, bourbon, moonshine

John McCulloch Distillery, Martinsville
www.greenriverwhiskey.com
Green River Whiskey, moonshine

Middle West Spirits, Columbus
www.middlewestspirits.com
Whiskey, bourbon

Mill St Distillery, Urica
www.millstdistillery.com
Moonshine, bourbon

Noble Cut Distillery, Gahanna
www.noblecutdistillery.com
Moonshine, bourbon

Red Eagle Distillery, Geneva
www.redeaglespirits.com
Bourbon, rye

Renaissance Artisan Distillers, Akron
www.renartisan.com
Whiskey

**Straitsville Special Moonshine
Distillery**, New Straitsville
www.straitsvillemoonshine.com
Moonshine

Tom's Foolery Distillery, Chagrin Falls
www.tomsfoolery.com
Whiskey, bourbon

Watershed Distillery, Columbus
www.watersheddistillery.com; Bourbon

Reserve Distillers, Lakewood
www.westernreservedistillers.com
Whiskey

Woodstone Creek Distillery, Cincinnati
www.woodstonecreek.com
Single barrel single malt whiskey

KENTUCKY
Barrel House Distillers, Lexington
www.barrelhousedistillery.com
Bourbon, moonshine

Bluegrass Distillers, Lexington
www.bluegrassdistillers.com
Bourbon, Kentucky Rye whiskey

Boone County Distilling, Independence
www.boonedistilling.com
Aged bourbon, unaged whiskey, rye

Casey Jones Distillery, Hopkinsville
www.caseyjonesdistillery.com
Casey's Cut 92 Moonshine

Corsair Distillery, Bowling Green
www.corsairdistillery.com
Whiskey, American Single Malt,
unaged rye

Dueling Grounds Distillery, Franklin
www.duelinggroundsdistillery.com
Bourbon, Kentucky Clear Bourbon

Jeptha Creed Distillery, Shelbyville;
www.jepthacreed.com; Bourbon

Kentucky Artisan Distillers, Crestwood
www.kentuckyartisandistillery.com
Bourbon, rye

Kentucky Mist Moonshine, Whitesburg
www.kentuckymist.com
Flavoured moonshine

Kentucky Peerless Distilling, Louisville
www.kentuckypeerless.com
Rye, bourbon, moonshine

Limestone Branch Distillery, Lebanon
www.limestonebranch.com
TJ Pottinger Whiskey, Richwood Bourbon,
flavored moonshine

Louisville Distilling, Louisville
www.angelsenvy.com
Angel's Envy Bourbon finished in port
casks

Lulbegrud Creek Distillery, Richmond
www.lulbegrudcreek.com
Organic whiskey, bourbon

MB Roland Distillery, Pembroke
www.mbroland.com; Bourbon, whiskey

New Riff Distilling, Newport
www.newriffdistilling.com; Bourbon, rye

Preservation Distillery, Bardstown
www.preservationdistillery.com
Whiskey, bourbon

Silent Brigade Distillery, Paducah
www.silentbrigadedistillery.com
Moonshine

The Old Pogue Distillery, Maysville
www.oldpogue.com; Limestone Landing
Single Malt Rye, Old Pogue Bourbon, Five
Fathers Pure Rye Malt Whiskey

Three Boys Farm Distillery, Graefenburg
www.threeboysfarmdistillery.com; Whiskey

Tyler Wood White Whiskey, Lewisburg
www.whitewhiskey.com; White whiskey

Wilderness Trail Distillery, Danville
www.wildernesstraildistillery.com
Straight bourbon, straight rye

TENNESSEE
Beechtree Distillery, Nashville
www.beechtreedistillery.com
Tenessee whiskey

Bootleggers Distillery, Hartford
www.bootleggerswhiskey.com; Whiskey

Chattanooga Whiskey, Chattanooga;
www.chattanoogawhiskey.com
Whiskey 1816 Reserve, 1816 Single Barrel

Collier & McKeel, Nashville
www.collierandmckeel.com
Tennessee whiskey, White dog, flavored
whiskeys

Corsair Distillery, Nashville
www.corsairartisan.com; Whiskey

Doc Collier Distillery, Gatlinburg
www.doccollier.com; Whiskey, moonshine

Duck River Distillery, Lewisburg
www.duckriverdistillery.com
White whiskey, moonshine

Fugitives Spirits, Nashville
www.fugitivesspirits.com; Whiskey

H Clark Distillery, W Thompson Station
www.hclarkdistillery.com
Tennessee New Whiskey, Tennessee
Bourbon, oatmeal stout whiskey

Jug Creek Distillery, Lascassas
www.jugcreekdistillery.com
Whiskey

Knoxville Whiskey Works, Knoxville
www.knoxvillewhiskeyworks.com
Whisky, bourbon, moonshine

Leiper's Fork Distillery, Franklin
www.leipersforkdistillery.com
White and barrel-aged whiskeys

Nashville Craft Distillery, Nashville
www.nashvillecraft.com
Manifesto Tennessee Nascent Whiskey

Nelson's Green Brier Distillery, Nashville
www.greenbrierdistillery.com
Belle Meade Bourbon, Tennessee whiskey

Old Dominick Distillery, Memphis
www.olddominick.com
Tennessee whiskey

Old Forge Distillery, Pigeon Forge
www.oldforgedistillery.com
Bourbon, moonshine

Old Glory Distilling, Clarksville
www.oldglorydistilling.com
White Hat Whiskey, moonshine

Popcorn Sutton, Newport
www.popcornsutton.com
Tennessee white whiskey

Prichard's Distillery, Kelso
www.prichardsdistillery.com
Whiskey

Short Mountain Distillery, Woodbury
www.shortmountaindistillery.com
Moonshine

Southern Pride Distillery, Fayetteville
www.southernpridedistillery.com
Moonshine, flavored moonshine

Speakeasy Spirits Distillery, Nashville
www.speakeasyspiritsdistillery.com
Whiskey, flavored rye, bourbon

Sugarlands Distilling, Gatlinburg
www.sugarlands.com
Whiskey, Sugarlands Shine, moonshine

Tenn South Distillery, Lynnville
www.tennsouthdistillery.com
Whiskey, moonshine; flavored moonshine

Thunder Road Distillery, Kodak
www.thunderroaddistillery.com
Whiskey, moonshine

ALABAMA
Big Escambia Spirits, Armore
bigespirits@gmail.com
Alabama Bourbon

Blue Pants Brewery, Madison
www.bluepantsbrew.com
Whiskey

High Ridge Spirits, Troy
www.highridgespirits.com
Whiskey, white whiskey

Irons One Distillery, Huntsville
www.ironsone.com
Bourbon

John Emerald Distilling Co., Opelika
www.johnemeralddistilling.com
Single malt whiskey

Mad County Winery, Cidery and Distillery, Madison
www.madcountywinery.com; Moonshine

Shelta Cavern Spirits, Huntsville
www.straighttoale.com; Whiskey

NEW YORK
Adirondack Distilling Co, Utica
www.adirondackdistilling.com
Bourbon, whiskey

Albany Distilling, Albany
www.albanydistilling.com; Coal Yard New
Make Whiskey, Ironweed Bourbon

Arcane Distilling, Brooklyn
www.arcanedistilling.com
Beer whiskey

Black Button Distillery, Rochester
www.blackbuttondistilling.com; Whiskey

Black Dirt Distillery, Warwick
www.blackdirtdistillery.com
Whiskey, bourbon

Breukelen Distilling Company, Brooklyn
www.brkdistilling.com
Whiskey

Buffalo Distilling Co., Buffalo
www.blfodistilling.com
One Foot Cock Bourbon, moonshine

Cacao Prieto Distillery, Brooklyn
www.widowjane.com; Straight bourbon

Catskill Distilling Company, Bethel
www.catskilldistilling.com
Bourbon, rye, buckwheat

Celk Distilling, Williamson
www.applecountryspirits.com; Whiskey

Clayton Distillery, Clayton
www.claytondistillery.com
Bourbon, moonshine, flavoured whiskeys

Cooperstown Distillery, Cooperstown
www.copperstowndistillery.com
Bourbon

Coppersea Distilling, New Paltz
www.coppersea.com
Whiskey

Cortland Distilling, Cortland
www.cortlandbeer.com; Whiskey,
moonshine

Dark Island Spirits, Alexandria Bay
www.darkislandspirits.com
Whiskey, flavored whiskey

Delaware Phoenix Distillery, Walton
www.delawarephoenix.com
Whiskey, bourbon

Denning's Point Distillery, Beacon
www.denningspointdistillery.com
Whiskey

Dragonfyre Distillery, Marathon
www.dragonfyredistillery.com
Whiskey

Dutch's Spirits, Pine Plains
www.dutchsspirits.com
Whiskey, moonshine

Finger Lakes Distilling, Burdett
www.fingerlakesdistilling.com
Rye, bourbon

Five & 20 Spirits, Westfield
www.fiveand20.com
Whiskey, bourbon

French Distillers & Alchemists, Lisle
phil34@gmail.com; Small batch whiskey

Good Shepherd Distillery, Mamaroneck
www.goodshepherddistillery.com
Bourbon, single malt whiskey

Grazin Spirits, Ghent;
www.grazinspirits.com
Corn whiskey, bourbon, flavoured whiskey

Gristmill Distillers, Keene
www.gristmilldistillers.com
Whiskey

High Peaks Distilling, Lake George
www.highpeakdistilling.com
Single malt whiskey

High Rock Distillery, Ballston Spa
www.highrockdistillery.com
Corn whiskey, moonshine

Hillrock Estate Distillery & Malthouse,
Ancram; www.hillrockdistillery.com
Bourbon

Iron Smoke Whiskey
www.ironsmokewhiskey.com
Straight Bourbon Whiskey

JW Overbey & Co, Brooklyn
www.jwoverbey.com; Bourbon

Kerrs Creek Distillery, Walton
www.kerrscreekdistillery.com; Bourbon

Kings County Distillery, Brooklyn
www.kingscountydistillery.com
Bourbon, moonshine

Krooked Tusker Distillery, Hammondport
www.krookedtusker.com
Bourbon, moonshine

Kymar Farm Distillery, Charlotteville
www.ky-mar.com
Whiskey, moonshine

Lake George Distilling Company,
Fort Ann
www.lakegeorgedistillingcompany.com
Bullhead Bourbon, moonshine

Last Shot Distillery, Skaneatele
www.lastshotdistillery.com
Whiskey, moonshine

Lockhouse Distillery, Buffalo
www.lockhousedistillery.com
Rye, white rye

Long Island Spirits, Baiting Hollow
www.lispirits.com
Bourbon, rye

Myer Farm Distillers, Ovid
www.myerfarmdistillers.com
Whiskey

Nahmias et Fils Distillery
www.nahmiasetfils.com
Whiskey

New York Distilling Company, Brooklyn
www.nydistilling.com
American rye

O'Begley Distillery, Dundee
www.obegley.com
Irish style whiskey

Old Home Distillers, Lebanon
www.oldhomedistillers.com
Bourbon, corn whiskey, malt whiskey,
flavored whiskeys

**Olde York Farm Distilling and
Cooperage**, Claverack
www.oldeyorkfarm.com; Whiskey

Orange County Distillery, Goshen
www.orangecountydistillery.com; Rye,
bourbon, single malt, flavoured whiskeys

Prohibition Distillery, Roscoe
www.prohibitiondistillery.com; Whiskey

Sagaponack Farm Distillery, Sagaponack
www.sagaponackfarmdistillery.com;
Whiskey, bourbon

Saint Lawrence Spirits, Clayton
www.saintlawrencespirits.com
Whiskey, bourbon

Saratoga Courage, Saratoga Springs
www.saratogadistilleries.com
Moonshine

Shady Knoll Orchards and Distillery, Millbrook
www.shadyknolldistillery.com
Rye

Southern Tier Distilling Co., Lakewood;
www.southerntierdistilling.com
Bourbon, American whiskey, hopped whiskey, rye

Springbrook Hollow Farm Distillery, Queensbury
www.springbrookhollow.com
Rye, bourbon, moonshine

Standard Wormwood Distillery, Brooklyn
www.standardwormwood.com
Rye, moonshine

StilltheOne Distillery, Port Chester
www.combvodka.com
Single malt whiskey

Taconic Distillery, Stanfordville
www.taconicdistillery.com
Whiskey, bourbon

Union Grove Distillery, Arkville
www.uniongrovedistillery.com
Rye

Upstate Distilling Co., Saratoga Springs
wwwupstatedistilling.com
Whiskey, rye

Van Brunt Stillhouse, Brooklyn
www.vanbruntstillhouse.com
American whiskey, rye bourbon, moonshine

VERMONT
Appalachian Gap Distillery, Middlebury;
www.appalachiangap.com
Whiskey

Mad River Distillers, Waitsfield
www.madriverdistillers.com;
Bourbon, rye, single malt

Saxtons River Distillery, Brattleboro
www.saplingliqueur.com

SILO Distillery, Windsor
www.americancraftedspirits.com
Whiskey, bourbon

Smugglers' Notch Distillery, Burlington
www.smugglersnotchdistillery.com
Whiskey, bourbon

Stonecutter Spirits, Middlebury
www.stonecutterspirits.com
Heritage Cask Whiskey

Vermont Spirits Distilling, Quechee
www.vermontspirits.com
Whiskey, bourbon

NEW HAMPSHIRE
Cold Garden Spirits, Canterbury
www.coldgardenspirits.com
Whiskey

Djinn Spirits Distillery, Nashua
www.djinnspirits.com
Whiskey

Flag Hill Distillery, Lee
www.flaghill.com
Whiskey, bourbon, rye

**New England Sweetwater
Farm & Distillery,** Winchester
www.newenglandsweetwater.com
Bourbon, American single malt whiskey

Smoky Quartz Distillery, Seabrook
www.smokyquartzdistilllery.com
Bourbon, moonshine

Stark Brewery & Distillery, Manchester
www.starkbrewingcompany.com
Bourbon

MAINE
**Doom Forest Distillery/
Chadwick's,** Pittston
www.chadwickscraftspirits.com
Chadwick's Maple Whiskey

Liquid Riot Bottling Co., Portland
www.liquidriot.com
White oak whiskey

Maine Craft Distilling, Portland
www.mainecraftdistilling.com
Single malt whiskey, American whiskey

New England Distilling, Portland
www.newenglanddistilling.com
Whiskey

Wiggly Bridge Distillery Barn, York
www.wigglybridgedistillery.com
Whiskey

MASSACHUSETTS
Berkshire Mountain Distillers, Sheffield
www.berkshiremountaindistillers.com
Bourbon, corn whiskey

Boston Harbor Distillery, Boston
www.bostonharbordistillery.com;
Single malt, rye

Bully Boy Distillers, Roxbury
www.bullyboydistillers.com
Whiskey

Damnation Alley Distillery, Newton
www.damnationalleydistillery.com
Whiskey, bourbon

Deacon Giles Distillery, Salem
www.deacongiles.com
Whiskey

McMillan Distillery, Watertown
www.mcmillandistillery.com
Whiskey

Ryan & Wood, Glucester
www.ryandandwood.com; Rye

Triple Eight Distillery, Nantucket
www.ciscobrewers.com
Whiskey

CONNECTICUT
Aylum Distillery, Bridgeport
www.asylumdistillery.com
Corn whiskey, flavored whiskey

**Full Moonshine by Hickory Ledges Farm
& Distillery,** Canton
www.fullmoonshine.com
Flavored monshine

Litchfield Distillery, Litchfield
www.litchfielddistillery.com
Bourbon, whiskey

Mine Hill Distillery, Roxbury
www.minehilldistillery.com; Bourbon, rye

Onyx Moonshine, East Hartford
www.onyxmoonshine.com
Moonshine

Powderman Spirits, Simsbury
www.powdermenspirits.com
Pot still whiskey, white whiskey

RHODE ISLAND
Sons of Liberty Spirits, South Kingstown
www.solspirits.com
Whiskey, single malt

PENNSYLVANIA
4Play Moonshine, Schuyllkill
www.4playmoonshine.com; Moonshine

Allegheny Distilling, Pittsburgh
www.maggiesfarmrum.com
Whiskey, bourbon

Big Spring Spirits, Belefonte
www.bigspringspirits.com
White whiskey

Bluebird Distillery, Phoenixville
www.bluebirddistilling.com
White whiskey

Cart/Horse Distillery, Edinboro
www.carthorsedistilling.com
Wheat whiskey, moonshine

CJ Spirits, Kane
www.cjspirits.com
White whiskey

Conneaut Cellars Distillery, Conneaut
Lake; www.conneautcellars.com
Whiskey

County Seat Spirits, Allentown
www.countyseatspirits.com; Whiskey

Disobedient Spirits, Homer City
www.disobdientspirits.com
Whiskey

DR Distillery, Slippery Rock
www.drdistillery.com
Whiskey, white whiskey

Eight Oaks Craft Distillers, New Tripoli
www.eightoaksdistillers.com
Bourbon

**Five Saints Distilling and
International Spirits,** Norristown
www.fivesaintsdistilling.com
White whiskey

Hewn Spirits, Pipersville
www.hewnspirits.com
Rye, moonshine

Liberty Pole Spirits, Washington
www.libertypolespirits.com
Whiskey, bourbon, peated bourbon rye, corn, single malt, white rye

Luminary Distilling, Eric
www.luminarydistilling.com
Wheat whiskey

Manatawny Still Works, Pottstown
www.manatawnystillworks.com
Whiskey

Mason Dixon Distillery, Gettysburg
www.masondixondistillery.com
Corn whiskey, rye

McHenry Whiskey, Benton
www.born1812.com; Rye

McLaughlin Distillery, Sewickley
www.mclaughlindistillery.com
Bourbon, moonshine, whiskey

Midnight Madness Distilling, Quakertown
www.paprivatelabelspirits.com; Whiskey

Midstate Distilling, Harrisburg
www.midstatedistilllery.com
Moonshine

Mountain Laurel Spirits, Bristol
www.dadshatrye.com; Dad's Hat Rye

Mountain Top Distillery, Williamsport
www.mountaintopdistillery.com
Moonshine, corn whiskey

**Mountain View Vineyard, Winery &
Distillery,** Stroudsburg
www.mountainviewvineyard.com
Moonshine

New Liberty Distillery, Philadelphia
www.newlibertydistillery.com
Malt whiskey, rye

Nittany Mountain Distillery, Lemont
www.nittanymountaindistillery.com
Moonshine

Red Brick Craft Distillery, Philadelphia
www.redbrickcraftdistillery.com
Single malt whiskey, barrel strength
whiskey

Ridge Runner Distillery, Chalk Hill
www.ridgerunnerdistillery.com
Moonshine

Social Still, Bethlehem
www.socialstill.com
Bourbon, rye, flavoured rye

Tall Pines Disillery, Salisbury
www.tallpinesdistillery.com
Whiskey, moonshine

Thistle Finch Distilling, Lancaster
www.thistlefinch.com
White rye

W.P. Palmer Distilling Co,
Philadelphia
www.palmerdistilling.com
Manayunk Moonshine

Wigle Whiskey, Pittsburgh
www.wiglewhiskey.com
Whiskey, bourbon

NEW JERSEY
Asbury Park Distilling, Asbury Park
www.apdistilling.com
Whiskey

Claremont Distilled Spirits,
Fairfield
www.claremontdistillery.com
Moonshine, whiskey

Cooper River Distillers, Camden
www.cooperriverdistillers.com
Cooper River Bourbon, Cooper
River Rye, Silver Fox Rye

Jersey Spirits Distilling, Fairfield
www.jerseyspirits.com
Bourbon, whiskey

Little Water Distillery, Atlantic City
www.littlewaterdistillery.com
Whitecap Whiskey

Milk Street Distillery, Branchville
www.milkstreetdistillery.com
Single malt, bourbon

Nauti Spirits Company
www.nautispirits.com
Whiskey

Res Natura, Newark
www.allpointswestdistillery.com
All Points West Whiskey

Silk City Distillers, Clifton
www.silkcitydistillers.com
Bourbon, Oat Bourbon, Millett Bourbon,
Corn Whiskey

Skunktown Distillery, Flemington
www.skunktowndistillery.com
Whiskey

MARYLAND
Dragon Distillery, Frederick
www.dragondistillery.com
Moonshine, bourbon, whiskey

Lost Ark Distilling Co., Columbia
www.lostarkdistilling.com
Whiskey, bourbon

Louthan Distillery, Baltimore
www.louthandistilling.com
Corn whiskey

Lyon Distilling Co., St Michaels
www.lyondistilling.com
Rye

McClintock Distilling, Frederick
www.mcclintockdistilling.com
Maryland Heritage White Whiskey

MISCellaneous Distillery, Mount Airey
www.miscdistillery.com
Whiskey

Old Line Spirits, Baltimore
www.oldlinespirits.com
Single malt whiskey, peated,
cask strength

Patapsco Distillery, Sykeville
www.patapscodistilling.com
Rye, bourbon

Sagamore Spirit, Baltimore
www.sagamorespirit.com

Seacrets Distilling, Ocean City
www.seacrets.com
American whiskey, bourbon

Skipjacks Spirits, Tilghman
Whiskey

Spirits of Patriots, Princess Anne
www.spiritsofpatriots.com
Moonshine

Springfield Manor Winery & Distillery
www.springfieldmanor.com
Bourbon, corn whiskey, rye

Tenth Ward Distilling Company,
Frederick; www.tenthwarddistilling.com
Caraway Rye, corn whiskey

Tobacco Barn Distillery, Hollywood
www.tobaccobarndistillery.com
Bourbon, whiskey

Twin Valley Distillers, Rockville
www.tvdistillers.com
Bourbon, whiskey

White Tiger Distillery, Stevensville
www.whitetigerdistillery.com
Laotian style rice whiskey

DELAWARE
Painted Stave Distilling, Smyrna
www.paintedstave.com
Straight bourbon, straight rye

VIRGINIA
8 Shires Distillery, Williamsburg;
www.8shires.com; Bourbon

Belle Isle Craft Spirits, Richmond
www.belleislecraftspirits.com; Moonshine

Belmont Farms of Virginia,
Culpeper
www.belmontfarmdistillery.com
Virginia Lightning Whiskey, Kopper Kettle
Bourbon, moonshine

Boar Creek Appalachian Whiskey,
Hillsville; www.boarcreekwhiskey.com
Whiskey

Cavalier Distillery, Virginia Beach
www.cavalierhotel.com
Whiskey

Copper Fox Distillery, Sperryville
www.copperfox.biz
Wasmund's Single Malt Whisky, rye

Davis Valley Distillery, Rural Retreat
www.davisvalleydistillery.com
Appalachian Corn Whiskey, moonshine

Dr Stoner's Spirits, Winchester
www.drstoners.net
Whiskey

Filibuster Distillery, Maurertown
www.filibusterbourbon.com
Bourbon, rye, whiskey

Five Mile Mountain Distillery,
Floyd
www.5milemountain.com
Flavored moonshine

**George Washington's
Mount Vernon Distillery**,
Mount Vernon
www.mountvernon.org
Aged and unaged small batch rye

Ironclad Distillery, Newport News
www.ironcladdidtillery.com
Bourbon

KO Distilling, Manassa
www.kodistilling.com
White whiskey, wheat whiskey,
bourbon, rye

Reservoir Distillery, Richmond
www.reservoirdistillery.com
Bourbon, wheat whiskey, rye,
speciality whiskey

Silverback Distillery, Afton
www.sbdistillery.com
Blackback Rye, Blackback Honey Rye

Three Bros. Distillery, Chesapeake
www.threebrotherswhiskey.com
KaBlam Unage Corn Whiskey, George
Straight Rye Whiskey

Twin Creeks Distillery, Rocky Mount
www.twincreeksdistillery.com
Moonshine, whiskey

Virginia Distillery Co., Lovingston
www.vadistillery.com
Virginia-Highland Whisky finished in
various casks

Virginia Sweetwater Distillery, Marion
Virginia Sweetwater Moonshine,
War Horn Whisky

Vitae Spirits Distillery, Charlottesville
www.vitaespirits.com
Whiskey

NORTH CAROLINA
Asheville Distilling Co., Asheville
www.troyandsons.com
Moonshine, corn whiskey

Blue Ridge Distillling Co., Bostic
www.blueridgedistilling.com
Whiskey, bourbon

Broad Branch Distillery, Winston Salem
www.broadbranchdistillery.com
Bourbon, blended whiskey

Broadslab Distillery, Benson
www.broadslabdistillery.com
Moonshine

Call Family Distillers, Wilkesboro
www.callfamilydistillers.com
Moonshine

Copper Barrel Distillery, North
Wilkesboro; www.copperbarrel.com
Moonshine

Diablo Distilleries, Jacksonville
www.diablodistilleries.com
Corn whiskey, Hell Hound Moonshine

Doc Porter's Distilling, Chalotte
www.docporters.com
Bourbon

Elevated Mountain Distilling Co.,
Maggie Valley
www.elevatedmountain.com
Whiskey

Fainting Goat Spirits by Greensboro Distilling, Greensboro
www.faintinggoatspirits.com
Bourbon, American Single malt whiskey, rye

Great Wagon Road Distilling, Charlotte
www.gwrdistilling.com
American single malt whiskey, moonshine

Howling Moon Distillery, Asheville
www.howlingmoonshine.com
Moonshine

Mayberry Spirits, Mount Airy
www.mayberryspirits.com
Whiskey, moonshine

Mother Earth Spirits, Kinston
www.motherearthspirits.com
Whiskey

Old Nick Williams Co., Lewisville
www.oldnickwhiskey.com
Whiskey, bourbon

Piedmont Distillers, Madison
www.piedmontdistillers.com
Moonshine, whiskey

Seven Jars Distillery, Charlotte
www.sevenjars.com
Bourbon

South Mountain Distilling Co.,
Rutherford College
www.southmountaindistillery.com
Whiskey, moonshine

Southern Artisan Spirits, Kings Mountain
www.southernartisanspirits.com
Turning Point Rye, Butcher Whiskey

Southern Distilling Company, Stateville
www.southernartisanspirits.com
Bourbon, rye

Southern Grace Distilleries, Mt Pleasant
www.southerngracedistilleries.com
Flavored corn whiskey

Top of the Hill Distillery, Chapel Hill
www.topodistillery.com
Whiskey

Walton's Distillery, Jacksonville
www.waltonsdistillery.com
Corn whiskey, moonshine

SOUTH CAROLINA
Carolina Moon Distillery, Edgefield
www.carolinamoondistillery.com
Corn whiskey

Charleston Distilling Co., Charleston
www.charlestondistilling.com
Whiskey

Chattooga Belle Farm Distillery,
Long Creek
www.chattoogabellefarm.com
Malt whiskey, corn whiskey, wheat whiskey

Copperhead Mountain Distillery,
Travelers Rest
www.copperheadmtn.com
Moonshine

Crouch Distilling, Columbia
www.crouchdistilling.com
Rye, bourbon, single malt, whiskey

Dark Corner Distillery, Greenville
www.darkcornerdistillery.com
Moonshine, whiskey

Gorget Distilling Co., Lugoff
www.gorgetdistilling.com
Corn whiskey, bourbon

High Wire Distilling Co., Charleston
www.highwiredistilling.squarespace.com
Sorghum whiskey

JAKAL Distillery, Lexington
www.jakaldistillery.com
Corn whiskey, moonshine

Lucky Duck Distillery, Yemassee
www.luckyduckdistillery.com
Corn whiskey, moonshine

Motte & Sons Bootlegging Co.,
Spartanburg
www.motteandsons.comWhiskey

Palmetto Moonshine, Anderson
www.palmettomoonshine.com
Moonshine

Rock Bottom Distillers, Spartanburg;
www.rockbottomdistillers.com
Appalachian moonshine

Six and Twenty Distillery, Piedmont
www.sixandtwentydistillery.com
Bourbon, whiskey

Straw Hat Distillery, Florence
www.strawhatdistillery.com
Corn whiskey, moonshine

Striped Pig Distillery, Charleston
www.stripedpigdistillery.com
Whiskey

Super Tit Moonshine, Reidville
www.sugartitmoonshine.com
Flavored moonshine

Tiger Juice Distillery, Hartsville
Whiskey

Yesternight Distillery, Lexington
Clear and flavoured moonshine

GEORGIA
American Spirit Whiskey, Atlanta
www.americanspiritwhiskey.com
Whiskey

Dalton Distillery, Dalton
www.addistillery.com
Raymond's Reserve Moonshine

Dawsonville Moonshine Distillery,
Dawsonville
www.dawsonvillemoonshinedistillery.com
Moonshine, corn whiskey

Georgia Distilling Company,
Milledgeville
www.georgiadistilling.com
Moonshine, rye, whiskey, bourbon

Ghost Coast Distillers, Savannah
www.ghostcoastdistillery.com
Flavored whiskey

Independent Distilling, Decatur
www.independentdistilling.com
Sour mash whiskey, White Dog

Lazy Guy Distillery, Kennesaw
www.lazyguydistillery.com
Straight bourbon, rye, American single malt

Lovell Bros. Distillery
www.lovellbroswhiskey.com
Georgia Sour Mash

Moonrise Distillery, Clayton
www.moonrisedistillery.com
James Henry Bourbon, James Henry Rye, moonshine

SpiritsUSA, Cumming
www.spiritsusa.com
Legends Whiskey

Stillhouse Creek Craft Distillery,
Dahlonega
Bourbon, whiskey

Thirteenth Colony Distilleries,
Americus; www.thirteenthcolony.com
Southern Corn Whiskey

FLORIDA
Alchemist Distillery, Miami
www.alchemistdistillery.com
Whiskey

Big Cypress Distillery, Miami
www.bigcypressdistillery.com
Whiskey

Citrus Distillers, Riviera Beach
www.citrusdistillers.com
Whiskey

Cotherman Distilling Co, Dunedin
www.cothermandistilling.com
American malt whiskey

Fish Hawk Spirits, Gainsville
www.fishhawkspirits.com
Sui Generia Whiskey

Florida Cane Distillery, Tampa
www.cane-vodka.com
Moonshine

Key West Distlling, Key West
www.keywestdistilling.com
Whiskey

Kozuba & Sons Distillery, St Petersburg
www.kozubadistilling.com
Whiskey

Manifest Distilling, Jacksonville
www.manifestdistilling.com
Bourbon, rye

NJoy Spirits, Weeki Wachee
www.wildbuckwhiskey.com
Wild Buck Whiskey

Peaden Brothers Distillery, Crestview
www.peadenbrothersdistillery.com
Flavored corn whiskey, moonshine

Scratch Ankle Distillery, Milton
www.scratchankledistillery.com
Whiskey, moonshine

St. Augustine Distillery Co.,
St. Augustine
www.staugustinedistillery.com
Bourbon

St. Petersburg's Craft Distillery,
St. Petersburg
www.stpetersburgdistillery.com
Whiskey

Timber Creek Distillery, Destin
www.timbercreekdistillery.com
Bourbon, black rye whiskey

Winter Park Distilling Co., Winter Park
www.wpdistilling.com
Whiskey

Yalaha Bootlegging Company
Yalaha
www.yalahabootleggingco.com
Moonshine

INDEX

GLOSSARY

ABV
An abbreviation for alcohol by volume. This is the standard way of measuring how much alcohol (ethanol) is in an alcoholic drink.

AMONTILLADO
A type of sherry that is named after the Montilla region of southern Spain where the style originated.

AMOROSO
A dark, rich, and sweet sherry, which is similar to Oloroso sherry.

"ANGELS' SHARE"
The name for the small volume of whiskey that is lost to evaporation during the maturation process.

BONDED WAREHOUSE
A place where stock, including whiskey, is stored "under bond" before duty is due to be paid on it.

BOURBON
American whiskey made with at least 51 per cent corn, as well as other grains, and matured in a new oak barrel.

BUTT
A wine cask that contains around two hogsheads (about 125–126 gallons, or 475–480 liters) of liquid.

CARAMEL
A dark brown sugar-based confectionery used by some whiskey-makers as a coloring agent.

CASK STRENGTH
The alcohol-by-volume (ABV) level of a whiskey once it has completed the maturation process. The cask strength of whiskey is typically around 60 to 65 per cent ABV before dilution.

CHARRING
Part of the barrel-making process whereby the inside is toasted with flame. This means that the taste of the whiskey will change as it matures in the barrel.

CHILL-FILTERING
A cosmetic method of removing residue from a whiskey by cooling and passing the whiskey through a filter.

COLUMN STILL
A long, tall still for making American whiskey, using steam under extreme pressure to separate spirit from a grain mash. This is also known as a continuous still.

CONGENERS
Chemical compounds formed during fermentation, distillation, and maturation of whiskey that affect its taste and smell.

CONTINUOUS STILL
See "Column Still".

DRAM
A Scottish term for a measure of whisky. A dram is typically around 25 ml.

DUMPING
The process of emptying the barrel of its whiskey.

FINO
A dry and very pale sherry from Spain.

FIRST-FILL CASK
The term used for an oak cask that is filled for the first time with new-make whiskey after it has been emptied of its previous contents.

GRIST
A coarse flour of malt and other grains that is used to make a whiskey.

HIGHBALL
A cocktail of whiskey mixed with club soda or ginger ale and served with ice in a tall glass.

HOGSHEAD ("HOGGIE")
A cask holding approximately 55 gallons (208 liters) of liquid.

MADEIRA
A fortified Portuguese wine made in the Madeira Islands in several different styles.

MARSALA
A wine made in the area around Marsala, Sicily.

MASH BILL
The mixture of different grains that go into a whiskey, also known as a grain bill.

MASHING
The process whereby grain(s) and water is combined and heated.

MASH TUN
The large vessel used for mashing. It typically features a stirring mechanism, known as a mash rake, and a heating device.

MOUTH-COATING
Moving the whiskey around the mouth to coat the four taste receptors and help release flavors.

MOUTHFEEL
A way of assessing a whiskey's intensity by holding it on the center of the tongue for a few seconds.

NONAGE STATEMENT (NAS)
Whiskey that is sold without a specific age on the label.

NEW-MAKE
The spirit produced by a distillery prior to maturation.

OLOROSO
A dark and nutty variety of sherry produced by oxidative aging.

PEDRO XIMÉNEZ
A type of white grape that is grown in certain parts of Spain.

PHENOLS
Chemical compounds introduced to a whiskey through a peat-heated fire. Phenols add a smoky aroma and flavor to the spirit.

POT STILL
A kettle-like still used to make batches of whiskey, normally single malt whiskey.

RYE
A spirit made with at least 51 per cent rye, as well as other grains, and matured in a new oak barrel.

SALADIN BOX
A nineteenth-century French invention in which barley germinates while being mechanically turned.

SINGLE MALT WHISKEY
A whiskey made using only malted barley, yeast and water at one distillery.

SOLERA
A process for aging liquids by fractional blending in such a way that the finished product is a mixture of ages.

SOUR MASH
The thin watery liquid containing spent grains that are stripped of all their sugars (hence sour), that are added back in at the start of the distilling process. This is also known as backset or stillage.

STAVES
The pieces of wood that form a barrel.

STRAIGHT BOURBON
A bourbon which has been matured in a new oak barrel for a minimum of two years.

WASH
The liquid produced at the end of the fermentation of the wort, after the yeast has been added.

WASH BACK
A large vat, usually made of wood, in which distillers ferment the wort to form wash.

WHEAT WHISKEY
A whiskey made up of at least 51 per cent wheat, as well as other grains.

WORT
The sugary liquid obtained during the mashing process. The sugars will ferment to form alcohol.

ACKNOWLEDGEMENTS

I don't think anyone could have foreseen what a huge undertaking Whiskey: America was going to be when I restarted work on it. American craft distilling is in a constant state of flux, with new distilleries opening on a weekly basis and, in some cases, closing down too. We have steered our way through uncharted territory, and have learned masses. There were no text books to refer to, so I had to turn to some unusual sources for help, information and inspiration.

These include the online teams at The Whisky Exchange and Masters of Malt. I regularly went to their websites to seek out the most recent American whiskey releases and to read their tasting notes just to check I wasn't going crazy. I would also like to give a huge thanks to Bill Owens and David Smith of the American Distilling Institute. They provided the directory that we used as a base for our distillery guide.

I would like to thank my editors for this project, Elspeth Beidas and latterly, Joe Hallsworth, who must have wondered what hit him when he inherited not one but two of my bigger book projects. Also Ruth Patrick for her consistent support in recent years.

I'd also like to thank Krzysztof, Ronnie and the whole team at my new employees, Stilnovisti. It's early days, and who knows where we will end up, but believing in me and giving me the chance to edit again means everything to me.

I'd like to thank the many distillers, blenders, warehouse workers, ambassadors, retailers, and public relations folk, who have always worked so hard to make my job as easy as possible in so many different ways. They are far too many to mention by name, but I am proud that I shared drams with wonderful people right across the world and that they have all made me feel that I am part of a huge and wonderful family. It never ceases to amaze me how humble the world of whisky is, and I am almost embarrassed by the attention we in the media receive while the real whiskey heroes go mostly unsung. My greatest respect to all of them.

I once described the world of whiskey as like a conveyor belt which has been moving for hundreds of years, and will move forward for hundreds of years more. Everyone involved with it steps onto the conveyor belt for some years

– decades if they're lucky – and then they step or fall off somewhere down the line, and on it moves. Inevitably, then, over a period of 10 years, some people have left the conveyor belt.

I want to mention just three of the less celebrated members of the whisky profession who are no longer with us.

The first is Henry Besant, who died very prematurely in 2013. He had a huge influence on me, and nurtured my love of bourbon, and his death was a huge shock. I will never forget him.

At the start of 2018 I heard that Carl Reavey had died. He worked at Bruichladdich Distillery and had a passion and love for Islay and his distillery which was infectious. He was full of ideas, was bursting with enthusiasm, and was generous with his time. He will be sadly missed.

As I write I have just heard of the passing of John Ryan, the man who introduced me to Irish whiskey in general, and Jameson in particular, long before I started writing about whisky for a living. John was a wonderful advocate for Irish whiskey and a proud Irishman.

As many people know, I became severely ill in 2013 and I have battled ever since with my health. I have pretty much won that battle, but it has been very tough. If you're reading this and you're struggling, please, please, please talk to someone about it. It might save your life.

I would like to thank those people who looked out for me during those dark days: in particular, my very good friend Tony Bagnall, Andrew Naylor Higgins, Chris Rodden, Doug McIvor, Ronnie Cox, Richard Paterson, and Mark Gillespie.

A special thank you to Joanna Seymour, and to my amazing and long suffering wife Sally, and my fantastic children Julian, Louie, and Madeleine. I am proud of them all.

Finally, since the last edition of the book, my beloved Leicester City have won the English Premiership and reached the Quarter Finals of The Champions League, and my beloved All Blacks have won the Rugby World Cup. Twice. Miracles can happen. This book is dedicated to the memory of my dad.

PICTURE CREDITS

The publishers would like to thank the distilleries, bars, picture libraries, and photographers for their kind permission to reproduce the works featured in this book. Every effort has been made to trace all copyright holders but if any have been inadvertently overlooked, the publishers would be pleased to make the necessary arrangements at the first opportunity.

13 Our Local Commons 17 Zachary Frank/Alamy Stock Photo 18 North Wind Picture Archives/Alamy Stock Photo 19l Old Paper Studios/Alamy Stock Photo 19r Antiqua Print Gallery/Alamy Stock Photo 20-21 age footstock/Alamy Stock Photo 23b Kristoffer Tripplaar/Alamy Stock Photo 24-25 Daniel Dempster Photography/Alamy Stock Photo 26l Jason Kolenda – Travel/Alamy Stock Photo 26r Daniel Dempster Photography/Alamy Stock Photo 27t Danita Delimont/Alamy Stock Photo 27b Andrew Woodley/Alamy Stock Photo 28 David Paul Morris/Bloomberg via Getty Images 29 Blaine Harrington III/Alamy Stock Photo 30 Radharc Images/Alamy Stock Photo 31t Ed Clark/The LIFE Picture Collection/Getty Images 31b Chris Howes/Wild Places Photography/Alamy Stock Photo 36-37 Michael Halberstadt/Alamy Stock Photo 38-40

Daniel Dempster Photography/Alamy Stock Photo 41 Scott Olson/Getty Images 42 B Christopher/Alamy Stock Photo 43t PAUL J.RICHARDS/AFP/Getty Images 43b Carl D. Walsh/Portland Press Herald via Getty Images 46 karenfoleyphotography/Alamy Stock Photo 47t ZUMA Press Inc/Alamy Stock Photo 47b Cayce Clifford/Bloomberg via Getty Images 48-49 ZUMA Press Inc/Alamy Stock Photo 50 karenfoleyphotography/Alamy Stock Photo 51 Laperruque/Alamy Stock Photo 52-53 Cayce Clifford/Bloomberg via Getty Images 54 LEON NEAL/AFP/Getty Images 55t LEON NEAL/AFP/Getty Images 55b Neil McAllister/Alamy Stock Photo 56 xxx 57 Leisa Tyler/LightRocket via Getty Images 58-59 Mike Groll/AP/REX/Shutterstock 59r Mike Di Paola/Bloomberg via Getty Images 67 Nicole Kandi 74 Carly Diaz 80t Maker Walk LA 80b Marc Royce 96 ZUMA Press Inc/Alamy Stock Photo 97 Urban Toad Media 112 Garry McMichael 116 The MKE Collection/Alamy Stock Photo 133 Middle West Spirits LLC 141 Shaun Wilson 171l Rick Martin 171r Kristen Dill 173t Our Local Commons 173b Ron Rammelkamp 210r 68 Huntley Multimedia 211l 68 Huntley Multimedia 213l The Whiskey Exchange 214r The Whiskey Exchange 218 The Whiskey Exchange 219r The Whiskey Exchange